CLASSIC TEXTS SERIES

# DIFFERENTIAL CALCULUS FOR BEGINNERS

JOSEPH EDWARDS

arihant
SUCCESS AND NOTHING LESS

ARIHANT PRAKASHAN (Series), MEERUT



**Administrative & Production Offices**

**Regd. Office**

'Ramchhaya' 4577/15, Agarwal Road, Darya Ganj, New Delhi -110002
Tele: 011- 47630600, 43518550

**Head Office**

Kalindi, TP Nagar, Meerut (UP) - 250002
Tel: 0121-7156203, 7156204

**Sales & Support Offices**

Agra, Ahmedabad, Bengaluru, Bareilly, Chennai, Delhi, Guwahati, Hyderabad, Jaipur, Jhansi, Kolkata, Lucknow, Nagpur & Pune.

**PRICE** ₹140.00

**PO No :** TXT-59-T065519-06-25

Published by Arihant Publications (India) Ltd.

For further information about the books published by Arihant, log on to www.arihantbooks.com or e-mail at info@arihantbooks.com

Follow us on

# PREFACE

The present small volume is intended to form a sound introduction to a study of the Differential Calculus suitable for the beginner. It does not therefore aim at completeness, but rather at the omission.of all portions which are usually considered best left for a later reading. At the same time it has been constructed to include those parts of the subject prescribed in Schedule I. of the Regulations for the Mathematical Tripos Examination for the reading of students for Mathematical Honours in the University of Cambridge.

Particular attention has been given to the examples which are freely interspersed throughout the text. For the most part they are of the simplest kind, requiring but little analytical skill. Yet it is hoped they will prove sufficient to give practice in the processes they are intended to illustrate.

It is assumed that in commencing to work at the Differential Calculus the student possesses a fair knowledge of Algebra as far as the Exponential and Logarithmic Theorems; of Trigonometry as far as Demoivre's Theorem, and of the rudiments of Cartesian Geometry as far as the equations of the several Conic Sections in their simplest forms.

Being to some extent an abbreviation of my larger Treatise my acknowledgments are due to the same authorities as there mentioned. My thanks are also due to several friends for useful suggestions with regard to the desirable scope of the book.

Any suggestions for its improvement or for its better adaptation to the requirements of junior students, or lists of errata, will be gratefully received.

JOSEPH EDWARDS.

80, Cambridge Gardens,
North Kensinton, W.

# CONTENTS

## INTEGRAL CALCULUS

# DIFFERENTIAL CALCULUS.

## CHAPTER I.

## LIMITING VALUES. ELEMENTARY UNDETERMINED FORMS.

**1. Object of the Differential Calculus.** When an increasing or decreasing quantity is made the subject of mathematical treatment, it often becomes necessary to estimate its rate of growth. It is our principal object to describe the method to be employed and to exhibit applications of the processes described.

**2. Explanation of Terms.** The frequently recurring terms "Constant," "Variable," "Function," will be understood from the following example:

Let the student imagine a triangle of which two sides $x$, $y$ are unknown but of which the angle ($A$) included between those sides is known. The area ($\Delta$) is expressed by $\Delta = \frac{1}{2} xy \sin A$.

The quantity $A$ is a "*constant*" for by hypothesis it retains the same value, though the sides $x$ and $y$ may change in length while the triangle is under observation. The quantities $x$, $y$ and $\Delta$ are therefore called *variables*. $\Delta$, whose value *depends upon* those of $x$ and $y$, is called the *dependent variable*; $x$ and $y$, whose values may be any whatever, and may either or both take up any values which may be assigned to them, are called *independent variables*.

The quantity $\Delta$ whose value thus depends upon those of $x$, $y$ and $A$ is said to be a *function* of $x$, $y$ and $A$.

**3. Definitions.** We are thus led to the following definitions :

(*a*) A CONSTANT *is a quantity which, during any set of mathematical operations, retains the same value.*

(*b*) A VARIABLE *is a quantity which, during any set of mathematical operations, does not retain the same value but is capable of assuming different values.*

(*c*) *An* INDEPENDENT VARIABLE *is one which may take up any arbitrary value that may be assigned to it.*

(*d*) A DEPENDENT VARIABLE *is one which assumes its value in consequence of some second variable or system of variables taking up any set of arbitrary values that may be assigned to them.*

(e) *When one quantity depends upon another or upon a system of others in such a manner as to assume a definite value when a system of definite values is given to the others it is called a* FUNCTION *of those others.*

**4. Notation.** The usual notation to express that one variable $y$ is a function of another $x$ is $y = f(x)$ or $y = F(x)$ or $y = \phi(x)$.

Occasionally the brackets are dispensed with when no confusion can thereby arise. Thus $fx$ may be sometimes written for $f(x)$. If $u$ be an unknown function of several variables $x, y, z$, we may express the fact by the equation $u = f(x, y, z)$.

**5.** It has become conventional to use the letters $x, b, c \ldots \alpha, \beta, \gamma \ldots$ from the beginning of the alphabet to denote constants and to retain later letters, such as $u, v, w, x, y, z$ and the Greek letters $\xi, \eta, \zeta$ for variables.

**6. Limiting Values.** The following illustrations will explain the meaning of the term "LIMITING VALUE" :

(1) We say $\cdot\dot{6} = \frac{2}{3}$, by which we mean that by taking enough sixes we can make $\cdot 666\ldots$ *differ by as little as we please* from $\frac{2}{3}$.

(2) The limit of $\frac{2x+3}{x+1}$ when $x$ is indefinitely diminished is 3.

For the difference between $\frac{2x+3}{x+1}$ and 3 is $\frac{x}{x+1}$, and by diminishing $x$ indefinitely this *difference can be made less than any assignable quantity however small.*

The expression can also be written $\dfrac{2+\frac{3}{x}}{1+\frac{1}{x}}$, which shews that if $x$ be increased indefinitely it can be made to continually approach and to differ *by less than any assignable quantity* from 2, which is therefore its limit in that case. It is useful to adopt the notation $Lt_{x=a}$ to denote the words "the Limit when $x = a$ of."

Thus $$Lt_{x=0} \frac{2x+3}{x+1} = 3; Lt_{x=\infty} \frac{2x+3}{x+1} = 2.$$

(3) If an equilateral polygon be inscribed in any closed curve and the sides of the polygon be decreased indefinitely, and at the same time their number be increased indefinitely, the polygon continually approximates to the form of the curve, and ultimately *differs from it in area by less than any assignable magnitude,* and the curve is said to be the *limit* of the polygon inscribed in it.

**7.** We thus arrive at the following general definition:

DEF. *The* LIMIT *of a function for an assigned value of the independent variable is that value from which the function may be made to differ by less than any assignable quantity however small by making the independent variable approach sufficiently near its assigned value.*

## 8. Undetermined forms.

When a function involves the independent variable in such a manner that for a certain assigned value of that variable its value *cannot be found by simply substituting* that value of the variable, the function is said to take an undetermined form.

One of the commonest cases occurring is that of a fraction whose numerator and denominator both vanish for the value of the variable referred to.

Let the student imagine a triangle whose sides are made of a material capable of shrinking indefinitely till they are smaller than any conceivable quantity. To fix the ideas suppose it to be originally a triangle whose sides are 3, 4 and 5 inches long, and suppose that the shrinkage is uniform. As the shrinkage proceeds the sides retain the same mutual ratio and may at any instant be written $3m, 4m, 5m$ and the angles remain unaltered. It thus appears that though each of these sides is ultimately immeasurably small, and to all practical purposes zero, they still retain the same mutual ratio 3 : 4 : 5 which they had before the shrinkage began.

These considerations should convince the student *that the ultimate ratio of two vanishing quantities is not necessarily zero or unity.*

**9.** Consider the fraction $\dfrac{x^2 - a^2}{x - a}$; what is its value when $x = a$? Both numerator and denominator vanish when $x$ is put $= a$. But it would be incorrect to assume that the fraction therefore takes the value unity. It is equally incorrect to suppose the value to be zero for the reason that its numerator is evanescent; or that it is infinite since its denominator is evanescent, as the beginner is often fallaciously led to believe. If we wish to evaluate this expression we must *never put $x$ actually equal to $a$.* We may however put $x = a + h$ where $h$ is anything other than zero.

Thus $\dfrac{x^2 - a^2}{x - a} = 2a + h,$

and it is now apparent that by making $h$ indefinitely small (so that the value of $x$ is made to approach indefinitely closely to its assigned value $a$) we may make the expression differ from $2a$ by less than any assignable quantity. Therefore $2a$ is the limiting value of the given fraction.

**10.** Two functions of the same independent variable are said to be *ultimately equal* when as the independent variable approaches indefinitely near its assigned value the *limit of their ratio* is unity.

Thus $Lt_{\theta=0} \dfrac{\sin\theta}{\theta} = 1$ by trigonometry, and therefore when an angle is indefinitely diminished its sine and its circular measure are ultimately equal.

## EXAMPLES

1. Find the limit when $x = 0$ of $\dfrac{y}{x^2}$,

   (*a*) when $y = mx$, (*b*) when $y = x^2/a$, (*c*) when $y = ax^2 + b$.

2. Find $Lt \dfrac{ax+b}{bx+a}$,

   (i) when $x = 0$,

   (ii) when $x = \infty$.

3. Find $Lt_{x=a} \dfrac{x^3 - a^3}{x - a}$; $Lt_{x=a} \dfrac{x^4 - a^4}{x - a}$; $Lt_{x=a} \dfrac{x^5 - a^5}{x^2 - a^2}$.

4. Find the limit of $\dfrac{ax + \dfrac{b}{x}}{cx + \dfrac{d}{x}}$,

   (i) when $x = 0$,

   (ii) when $x = \infty$.

5. Find $Lt_{x=1} \dfrac{3x^2 - 4x + 1}{x^2 - 4x + 3}$.

6. The opposite angles of a cyclic quadrilateral are supplementary. What does this proposition become in the limit when two angular points coincide?

7. Evaluate the fraction $\dfrac{x^3 - 6x^2 + 11x - 6}{x^{-3} - 6x^{-2} + 11x^{-1} - 6}$ for the values $x = \infty$, 3, 2, 1, $\dfrac{1}{2}$, $\dfrac{1}{3}$, 0, $-\infty$.

8. Evaluate $Lt_{x=1} \dfrac{\sqrt{x} - 1}{\sqrt[3]{x} - 1}$ and $Lt_{x=0} \dfrac{\sqrt{1+x} - 1}{x}$.

**11. Four Important Limits.** The following limits are important :

(I) $Lt_{\theta=0} \dfrac{\sin\theta}{\theta} = 1$; $Lt_{\theta=0} \cos\theta = 1$,

(II) $Lt_{x=1} \dfrac{x^n - 1}{x - 1} = n$,

(III) $Lt_{x=\infty} \left(1 + \dfrac{1}{x}\right)^x = e$, where $e$ is the base of the Napierian logarithms,

(IV) $Lt_{x=0} \dfrac{a^x - 1}{x} = \log_e a$.

**12.** (I) The limits (I) can be found in any standard text-book on Plane Trigonometry.

**13.** (II) To prove $Lt_{x=1} \dfrac{x^n - 1}{x - 1} = n$. Let $x = 1 + z$. Then when $x$ approaches unity $z$ approaches zero. Hence we can consider $z$ to be less than 1, and we may therefore apply the Binomial to the expansion of $(1 + z)^n$ whatever $n$ may be.

Thus
$$Lt_{x=1} \frac{x^n - 1}{x - 1} = Lt_{z=0} \frac{(1+z)^n - 1}{z}$$
$$= Lt_{z=0} \frac{nz + \dfrac{n(n-1)}{1\cdot 2} z^2 + \ldots}{z}$$
$$= Lt_{z=0} \left\{ n + \frac{n(n-1)}{1\cdot 2} z + \ldots \right\} = n.$$

**14.** (III) To prove $Lt_{x=\infty} \left(1 + \dfrac{1}{x}\right)^x = e$.

Let $y = \left(1 + \dfrac{1}{x}\right)^x$, then $\log_e y = x \log_e \left(1 + \dfrac{1}{x}\right)$.

Now $x$ is about to become infinitely large, and therefore $\dfrac{1}{x}$ may be throughout regarded as *less than unity*, and we may expand by the Logarithmic Theorem.

Thus $\log_e y = x\left\{\dfrac{1}{x} - \dfrac{1}{2x^2} + \dfrac{1}{3x^3} - \ldots\right\} = 1 - \dfrac{1}{2x} + \dfrac{1}{3x^2} - \ldots$

$$= 1 - \frac{1}{x} \times [\text{a } \textit{convergent series}].$$

Thus when $x$ becomes infinitely large

$$Lt \log_e y = 1,$$

and $$Lt\, y = e,$$

i.e. $$Lt_{x=\infty}\left(1+\frac{1}{x}\right)^x = e.$$

COR. $$Lt_{x=\infty}\left(1+\frac{a}{x}\right)^x = Lt_{\frac{x}{a}=\infty}\left\{\left(1+\frac{a}{x}\right)^{\frac{x}{a}}\right\}^a = e^a.$$

**15.** (IV) To prove $Lt_{x=0}\dfrac{a^x-1}{x} = \log_e a.$

Assume the expansion for $a^x$, viz.

$$a^x = 1 + x\log_e a + \frac{x^2}{2!}(\log_e a)^2 + \ldots,$$

which is shewn in Algebra to be a *convergent series.*

Hence $$\frac{a^x-1}{x} = \log_e a + x\frac{(\log_e a)^2}{2!} + \ldots$$
$$= \log_e a + x \times [\text{a } \textit{convergent series}].$$

And the limit of the right-hand side, when $x$ is indefinitely diminished, is clearly $\log_e a$.

## 16. Method of Procedure.

The rule for evaluating a function which takes the undetermined form $\frac{0}{0}$ when the independent variable $x$ ultimately coincides with its assigned value $a$ is as follows:—

Put $x = a + h$ and *expand both numerator and denominator* of the fraction. It will now become apparent that the reason why both numerator and denominator ultimately vanish is that some power of $h$ is a common factor of each. This should now be *divided out.* Finally let $h$ diminish indefinitely so that $x$ becomes ultimately $a$, and the true limiting value of the function will be clear.

In the particular case in which $x$ is to become *zero* the expansion of numerator and denominator in powers of $x$ should be at once proceeded with without any preliminary substitution for $x$.

In the case in which $x$ is to become infinite, put

$$x = \frac{1}{y},$$

so that when $x$ becomes $\infty$, $y$ becomes 0.

Several other undetermined forms occur, *viz.* $0 \times \infty, \frac{\infty}{\infty}, \infty - \infty, 0^0, \infty^0, 1^\infty$, but they may be made to depend upon the form $\frac{0}{0}$ by special artifices.

The method thus indicated will be best understood by examining the mode of solution of the following examples :—

**Ex. 1.** *Find* $Lt_{x=1} \dfrac{x^7 - 2x^5 + 1}{x^3 - 3x^2 + 2}$.

This is of the form $\frac{0}{0}$ if we put $x = 1$. Therefore we put $x = 1 + h$ and expand. We thus obtain

$$Lt_{x=1} \frac{x^7 - 2x^5 + 1}{x^3 - 3x^2 + 2} = Lt_{h=0} \frac{(1+h)^7 - 2(1+h)^5 + 1}{(1+h)^3 - 3(1+h)^2 + 2}$$

$$= Lt_{h=0} \frac{(1 + 7h + 21h^2 + ...) - 2(1 + 5h + 10h^2 + ...) + 1}{(1 + 3h + 3h^2 + ...) - 3(1 + 2h + h^2) + 2}$$

$$= Lt_{h=0} \frac{-3h + h^2 + ...}{-3h + ...}$$

$$= Lt_{h=0} \frac{-3 + h + ...}{-3 + ...}$$

$$= \frac{-3}{-3} = 1.$$

It will be seen from this example that in the process of expansion it is only necessary in general *to retain a few of the lowest powers of h*.

**Ex. 2.** *Find* $Lt_{x=0} \dfrac{a^x - b^x}{x}$.

Here numerator and denominator both vanish if $x$ be put equal to 0. We therefore expand $a^x$ and $b^x$ by the exponential theorem.

Hence $Lt_{x=0} \dfrac{a^x - b^x}{x}$

$$= Lt_{x=0} \frac{\left\{1 + x\log_e a + \frac{x^2}{2!}(\log_e a)^2 + ...\right\} - \left\{1 + x\log_e b + \frac{x^2}{2!}(\log_e b)^2 + ...\right\}}{x}$$

$$= Lt_{x=0} \left\{\log_e a - \log_e b + \frac{x}{2!}(\overline{\log_e a}|^2 - \overline{\log_e b}|^2) + ...\right\}$$

$$= \log_e a - \log_e b = \log_e \frac{a}{b}.$$

**Ex. 3.** Find $Lt_{x=0} \left(\dfrac{\tan x}{x}\right)^{\frac{1}{x^2}}$.

Since $\dfrac{\tan x}{x} = \dfrac{1}{\cos x} \cdot \dfrac{\sin x}{x}$,

we have $Lt_{x=0} \dfrac{\tan x}{x} = 1$.

Hence the form assumed by $\left(\frac{\tan x}{x}\right)^{\frac{1}{x^2}}$ is an undetermined form $1^\infty$ when we put $x = 0$.

Expand $\sin x$ and $\cos x$ in powers of $x$. This gives

$$Lt_{x=0}\left(\frac{\tan x}{x}\right)^{\frac{1}{x^2}} = Lt_{x=0}\left(\frac{x - \frac{x^3}{3!} + \ldots}{x - \frac{x^3}{2!} + \ldots}\right)^{\frac{1}{x^2}}$$

$$= Lt_{x=0}\left(1 + \frac{x^2}{3} + \text{higher powers of } x\right)^{\frac{1}{x^2}}$$

$$= Lt_{x=0}\left\{1 + \frac{x^2}{3}(1 + \ldots)\right\}^{\frac{1}{x^2}}$$

$$= Lt_{x=0}\left(1 + \frac{x^2 l}{3}\right)^{\frac{1}{x^2}},$$

where $l$ is a series in ascending powers of $x$ whose first term (and therefore whose limit when $x = 0$) is unity. Hence

$$Lt_{x=0}\left(\frac{\tan x}{x}\right)^{\frac{1}{x^2}} = Lt_{x=0}\left\{\left(1 + \frac{x^2 l}{3}\right)^{\frac{3}{lx^2}}\right\}^{\frac{l}{3}} = e^{\frac{1}{3}}, \text{ by Art. 14.}$$

**Ex. 4.** *Find* $Lt_{x=1} x^{\frac{1}{1-x}}$.

This expression is of the undetermined form $1^\infty$.

Put $1 - x = y$,

and therefore, if $x = 1$, $y = 0$;

therefore Limit required $= Lt_{y=0}(1 - y)^{\frac{1}{y}} = e^{-1}$ (Art. 14).

**Ex. 5.** $Lt_{x=\infty} x(a^{\frac{1}{x}} - 1)$.

This is of the undetermined form $\infty \times 0$.

Put $x = \frac{1}{y}$;

therefore, if $x = \infty$, $y = 0$,

and Limit required $= Lt_{y=0}\frac{a^y - 1}{y} = \log_e a$ (Art. 15).

**17.** The following Algebraical and Trigonometrical series are added, as they are wanted for immediate use. They should be learnt thoroughly.

$$(1+x)^n = 1 + nx + \frac{n(n-1)}{1\cdot 2}x^2 + \frac{n(n-1)(n-2)}{1\cdot 2\cdot 3}x^3 + \ldots$$

$$(1-x)^{-n} = 1 + nx + \frac{n(n+1)}{1\cdot 2}x^2 + \frac{n(n+1)(n+2)}{1\cdot 2\cdot 3}x^3 + \ldots$$

$$a^x = 1 + x\log_e a + \frac{x^2(\log_e a)^2}{2!} + \frac{x^3(\log_e a)^3}{3!} + \ldots$$

$$e^x = 1 + x + \frac{x^2}{2!} + \frac{x^3}{3!} + \ldots$$

$$\log_e(1+x) = x - \frac{x^2}{2} + \frac{x^3}{3} - \frac{x^4}{4} + \ldots.$$

$$\log_e(1-x) = -x - \frac{x^2}{2} - \frac{x^3}{3} - \frac{x^4}{4} - \ldots.$$

$$\frac{1}{2}\log_e\frac{1+x}{1-x} = x + \frac{x^3}{3} + \frac{x^5}{5} + \ldots$$

$$\tan^{-1}x = x - \frac{x^3}{3} + \frac{x^5}{5} - \ldots$$

$$\cos x = 1 - \frac{x^2}{2!} + \frac{x^4}{4!} - \ldots$$

$$\sin x = x - \frac{x^3}{3!} + \frac{x^5}{5!} - \ldots$$

$$\cosh x\left[\text{which} \equiv \frac{e^x + e^{-x}}{2}\right] = 1 + \frac{x^2}{2!} + \frac{x^4}{4!} + \ldots$$

$$\sinh x\left[\text{which} \equiv \frac{e^x - e^{-x}}{2}\right] = x + \frac{x^3}{3!} + \frac{x^5}{5!} + \ldots$$

## EXAMPLES

*Find the values of the following limits:*

**1.** $Lt_{x=0}\dfrac{a^x - 1}{b^x - 1}$.

**2.** $Lt_{x=1}\dfrac{x^{\frac{3}{2}} - 1}{x^{\frac{5}{2}} - 1}$.

**3.** $Lt_{x=1}\dfrac{x^m - 1}{x^n - 1}$.

**4.** $Lt_{x=0}\dfrac{(1+x)^{\frac{1}{n}} - 1}{x}$.

**5.** $Lt_{x=1}\dfrac{x^4 + x^3 - x^2 - 5x + 4}{x^3 - x^2 - x + 1}$.

6. $Lt_{x=1} \dfrac{x^5 - 2x^3 - 4x^2 + 9x - 4}{x^4 - 2x^3 + 2x - 1}$. 7. $Lt_{x=0} \dfrac{e^x - e^{-x}}{x}$.

8. $Lt_{x=0} \dfrac{e^x + e^{-x} - 2}{x^2}$. 9. $Lt_{x=0} \dfrac{x \cos x - \log_e (1+x)}{x^2}$.

10. $Lt_{x=0} \dfrac{xe^x - \log_e (1+x)}{x^2}$. 11. $Lt_{x=0} \dfrac{x - \sin x \cos x}{x^3}$.

12. $Lt_{x=0} \dfrac{\sin^{-1} x - x}{x^3 \cos x}$. 13. $Lt_{x=0} \dfrac{\cosh x - \cos x}{x \sin x}$.

14. $Lt_{x=0} \dfrac{\sin^{-1} x}{\tan^{-1} x}$. 15. $Lt_{x=0} \dfrac{\sin^{-1} x - \sinh x}{x^5}$.

16. $Lt_{x=0} \dfrac{x \cos^3 x - \log_e (1+x) - \sin^{-1} \dfrac{x^2}{2}}{x^3}$.

17. $Lt_{x=0} \dfrac{2 \sin x + \dfrac{1}{2} \log_e \dfrac{1+x}{1-x} - 3x}{x^5}$.

18. $Lt_{x=0} \dfrac{e^x \sin x - x - x^2}{x^2 + x \log_e (1-x)}$. 19. $Lt_{x=0} \dfrac{x^3 e^{\frac{x^4}{4}} - \sin^{\frac{3}{2}} x^2}{x^7}$.

20. $Lt_{x=0} \left( \dfrac{\tan x}{x} \right)^{\frac{1}{x}}$. 21. $Lt_{x=0} \left( \dfrac{\tan x}{x} \right)^{\frac{1}{x^3}}$.

22. $Lt_{x=0} \left( \dfrac{\sin x}{x} \right)^{\frac{1}{x}}$. 23. $Lt_{x=0} \left( \dfrac{\sin x}{x} \right)^{\frac{1}{x^2}}$.

24. $Lt_{x=0} \left( \dfrac{\sin x}{x} \right)^{\frac{1}{x^3}}$. 25. $Lt_{x=0} (\text{covers } x)^{\frac{1}{x}}$.

26. $Lt_{x=\frac{\pi}{2}} (\text{cosec } x)^{\tan^2 x}$.

# CHAPTER II.

# DIFFERENTIATION FROM THE DEFINITION.

## 18. Tangent of a Curve; Definition; Direction.

Let $AB$ be an arc of a curve traced in the plane of the paper, $OX$ a fixed straight line in the same plane.

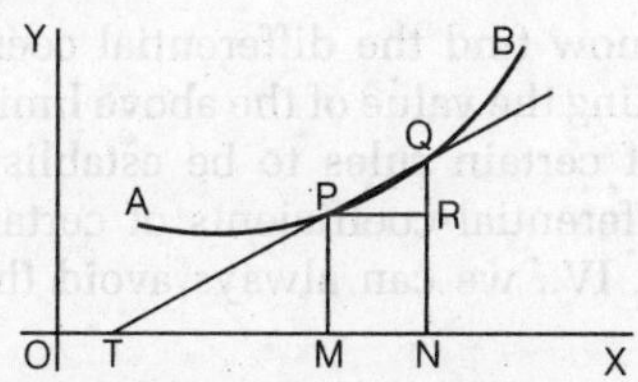


Let $P, Q$, be two points on the curve; $PM, QN$, perpendiculars on $OX$, and $PR$ the perpendicular from $P$ on $QN$. Join $P, Q$, and let $QP$ be produced to cut $OX$ at $T$.

When $Q$, *travelling along the curve*, approaches indefinitely near to $P$, the limiting position of chord $QP$ is called the TANGENT at $P$. $QR$ and $PR$ both ultimately vanish, but the limit of their ratio is in *general finite*; for $Lt\ \dfrac{RQ}{PR} = Lt \tan RPQ = Lt \tan XTP =$ *tangent of the angle which the tangent at P to the curve makes with OX*.

If $y = \phi(x)$ be the equation of the curve and $x, x + h$ the abscissae of the points $P, Q$ respectively; then $MP = \phi(x)$, $NQ = \phi(x + h)$, $RQ = \phi(x + h) - \phi(x)$ and $PR = h$.

Thus $$Lt\ \frac{RQ}{PR} = Lt_{h=0} \frac{\phi(x+h) - \phi(x)}{h}$$

Hence, to draw the tangent at any point $(x, y)$ on the curve $y = \phi(x)$, we must draw a line through that point, making with the axis of $x$ an angle whose tangent is

$$Lt_{h=0} \frac{\phi(x+h) - \phi(x)}{h};$$

and if this limit be called $m$, the equation of the tangent at $P(x, y)$ will be $Y - y = m(X - x)$,

$X, Y$ being the current co-ordinates of any point on the tangent ; for the line represented by this equation goes through the point $(x, y)$, and makes with the axis of $x$ and angle whose tangent is $m$.

## 19. DEF.—DIFFERENTIAL COEFFICIENT.

*Let $\phi(x)$ denote any function of x, and $\phi(x+h)$ the same function of x + h; then* $Lt_{h=0}\dfrac{\phi(x+h)-\phi(x)}{h}$ *is called* the FIRST DERIVED FUNCTION *or DIFFERENTIAL COEFFICIENT of $\phi(x)$ with respect to x.*

The operation of finding this limit is called *differentiating* $\phi(x)$.

## 20. Geometrical meaning.

The geometrical meaning of the above limit is indicated in the last article, where it is shewn to be *the tangent of the angle ψ which the tangent at any definite point (x, y) on the curve $y = \phi(x)$ makes with the axis of x.*

## 21.

We can now find the differential coefficient of any proposed function by investigating the value of the above limit; but it will be seen later on that, by means of certain rules to be established in Chap. III. and a knowledge of the differential coefficients of certain standard forms to be investigated in Chap. IV., we can always avoid the labour of an *ab initio* evaluation.

**Ex. 1.** Find from the definition the differential coefficient of $\dfrac{x^2}{a}$, where $a$ is constant; and the equation of the tangent to the curve $ay = x^2$.

Here $\qquad \phi(x) = \dfrac{x^2}{a},\ \phi(x+h) = \dfrac{(x+h)^2}{a},$

therefore
$$Lt_{h=0}\frac{\phi(x+h)-\phi(x)}{h} = Lt_{h=0}\frac{(x+h)^2-x^2}{ha}$$
$$= Lt_{h=0}\frac{2xh+h^2}{ha} = Lt_{h=0}\frac{(2x+h)}{a} = \frac{2x}{a}.$$

The geometrical interpretation of this result is that, if a tangent be drawn to the parabola $ay = x^2$ at the point $(x, y)$, it will be inclined to the axis of $x$ at the angle $\tan^{-1}\dfrac{2x}{a}$.

The equation of the tangent is therefore
$$Y - y = \frac{2x}{a}(X - x).$$

**Ex. 2.** Find from the definition the differential coefficient of $\log_e \sin\dfrac{x}{a}$, where $a$ is a constant.

Here $\qquad \phi(x) = \log_e \sin\dfrac{x}{a},$

and
$$Lt_{h=0}\frac{\phi(x+h)-\phi(x)}{h} = Lt_{h=0}\frac{\log_e \sin\dfrac{x+h}{a} - \log_e \sin\dfrac{x}{a}}{h}$$

$$= Lt_{h=0} \frac{1}{h} \log_e \frac{\sin\frac{x}{a}\cos\frac{h}{a} + \cos\frac{x}{a}\sin\frac{h}{a}}{\sin\frac{x}{a}}$$

$$= Lt_{h=0} \frac{1}{h} \log_e \left(1 + \frac{h}{a}\cot\frac{x}{a} + \text{higher powers of } h\right)$$

$\left[\text{by substituting for } \sin\frac{h}{a} \text{ and } \cos\frac{h}{a} \text{ their expansions in powers of } \frac{h}{a}\right]$

$$= Lt_{h=0} \frac{\frac{h}{a}\cot\frac{x}{a} - \text{higher powers of } h}{h}$$

[by expanding the logarithm]

$$= \frac{1}{a}\cot\frac{x}{a}.$$

Hence the tangent at any point on the curve $\frac{y}{a} = \log_e \sin\frac{x}{a}$ is inclined to the axis of $x$ at an angle whose tangent is $\cot\frac{x}{a}$; that is at an angle $\frac{\pi}{2} - \frac{x}{a}$, and the equation of the tangent at the point $x, y$ is

$Y - y = \cot\frac{x}{a}(X - x).$

# EXAMPLES

*Find the equation of the tangent at the point (x, y) on each of the following curves :*

**1.** $y = x^3$. **2.** $y = x^4$.

**3.** $y = \sqrt{x}$. **4.** $y = x^2 + x^3$.

**5.** $y = \sin x$. **6.** $y = e^x$.

**7.** $y = \log_e x$. **8.** $y = \tan x$.

**9.** $x^2 + y^2 = c^2$. **10.** $x^2/a^2 + y^2/b^2 = 1$.

**22. Notation.** It is convenient to use the notation $\delta x$ for the same quantity which we have denoted by $h$, viz. a small but finite increase in the value of $x$. We may similarly denote by $\delta y$ the *consequent* change in the value of $y$. Thus if $(x, y)$, $(x + \delta x, y + \delta y)$ be contiguous points upon a given curve $y = \phi(x)$, we have

$$y + \delta y = \phi(x + \delta x),$$

and

$$\delta y = \phi(x + \delta x) - \phi(x).$$

Thus the differential coefficient

$$Lt_{\delta x=0}\frac{\phi(x+\delta x)-\phi(x)}{\delta x}$$

may be written $\quad Lt_{\delta x=0}\dfrac{\delta y}{\delta x},$

which more directly indicates the geometrical meaning $Lt_{PR=0}\dfrac{RQ}{PR}$ pointed out in Art. 18.

The result of the operation expressed by

$$Lt_{h=0}\frac{\phi(x+h)-\phi(x)}{h},$$

or by $\quad Lt_{\delta x=0}\dfrac{\delta y}{\delta x}$, is denoted by $\dfrac{d}{dx}y$ or $\dfrac{dy}{dx}$.

The student must *guard against the fallacious notion that dx and dy are separate small quantities*, as $\delta x$ and $\delta y$ are. He must remember that $\dfrac{d}{dx}$ is a *symbol of operation* which when applied to any function $\phi(x)$ means that we are

(1) *to increase x to x + h,*

(2) *to subtract the original value of the function,*

(3) *to divide the remainder by h,*

(4) *to evaluate the limit when h ultimately vanishes.*

Other notations expressing the same thing are

$$\frac{d\phi(x)}{dx},\frac{d\phi}{dx},\phi'(x),\phi',\dot{\phi},\phi_x,y',\dot{y},y_1.$$

## EXAMPLES

*Find $\dfrac{dy}{dx}$ in the following cases:*

**1.** $y=2x$. **2.** $y=2+x$.

**3.** $y=2+3x$. **4.** $y=2+3x^2$.

**5.** $y=\dfrac{1}{x}$. **6.** $y=\dfrac{1}{x}+a$.

**7.** $y=\dfrac{1}{x^2}+a$. **8.** $y=a\sqrt{x}$.

**9.** $y=\sqrt{x^2+a^2}$. **10.** $y=e^{\sqrt{x}}$.

**11.** $y=e^{\sin x}$. **12.** $y=\log_e \sec x$.

**13.** $y=x\sin x$. **14.** $y=\dfrac{\sin x}{x}$.

**15.** $y=x^x$.

**23. Aspect of the Differential Coefficient as a Rate- Measurer.** When a particle is in motion in a given manner the space described is a function of the time of describing it. We may consider the time as an independent variable, and the space described in that time as the dependent variable.

The rate of change of position of the particle is called its velocity.

If *uniform* the velocity is measured by the space described in one second; if *variable*, the velocity at any instant is measured by the space which would be described in one second if, for that second, the velocity remained unchanged.

Suppose a space $s$ to have been described in time $t$ with varying velocity, and an additional space $\delta s$ to be described in the additional time $\delta t$. Let $v_1$ and $v_2$ be the greatest and least values of the velocity during the interval $\delta t$; then the spaces which would have been described with uniform velocities $v_1$, $v_2$, in time $\delta t$ are $v_1 \delta t$ and $v_2 \delta t$, and are respectively greater and less than the actual space $\delta s$.

Hence $v_1, \dfrac{\delta s}{\delta t}$, and $v_2$ are in descending order of magnitude.

If then $\delta t$ be diminished indefinitely, we have in the limit $v_1 = v_2 =$ the velocity at the instant considered, which is therefore represented by $Lt \dfrac{\delta s}{\delta t}$, i.e. by $\dfrac{ds}{dt}$.

**24.** It appears therefore that we may give another interpretation to a differential coefficient, viz. that $\dfrac{ds}{dt}$ means the *rate of increase of s in point of time.* Similarly $\dfrac{dx}{dt}, \dfrac{dy}{dt}$, mean the *rates of change* of $x$ and $y$ respectively in point of time, and *measure the velocities,* resolved parallel to the axes, of a moving particle whose co-ordinates at the instant under consideration are $x, y$. If $x$ and $y$ be given functions of $t$, and therefore the path of the particle defined, and if $\delta x, \delta y, \delta t$, be simultaneous infinitesimal increments of $x, y, t$, then

$$\frac{dy}{dx} = Lt \frac{\delta y}{\delta x} = Lt \frac{\dfrac{\delta y}{\delta t}}{\dfrac{\delta x}{\delta t}} = \frac{\dfrac{dy}{dt}}{\dfrac{dx}{dt}}$$

and therefore represents *the ratio of the rate of change of y to that of x.* The rate of change of $x$ is arbitrary, and if we choose it to be unit velocity, then $\dfrac{dy}{dx} = \dfrac{dy}{dt} =$ absolute rate of change of $y$.

## 25. Meaning of Sign of Differential Coefficient.

If $x$ be increasing with $t$, the $x$-velocity is positive, whilst, if $x$ be decreasing while $t$ increases, that velocity is negative. Similarly for $y$.

Moreover, since $\dfrac{dy}{dx} = \dfrac{\frac{dy}{dt}}{\frac{dx}{dt}}$, $\dfrac{dy}{dx}$ is *positive when $x$ and $y$ increase or decrease together, but negative when one increases as the other decreases.*

This is obvious also from the geometrical interpretation of $\dfrac{dy}{dx}$. For, if $x$ and $y$ are *increasing together*. $\dfrac{dy}{dx}$ is the *tangent of an acute angle and therefore positive*, while if, as *$x$ increases $y$ decreases*, $\dfrac{dy}{dx}$ represents the *tangent of an obtuse angle and is negative.*

## 26.

The above article frequently affords important information with regard to the sign of a given expression. For if, for instance, $\phi(x)$ be a continuous function which is positive when $x = a$ and when $x = b$, and if $\phi'(x)$ be of one sign for all values of $x$ lying between $a$ and $b$ so that it is known that $\phi(x)$ is always increasing or always decreasing from the one value $\phi(a)$ to the other $\phi(b)$, it will follow that $\phi(x)$ must be positive for all intermediate values of $x$.

**Ex.** Let $\phi(x) = (x-1)e^x + 1$.

Here $\phi(0) = 0$ and $\phi'(x) = Lt_{h=0}\dfrac{(x+h-1)e^{x+h} - (x-1)e^x}{h}$

$$= Lt_{h=0}\frac{(x+h-1)\left(1+h+\frac{h^2}{2!}+\ldots\right)-(x-1)}{h}e^x$$

$$= Lt_{h=0}\frac{hx + \text{higher powers of } h}{h}e^x = xe^x.$$

So that $\phi'(x)$ is positive for all positive values of $x$. Therefore as $x$ increases from 0 to $\infty$, $\phi(x)$ is always increasing. Hence since its initial value is zero the expression is positive for all positive values of $x$.

## EXAMPLES

1. Differentiate the following expressions, and shew that they are each positive for all positive values of $x$ :

(i) $(x-2)e^x + x + 2$, (ii) $(x-3)e^x + \frac{x^2}{2} + 2x + 3$,

(iii) $x - \log_e(1+x)$.

2. In the curve $y = ce^{\frac{x}{c}}$, if $\psi$ be the angle which the tangent at any point makes with the axis of $x$, then prove $y = c\tan\psi$.

3. In the curve $y = c\cosh\frac{x}{c}$, prove $y = c\sec\psi$.

4. In the curve $3b^2y = x^3 - 3ax^2$ find the points at which the tangent is parallel to the axis of $x$. [N.B.—This requires that $\tan\psi = 0$.]

5. Find at what points of the ellipse $\frac{x^2}{a^2} + \frac{y^2}{b^2} = 1$ the tangent cuts off equal intercepts from the axes.
[N.B.—This requires that $\tan\psi = \pm 1$.]

6. Prove that if a particle move so that the space described is proportional to the square of the time of description, the velocity will be proportional to the time, and the rate of increase of the velocity will be constant.

7. Shew that if a particle moves so that the space described is given by $s \propto \sin\mu t$, where $\mu$ is a constant, the rate of increase of the velocity is proportional to the distance of the particle measured along its path from a fixed position.

8. Shew that the function $x\sin x + \cos x + \cos^2 x$

continually diminishes as $x$ increases from 0 to $\pi/3$.

9. If $y = 2x - \tan^{-1}x - \log_e(x + \sqrt{1+x^2})$,
shew that $y$ continually increases as $x$ changes from zero to positive infinity.

10. A triangle has two of its angular points at $(a, 0), (0, b)$, and the third $(x, y)$ is moveable along the line $y = x$. Shew that if $A$ be its area $2\frac{dA}{dx} = a + b$, and interpret this result geometrically.

11. If $A$ be the area of a circle of radius $x$, shew that the circumference is $\frac{dA}{dx}$. Interpret this geometrically.

12. $O$ is a given point and $NP$ a given straight line upon which $ON$ is the perpendicular. The radius $OP$ rotates about $O$ with the constant angular velocity $\omega$. Shew that $NP$ increases at the rate

$$\omega \cdot ON\sec^2 NOP.$$

# CHAPTER III.

# FUNDAMENTAL PROPOSITIONS.

**27.** IT will often be convenient in proving standard results to denote by a small letter the function of $x$ considered, and by the corresponding capital the same function of $x+h$, e.g. if $u=\phi(x)$, then $U=\phi(x+h)$, or if $u=a^x$, then $U=a^{x+h}$.

Accordingly we shall have $\frac{du}{dx}=Lt_{h=0}\frac{U-u}{h}$,

$$\frac{dv}{dx}=Lt_{h=0}\frac{V-v}{h}, \text{ etc.}$$

We now proceed to the consideration of several important propositions.

**28.** PROP. I. **The Differential Coefficient of any Constant is zero.** This proposition will be obvious when we refer to the definition of a constant quantity. A constant is essentially a quantity of which there is no variation, so that if $y=c$, $\delta y=$ absolute zero whatever may be the value of $\delta x$. Hence $\frac{\delta y}{\delta x}=0$ and $\frac{dy}{dx}=0$ when the limit is taken.

Or geometrically : $y=c$ is the equation of a straight line parallel to the x-axis. At each point of its length it is its own tangent and makes an angle whose tangent is zero with the x-axis.

**29.** PROP. II. **Product of Constant and Function.** *The differential coefficient of a product of a constant and a function of x is equal to the product of the constant and the differential coefficient of the function*, or, stated algebraically,

$$\frac{d}{dx}(cu)=c\frac{du}{dx}.$$

For $$\frac{d}{dx}(cu)=Lt_{h=0}\frac{cU-cu}{h}=cLt_{h=0}\frac{U-u}{h}$$

$$=c\frac{du}{dx}.$$

**30.** PROP. III. **Differential Coefficient of a Sum.**

The differential coefficient of the sum of a set of functions of $x$ is the sum of the differential coefficients of the several functions.

Let $u, v, w, \ldots$, be the functions of $x$ and $y$ their sum.

Let $U, V, W, \ldots, Y$ be what these expressions severally become when $x$ is changed to $x + h$

Then
$$y = u + v + w + \ldots$$
$$Y = U + V + W + \ldots,$$

and therefore $Y - y = (U - u) + (V - v) + (W - w) + \ldots;$

dividing by $h$, $\dfrac{Y-y}{h} = \dfrac{U-u}{h} + \dfrac{V-v}{h} + \dfrac{W-w}{h} + \ldots$

and taking the limit $\dfrac{dy}{dx} = \dfrac{du}{dx} + \dfrac{dv}{dx} + \dfrac{dw}{dx} + \ldots$

If some of the connecting signs had been $-$ instead of $+$ a corresponding result would immediately follow, e.g. if $y = u + v - w + \ldots$

then
$$\frac{dy}{dx} = \frac{du}{dx} + \frac{dv}{dx} - \frac{dw}{dx} + \ldots,$$

## 31. PROP. IV. The Differential Coefficient of the product of two functions is

(*First Function*) × (*Diff. Coeff. of Second*) + (*Second Function*) × (*Diff. Coeff. of First*),

or, stated algebraically,

$$\frac{d(uv)}{dx} = u\frac{dv}{dx} + v\frac{du}{dx}.$$

With the same notation as before, let

$$y = uv, \text{ and therefore } Y = UV;$$

whence,
$$Y - y = UV - uv$$
$$= u(V - v) + V(U - u);$$

therefore
$$\frac{Y-y}{h} = u\frac{V-v}{h} + V\frac{U-u}{h},$$

and taking the limit $\dfrac{dy}{dx} = u\dfrac{dv}{dx} + v\dfrac{du}{dx}.$

## 32. On division by $uv$ the above result may be written

$$\frac{1}{y}\frac{dy}{dx} = \frac{1}{u}\frac{du}{dx} + \frac{1}{v}\frac{dv}{dx}.$$

Hence, it is clear that the rule may be extended to products of more functions than two.

For example, if $y = uvw$; let $vu = z$, then $y = uz$.

whence
$$\frac{1}{y}\frac{dy}{dx} = \frac{1}{u}\frac{du}{dx} + \frac{1}{z}\frac{dz}{dw},$$

but
$$\frac{1}{z}\frac{dz}{dx} = \frac{1}{v}\frac{dv}{dx} + \frac{1}{w}\frac{dw}{dx},$$

whence by substitution

$$\frac{1}{y}\frac{dy}{dx}=\frac{1}{u}\frac{du}{dx}+\frac{1}{v}\frac{dv}{dx}+\frac{1}{w}\frac{dw}{dx}.$$

Generally, if $y = uvwt...$

$$\frac{1}{y}\frac{dy}{dx}=\frac{1}{u}\frac{du}{dx}+\frac{1}{v}\frac{dv}{dx}+\frac{1}{w}\frac{dw}{dx}+\frac{1}{t}\frac{dt}{dx}+\ldots,$$

and if we multiply by $uvwt...$ we obtain

$$\frac{dy}{dx}=(vwt\ldots)\frac{du}{dx}+(uwt\ldots)\frac{dv}{dx}+(uvt\ldots)\frac{dw}{dx}+\ldots,$$

i.e. *multiply the differential coefficient of each separate function by the product of all the remaining functions and add up all the results*; the sum will be the differential coefficient of the product of all the functions.

## 33. PROP. V. The Differential Coefficient of a quotient of two functions is

$$\frac{(\textit{Diff. Coeff. of Num.}^r)(\textit{Den}^r.)-(\textit{Diff. Coeff. of Den.}^r)(\textit{Num.}^r)}{\textit{Square of Denominator}}$$

or, stated algebraically, $\dfrac{d}{dx}\left(\dfrac{u}{v}\right)=\dfrac{\dfrac{du}{dx}v-\dfrac{dv}{dx}u}{v^2}.$

With the same notation as before, let $y=\dfrac{u}{v}$, and therefore $Y=\dfrac{U}{V}$,

whence $$Y-y=\frac{U}{V}-\frac{u}{v}=\frac{Uv-Vu}{Vv};$$

therefore $$\frac{Y-y}{h}=\frac{\dfrac{U-u}{h}v-\dfrac{V-v}{h}u}{Vv},$$

and taking the limit

$$\frac{dy}{dx}=\frac{\dfrac{du}{dx}v-\dfrac{dv}{dx}u}{v^2}.$$

**34.** To illustrate these rules let the student recall to memory the differential coefficients of $x^2$ and $a\log_e\sin\dfrac{x}{a}$ established in Art. 21, viz. $2x$ and $\cot\dfrac{x}{a}$ respectively.

**Ex. 1.** Thus if $y = x^2 + a\log_e\sin\dfrac{x}{a}$,

we have by Prop. III. $\dfrac{dy}{dx}=2x+\cot\dfrac{x}{a}.$

**Ex. 2.** If $y = x^2 \times a \log_e \sin \frac{x}{a}$,

we have by Prop. IV. $\frac{dy}{dx} = 2x \times a \log_e \sin\frac{x}{a} + x^2 \cot\frac{x}{a}$.

**Ex. 3.** If $y = \frac{a \log_e \sin \frac{x}{a}}{x^2}$,

we have by Prop. V. $\frac{dy}{dx} = \frac{x^2 \cdot \cot\frac{x}{a} - 2x \cdot a \log_e \sin\frac{x}{a}}{x^4}$.

# EXAMPLES

The following differential coefficients obtained as results of preceding examples may for *present purposes* be assumed :

$y = x^3, \quad y_1 = 3x^2. \quad y = e^x, \; y_1 = e^x. \qquad y = x^4, \quad y_1 = 4x^3.$

$y = \log_e x, y_1 = \frac{1}{x}. \quad y = \sqrt{x}, y_1 = \frac{1}{2\sqrt{x}}. \qquad y = \tan x, y_1 = \sec^2 x.$

$y = \sin x, \quad y_1 = \cos x. \; y = \log_e \sin x, \qquad y_1 = \cot x.$]

Differentiate the following expressions by aid of the foregoing rules:

**1.** $x^3 \sin x, x^3 e^x, x^3 \log_e x, x^3 \tan x, x^3 \log_e \sin x.$

**2.** $x^4 / \sin x, \sin x / x^4, \sin x / e^x, \; e^x / \sin x.$

**3.** $\tan x \cdot \log_e \sin x, e^x \log_e x, \; \sin^2 x / \cos x.$

**4.** $x^3 e^x \sin x, x \tan x \log_e x.$

**5.** $x^3 \sin x / e^x, x^3 / e^x \sin x, 1 / x^3 e^x \sin x.$

**6.** $2\sqrt{x} \cdot \sin x, 3 \tan x / \sqrt{x}, 5 + 4e^x / \sqrt{x}.$

**7.** $e^x (x^3 + \sqrt{x}), (x^3 + x^4)(e^x \log_e x).$

## 35. Function of a Function.

Suppose $\quad u = f'(v)$ ...(1),

where $\quad v = \phi(x)$ ...(2).

If $x$ be changed to $x + \delta x$, $v$ will become $v + \delta v$, and in consequence $u$ will become $u + \delta u$.

Now if $v$ had been first eliminated between equations (1) and (2) we should have a result of the form

$$u = F'(x) \qquad ...(3).$$

This equation will be satisfied by the same simultaneous values $x + \delta x, u + \delta u$, which satisfy equations (1) and (2) . Also

$$\frac{\delta u}{\delta x} = \frac{\delta u}{\delta v} \cdot \frac{\delta v}{\delta x};$$

and proceeding to the Limit

$$Lt_{\delta x=0} \frac{\delta u}{\delta x} = \frac{du}{dx} \text{ as obtained from equation (3),}$$

$$Lt_{\delta v=0} \frac{\delta u}{\delta v} = \frac{du}{dv} \text{ as obtained from equation (1),}$$

$$Lt_{\delta x=0} \frac{\delta v}{\delta x} = \frac{dv}{dx} \text{ as obtained from equation (2).}$$

Thus $$\frac{du}{dx} = \frac{du}{dv} \cdot \frac{dv}{dx}.$$

**36.** For instance, the diff. coeff. of $x^2$ is $2x$, and of $\log_e \sin x$ is $\cot x$. } Art .21.

Suppose $u = (\log_e \sin x)^2$, i.e. $v^2$ where $v = \log_e \sin x$, then

$$\frac{du}{dx} = \frac{du}{dv} \cdot \frac{dv}{dx} = 2v \cdot \cot x = 2 \cot x \cdot \log_e \sin x.$$

**37.** It is obvious that the above result may be extended. For, if

$u = \phi(v), v = \psi(w), w = f(x)$, we have

$$\frac{du}{dx} = \frac{du}{dv} \cdot \frac{dv}{dx},$$

but $$\frac{dv}{dx} = \frac{dv}{dw} \cdot \frac{dw}{dx};$$

and therefore $$\frac{du}{dx} = \frac{du}{dv} \cdot \frac{dv}{dw} \cdot \frac{dw}{dx},$$

and a similar result holds however many functions there may be.

*The rule may be expressed thus :*

$$\frac{d(\text{1st Func.})}{dx} = \frac{d(\text{1st Func.})}{d(\text{2nd Func.})} \cdot \frac{d\,(\text{2nd Func.})}{d\,(\text{3rd Func.})} \cdots \frac{d\,(\text{Last Func.})}{dx}$$

or if $u = \phi\,[\psi\,\{F\,(fx)\}]$,

$$\frac{du}{dx} = \phi'\,[\psi\,\{F\,(fx)\}] \times \psi'\,\{F\,(fx)\} \times F'\,(fx) \times f'\,x.$$

Thus in the preceding Example

$$\frac{d\,(\log_e \sin x)^2}{dx} = \frac{d(\log_e \sin x)^2}{d(\log_e \sin x)} \cdot \frac{d \log_e \sin x}{dx} = 2 \log_e \sin x \cdot \cot x.$$

Again,

$$\frac{d\,(\log_e \sin x^2)}{dx} = \frac{d\,(\log_e \sin x^2)}{d\,(\sin x^2)} \cdot \frac{d \sin x^2}{dx^2} \cdot \frac{dx^2}{dx}$$

$$= \frac{1}{\sin x^2} . \cos x^2 \cdot 2x = 2x \cot x^2.$$

## 38. Interchange of the dependent and independent variable.

If in the theorem $\dfrac{du}{dx}=\dfrac{du}{dy}\dfrac{dy}{dx}$

we put $u=x$, then $\dfrac{du}{dx}=\dfrac{dx}{dx}=Lt_{h=0}\dfrac{(x+h)-x}{h}=1,$

and we obtain the result $\dfrac{dy}{dx}\cdot\dfrac{dx}{dy}=1$, or $\dfrac{dy}{dx}=\dfrac{1}{\dfrac{dx}{dy}}$.

**39.** The truth of this is also manifest geometrically, for $\dfrac{dy}{dx}$ and $\dfrac{dx}{dy}$ are respectively the tangent and the cotangent of the angle $\psi$ which the tangent to the curve $y=f(x)$ makes with the $x$- axis.

**40.** This formula is very useful in the differentiation of an inverse function.

Thus if we have $y=f^{-1}(x), x=f(y)$, and $\dfrac{dx}{dy}=f'(y)$,

a form which we are supposing to have been investigated.

Thus $$\frac{dy}{dx}=\frac{1}{f'(y)}=\frac{1}{f'[f^{-1}(x)]}.$$

## EXAMPLES

Assuming as before for *present purposes* the following differential coefficients,

$$\frac{d}{dx}x^3=3x^2,\ \frac{d}{dx}\sqrt{x}=\frac{1}{2\sqrt{x}},\ \frac{d}{dx}\sin x=\cos x,$$

$$\frac{d}{dx}e^x=e^x,\ \frac{d}{dx}\log_e x=\frac{1}{x},\ \frac{d}{dx}\tan x=\sec^2 x,$$

*write down* the differential coefficients of the following combinations:

1. $e^{3x}, e^{-x}, \sin^3 x, \sqrt{\sin x}, \sqrt{\log_e x}, \sqrt{\tan x}, \sin\sqrt{x}$.
2. $e^{\sin x}, e^{\tan x}, e^{x^3}, e^{\sqrt{x}}, e^{\log_e x}$.
3. $\log_e \sin x, \log_e \tan x, \log_e \sqrt{x}, \log_e x^3$.
4. $\sin \log_e x, \tan \log_e x, \sqrt{\sin \log_e x}, \sqrt{\sin\sqrt{x}}, \log_e \sin\sqrt{x}$.
5. $\log_e \sqrt{\sin\sqrt{e^x}}, \tan \log_e \sin e^{\sqrt{x}}$.

# CHAPTER IV.
# STANDARD FORMS.

**41.** IT is the object of the present Chapter to investigate and tabulate the results of differentiating the several standard forms referred to in Art. 21.

We shall always consider angles to be measured in circular measure, and all logarithms to be Napierian, unless the contrary is expressly stated.

It will be remembered that if $u = \phi(x)$, then, by the definition of a differential coefficient,

$$\frac{du}{dx} = Lt_{h=0} \frac{\phi(x+h) - \phi(x)}{h}.$$

## 42. Differential Coefficient of $x^n$.

If $u = \phi(x) = x^n$,

then $\phi(x+h) = (x+h)^n$,

$$\text{and } \frac{du}{dx} = Lt_{h=0} \frac{(x+h)^n - x^n}{h} = Lt_{h=0}\, x^n \frac{\left(1+\frac{h}{x}\right)^n - 1}{h}.$$

Now, since $h$ is to be ultimately zero, we may consider $\frac{h}{x}$ to be less than unity, and we can therefore apply the Binomial Theorem to expand $\left(1+\frac{h}{x}\right)^n$, whatever be the value of $n$; hence

$$\frac{du}{dx} = Lt_{h=0} \frac{x^n}{h}\left\{n\frac{h}{x} + \frac{n(n-1)}{2!}\frac{h^2}{x^2} + \frac{n(n-1)(n-2)}{3!}\frac{h^3}{x^3} + \dots\right\}$$

$$= Lt_{h=0}\, nx^{n-1}\left\{1 + \frac{h}{x} \times (a \text{ convergent series})\right\}$$

$$= nx^{n-1}.$$

**43.** It follows by Art. 35 that if $u = [\phi(x)]^n$ then

$$\frac{du}{dx} = n[\phi(x)]^{n-1}\, \phi'(x).$$

# EXAMPLES

*Write down the differential coefficients of*

**1.** $x, x^{10}, x^{-1}, x^{-10}, x^{\frac{3}{2}}, x^{\frac{1}{2}}, x^{\frac{1}{3}}, x^{-\frac{5}{6}}, \sqrt[4]{x^{-5}}$.

**2.** $(x+a)^n, x^n + a^n, x^{\frac{1}{2}} + a^{\frac{1}{2}}, \frac{1}{x+a}, \frac{1}{\sqrt{x+a}}$.

**3.** $(ax+b)^n, ax^n + b, (ax)^n + b, a\,(x+b)^n, a^n\,(x+b)$.

**4.** $1 + x + \frac{x^2}{2!} + \frac{x^3}{3!} + \frac{x^4}{4!} + \frac{x^5}{5!} + \dots$

**5.** $\frac{a+b\sqrt[3]{x}}{c\sqrt[4]{x^5}}, \frac{\sqrt{a}+\sqrt{x}}{\sqrt{a}-\sqrt{x}}, \frac{\sqrt[3]{a}+\sqrt[3]{x}}{\sqrt[3]{a}-\sqrt[3]{x}}, \sqrt{\frac{a+x}{a-x}}, \sqrt[3]{\frac{a+x}{a-x}}$.

**6.** $\frac{ax^2+bx+c}{cx^2+bx+a}, (x+a)^p\,(x+b)^q, (x+a)^p/(x+b)^q$.

## 44. Differential Coefficient of $a^x$.

If $$u = \phi(x) = a^x,\ \phi(x+h) = a^{x+h},$$

and $$\frac{du}{dx} = Lt_{h=0}\frac{a^{x+h}-a^x}{h} = a^x\,Lt_{h=0}\frac{a^h-1}{h}$$

$$= a^x \log_e a. \qquad \text{[Art. 15.]}$$

**COR. 1.** If $u = e^x, \frac{du}{dx} = e^x \log_e e = e^x$.

**COR. 2.** It follows by Art. 35 that if $u = e^{\phi(x)}$, then $\frac{du}{dx} = e^{\phi(x)} \cdot \phi'(x)$.

## 45. Differential Coefficient of $\log_a x$.

If $$u = \phi(x) = \log_a x,$$

$$\phi(x+h) = \log_a (x+h),$$

and $$\frac{du}{dx} = Lt_{h=0}\frac{\log_a (x+h) - \log_a x}{h}$$

$$= Lt_{h=0}\frac{1}{h}\log_a\left(1+\frac{h}{x}\right).$$

Let $\frac{x}{h} = z$, so that if $h = 0$, $z = \infty$; therefore

$$\frac{du}{dx} = Lt_{z=\infty}\frac{z}{x}\log_a\left(1+\frac{1}{z}\right) = \frac{1}{x}Lt_{z=\infty}\log_a\left(1+\frac{1}{z}\right)^z$$

$$= \frac{1}{x}\log_a e. \qquad \text{[Art. 14.]}$$

**COR. 1.** If $u = \log_e x, \dfrac{du}{dx} = \dfrac{1}{x} \log_e e = \dfrac{1}{x}$.

**COR. 2.** And it follows as before that if

$$u = \log_e \phi(x),$$

then
$$\frac{du}{dx} = \frac{\phi'(x)}{\phi(x)}$$

## EXAMPLES

*Write down the differential coefficients of*

**1.** $e^{2x}, e^{-x}, e^{nx}$, $\cosh x$, $\sinh x$, $\dfrac{e^{2x}+e^{3x}}{1+e^{-x}}$.

**2.** $\log \sqrt{x}$, $\log(x+a)$, $\log(ax+b)$, $\log(ax^2+bx+c)$, $\log \dfrac{1+x}{1-x}$,

$\log \dfrac{1+x^2}{1-x^2}$, $\log_x a$.

**3.** $\phi(e^x)$, $\phi(\log x)$, $[\phi(x)]^{\frac{1}{2}}$, $[\phi(a+x)]^n$, $\phi[(a+x)^n]$.

**4.** $e^x \log(x+a)$, $x^n e^x$, $a^x . e^x$, $2^x$, $x°$(degrees).

**5.** $\log(x+e^x)$, $e^x + \log x$, $e^x / \log x$.

**6.** $e^{x \log x}$, $\log(xe^x)$, $\log x^x$.

## 46. Differential Coefficient of sin *x*.

If
$$u = \phi(x) = \sin x,$$
$$\phi(x+h) = \sin(x+h),$$

and
$$\frac{du}{dx} = Lt_{h=0} \frac{\sin(x+h) - \sin x}{h}$$

$$= Lt_{h=0} \frac{2\sin\frac{h}{2}\cos\left(x+\frac{h}{2}\right)}{h}$$

$$= Lt_{h=0} \frac{\sin\frac{h}{2}}{\frac{h}{2}} \cos\left(x+\frac{h}{2}\right)$$

$$= \cos x.$$ [Art. 11; I.]

## 47. Differential Coefficient of cos x.

If $$u=\phi(x)=\cos x,$$

$$\phi(x+h)=\cos(x+h),$$

and $$\frac{du}{dx}=Lt_{h=0}\frac{\cos(x+h)-\cos x}{h}$$

$$=-Lt_{h=0}\frac{\sin\frac{h}{2}}{\frac{h}{2}}\sin\left(x+\frac{h}{2}\right)=-\sin x.$$

COR. And as in previous cases the differential coefficients of $\sin\phi(x)$ and $\cos\phi(x)$ are respectively

$$\cos\phi(x)\cdot\phi'(x), \text{ and } -\sin\phi(x)\cdot\phi'(x).$$

## EXAMPLES

*Write down the differential coefficients of*

1. $\sin 2x, \sin nx, \sin^n x, \sin x^n, \sin\sqrt{x}$.
2. $\sqrt{\sin\sqrt{x}}, \log\sin x, \log\sin\sqrt{x}, e^{\sin x}, e^{\sqrt{\sin x}}$.
3. $\sin^m x\cos^n x, \sin^m x/\cos^n x, \sin^n(nx^n), e^{ax}\sin bx$.
4. $\sin x\sin 2x\sin 3x, \sin x\cdot\sin 2x/\sin 3x$.
5. $\cos x\cos 2x\cos 3x, \cos^p ax\cdot\cos^q bx\cdot\cos^r cx$.

**48.** The remaining circular functions can be differentiated from the definition in the same way. It is a little quicker however to proceed thus after obtaining the above results.

(i) If $y=\tan x=\dfrac{\sin x}{\cos x}$,

$$\frac{dy}{dx}=\frac{\frac{d}{dx}(\sin x)\cdot\cos x-\frac{d}{dx}(\cos x)\sin x}{\cos^2 x}$$

$$=\frac{\cos^2 x+\sin^2 x}{\cos^2 x}=\sec^2 x.$$

(ii) If $y=\cot x=\dfrac{\cos x}{\sin x}, \dfrac{dy}{dx}=\dfrac{(-\sin x)\sin x-\cos x(\cos x)}{\sin^2 x}$

$$=-\text{cosec}^2 x.$$

(iii) If $y=\sec x=(\cos x)^{-1}, \dfrac{dy}{dx}=(-1)(\cos x)^{-2}\dfrac{d}{dx}(\cos x)$

$$=\frac{\sin x}{\cos^2 x}=\sec x\tan x.$$

(iv) If $y = \text{cosec}\, x = (\sin x)^{-1}, \frac{dy}{dx} = (-1)(\sin x)^{-2} \frac{d}{dx}(\sin x)$

$$= -\frac{\cos x}{\sin^2 x} = -\text{cosec}\, x \cot x.$$

(v) If $y = \text{vers}\, x = 1 - \cos x, \frac{dy}{dx} = \sin x.$

(vi) If $y = \text{covers}\, x = 1 - \sin x \frac{dy}{dx} = -\cos x.$

## 49. Differentiation of the inverse functions.

We may deduce the differential coefficients of all the inverse functions directly from the definition as shewn below.

For this method it seems useful to recur to the notation of Art. 27 and to denote $\phi(x+h)$ by $U$.

**50.** Then if $u = \phi(x) = \sin^{-1} x,$

$$U = \phi(x+h) = \sin^{-1}(x+h).$$

Hence $x = \sin u$, and $x + h = \sin U$;

therefore $h = \sin U - \sin u$,

and $$\frac{du}{dx} = Lt_{h=0} \frac{U-u}{h} = Lt_{U=u} \frac{U-u}{\sin U - \sin u}$$

$$= Lt_{U=u} \left\{ \frac{\frac{U-u}{2}}{\sin \frac{U-u}{2}} \right\} \frac{1}{\cos \frac{U+u}{2}} = \frac{1}{\cos u} = \frac{1}{\sqrt{1-\sin^2 u}} = \frac{1}{\sqrt{1-x^2}};$$

and the remaining inverse ions may be differentiated similarly.

**51.** But the method in in the preceding chapter (Art. 40) for inverse functions simplif s and shortens the work considerably.

Thus :—

(i) If $u = \sin^{-1} x,$

we have $= \sin u$; whence $\frac{dx}{du}$ s $u$;

and therefore $$\frac{du}{dx} = \frac{1}{\frac{dx}{du}} = \frac{1}{\cos u} = \frac{1}{\sqrt{1-\sin^2 u}} = \frac{1}{\sqrt{1-x^2}};$$

and since $\cos^{-1} x = \frac{\pi}{2} - \sin^{-1} x,$

we have $$\frac{d \cos^{-1} x}{dx} = -\frac{1}{\sqrt{1-x^2}}.$$

(ii) If $u = \tan^{-1} x$,

we have $x = \tan u$;

whence $\frac{dx}{du} = \sec^2 u$;

and therefore $\frac{du}{dx} = \frac{1}{\sec^2 u} = \frac{1}{1 + \tan^2 u} = \frac{1}{1 + x^2}$;

and since $\cot^{-1} x = \frac{\pi}{2} - \tan^{-1} x$,

we have $\frac{d \cot^{-1} x}{dx} = -\frac{1}{1 + x^2}$.

(iii) If $u = \sec^{-1} x$,

we have $x = \sec u$;

whence $\frac{dx}{du} = \sec u \tan u$;

and therefore $\frac{du}{dx} = \frac{\cos^2 u}{\sin u} = \frac{1}{x^2\sqrt{1 - \frac{1}{x^2}}} = \frac{1}{x\sqrt{x^2 - 1}}$;

and since $\operatorname{cosec}^{-1} x = \frac{\pi}{2} - \sec^{-1} x$;

we have $\frac{d(\operatorname{cosec}^{-1} x)}{dx} = -\frac{1}{x\sqrt{x^2 - 1}}$.

(iv) If $u = \operatorname{vers}^{-1} x$

we have $x = \operatorname{vers} u = 1 - \cos u$;

whence $\frac{dx}{du} = \sin u$;

and therefore $\frac{du}{dx} = \frac{1}{\sin u} = \frac{1}{\sqrt{1 - \cos^2 u}} = \frac{1}{\sqrt{2x - x^2}}$;

whence also $\frac{d \operatorname{covers}^{-1} x}{dx} = -\frac{1}{\sqrt{2x - x^2}}$.

# EXAMPLES

*Write down the differential coefficients of each of the following expressions:*

1. $\sec x^2, \sec^{-1} x^2, \tan x^2, \tan^{-1} x^2, \text{vers}\, x^2, \text{vers}^{-1} x^2.$
2. $\tan^{-1} e^x, \tan e^x, \log \tan x, \log \tan^{-1} x, \log (\tan x)^{-1}.$
3. $\text{vers}^{-1} \dfrac{x}{a}, \text{vers}^{-1}(x+a), \tan^{-1} \dfrac{x}{a}, \cos^{-1} \dfrac{1-x^2}{1+x^2}.$
4. $\sqrt{\text{covers}\, x}, \tan^p x^q, (\tan^{-1} x^p)^q, x \log \tan^{-1} x.$
5. $\tan x \cdot \sin^{-1} x, \sec^{-1} \tan x, \tan^{-1} \sec x, e^x \sin^{-1} x.$

## 52. TABLE OF RESULTS TO BE COMMITTED TO MEMORY.

| | | | |
|---|---|---|---|
| $u = x^n.$ | $\dfrac{du}{dx} = nx^{n-1}.$ | $u = \text{cosec}\, x.$ | $\dfrac{du}{dx} = -\dfrac{\cos x}{\sin^2 x}.$ |
| $u = a^x.$ | $\dfrac{du}{dx} = a^x \log_e a.$ | $u = \sin^{-1} x.$ | $\dfrac{du}{dx} = \dfrac{1}{\sqrt{1-x^2}}$ |
| $u = e^x.$ | $\dfrac{du}{dx} = e^x.$ | $u = \cos^{-1} x.$ | $\dfrac{du}{dx} = -\dfrac{1}{\sqrt{1-x^2}}$ |
| $u = \log_a x.$ | $\dfrac{du}{dx} = \dfrac{1}{x} \log_a e.$ | $u = \tan^{-1} x.$ | $\dfrac{du}{dx} = \dfrac{1}{1+x^2}$ |
| $u = \log_e x.$ | $\dfrac{du}{dx} = \dfrac{1}{x}.$ | $u = \cot^{-1} x.$ | $\dfrac{du}{dx} = -\dfrac{1}{1+x^2}$ |
| $u = \sin x.$ | $\dfrac{du}{dx} = \cos x.$ | $u = \sec^{-1} x.$ | $\dfrac{du}{dx} = \dfrac{1}{x\sqrt{x^2-1}}$ |
| $u = \cos x.$ | $\dfrac{du}{dx} = -\sin x.$ | $u = \text{cosec}^{-1} x.$ | $\dfrac{du}{dx} = -\dfrac{1}{x\sqrt{x^2-1}}$ |
| $u = \tan x.$ | $\dfrac{du}{dx} = \sec^2 x.$ | $u = \text{vers}^{-1} x.$ | $\dfrac{du}{dx} = \dfrac{1}{\sqrt{2x-x^2}}$ |
| $u = \cot x.$ | $\dfrac{du}{dx} = -\text{cosec}^2 x.$ | $u = \text{covers}^{-1} x.$ | $\dfrac{du}{dx} = -\dfrac{1}{\sqrt{2x-x^2}}$ |
| $u = \sec x.$ | $\dfrac{du}{dx} = \dfrac{\sin x}{\cos^2 x}.$ | | |

## 53. The Form $u^v$. Logarithmic Differentiation.

In functions of the form $u^v$, where both $u$ and $v$ are functions of $x$, it is generally advisable to *take logarithms* before proceeding to differentiate.

Let $\qquad y = u^v,$

then $\qquad \log_e y = v \log_e u;$

therefore $\qquad \frac{1}{y}\frac{dy}{dx} = \frac{dv}{dx}\cdot \log_e u + v \cdot \frac{1}{u}\frac{du}{dx}$, Arts. 31, 45,

or $\qquad \frac{dy}{dx} = u^v \left( \log_e u \cdot \frac{dv}{dx} + \frac{v}{u}\frac{du}{dx} \right).$

Three cases of this proposition present themselves.

I. If *v be a constant* and *u* a function of $x$, $\frac{dv}{dx} = 0$ and the above reduces to

$$\frac{dy}{dx} = v \cdot u^{v-1} \frac{du}{dx},$$

as might be expected from Art. 43.

II. If $u$ be a *constant* and $v$ a function of $x$, $\frac{du}{dx} = 0$ and the general form proved above reduces to

$$\frac{dy}{dx} = u^v \log_e u. \frac{dv}{dx},$$

as might be expected from Art. 44.

III. If $u$ and $v$ be *both functions of x*, it appears that the general formula

$$\frac{dy}{dx} = u^v \log_e u \frac{dv}{dx} + vu^{v-1}\frac{du}{dx}$$

is the sum of the two special forms in I. and II., and therefore we may, instead of taking logarithms in any particular example, *consider first u constant and then v constant and add the results obtained on these suppositions.*

**Ex. 1.** Thus if $y = (\sin x)^x$

$$\log y = x \log \sin x;$$

therefore $\frac{1}{y}\frac{dy}{dx} = \log \sin x + x \cot x,$

and $\frac{dy}{dx} = (\sin x)^x \{\log \sin x + x \cot x\}.$

**Ex. 2.** In cases such as $y = x^{x^x} + (\sin x)^x$, we cannot take logarithms directly.

Let $\qquad u = x^{x^x}$ and $v = (\sin x)^x$.

Then $\qquad \frac{dy}{dx} = \frac{du}{dx} + \frac{dv}{dx}.$

But $\qquad \log u = x \log x,$

and $\qquad \log v = x \log \sin x;$

whence $\qquad \frac{du}{dx} = x^x \{1 + \log x\},$

$$\text{and} \qquad \frac{dv}{dx} = (\sin x)^x \{\log \sin x + x \cot x\},$$

$$\therefore \qquad \frac{dy}{dx} = x^x \{1 + \log x\} + (\sin x)^x \{\log \sin x + x \cot x\}.$$

The above compound process is called **Logarithmic differentiation** and is useful whenever variables occur as an index or when the expression to be differentiated consists of a product of several involved factors.

## EXAMPLES

**1.** Differentiate $x^{\sin x}, (\sin^{-1} x)^x, x^{x^2} x^{2x}$.

**2.** Differentiate $(\sin x)^{\cos x} + (\cos x)^{\sin x}, (\tan x)^x + x^{\tan x}$.

**3.** Differentiate $\tan x \times \log x \times e^x \times x^x \times \sqrt{x}$.

**54. Transformations.** Occasionally an Algebraic or Trigonometrical transformation before beginning to differentiate will much shorten the work.

(i) For instance, suppose $y = \tan^{-1} \dfrac{2x}{1-x^2}$.

We observe that $y = 2 \tan^{-1} x$;

whence $\dfrac{dy}{dx} = \dfrac{2}{1+x^2}$.

(ii) Suppose $y = \tan^{-1} \dfrac{1+x}{1-x}$.

Here $y = \tan^{-1} x + \tan^{-1} 1$,

and therefore $\dfrac{dy}{dx} = \dfrac{1}{1+x^2}$.

(iii) If $y = \tan^{-1} \dfrac{\sqrt{1+x^2} - \sqrt{1-x^2}}{\sqrt{1+x^2} + \sqrt{1-x^2}}$

$$\text{we have } y = \tan^{-1} \frac{1 - \sqrt{\dfrac{1-x^2}{1+x^2}}}{1 + \sqrt{\dfrac{1-x^2}{1+x^2}}} = \frac{\pi}{4} - \tan^{-1} \sqrt{\frac{1-x^2}{1+x^2}} = \frac{\pi}{4} - \frac{1}{2} \cos^{-1} x^2;$$

$$\therefore \qquad \frac{dy}{dx} = \frac{x}{\sqrt{1-x^4}}.$$

## EXAMPLES

*Differentiate :*

1. $\tan^{-1}\dfrac{3x-x^3}{1-3x^2}$.

2. $\tan^{-1}\dfrac{p-qx}{q+px}$.

3. $\tan^{-1}\dfrac{\sqrt{1+x^2}-1}{x}$.

4. $\tan^{-1}\dfrac{x}{\sqrt{1-x^2}}$.

5. $e^{\log x}$.

6. $\sec^{-1}\dfrac{1}{1-2x^2}$.

7. $\sec\tan^{-1}x$.

8. $\cos^{-1}\dfrac{x-x^{-1}}{x+x^{-1}}$.

9. $\sin^{-1}(3x-4x^3)$.

10. $\tan^{-1}\dfrac{\sqrt{x}-x}{1+x^{\frac{3}{2}}}$.

11. $\cos^{-1}(1-2x^2)$.

12. $\log\left\{e^x\left(\dfrac{x-2}{x+2}\right)^{\frac{3}{4}}\right\}$.

## 55. Examples of Differentiation.

**Ex. 1.** Let $y=\sqrt{z}$, where $z$ is a known function of $x$.

Here, $\quad y=z^{\frac{1}{2}}, \quad$ and $\dfrac{dy}{dz}=\dfrac{1}{2}z^{-\frac{1}{2}}=\dfrac{1}{2\sqrt{z}}$,

whence $\dfrac{dy}{dx}=\dfrac{dy}{dz}\cdot\dfrac{dz}{dx}$, (Art. 35)

$$=\frac{1}{2\sqrt{z}}\cdot\frac{dz}{dx}.$$

This form *occurs so often that it will be found convenient to commit it to memory.*

**Ex. 2.** Let $y=e^{\sqrt{\cot x}}$.

Here $\dfrac{d(e^{\sqrt{\cot x}})}{dx}=\dfrac{d(e^{\sqrt{\cot x}})}{d(\sqrt{\cot x})}\cdot\dfrac{d(\sqrt{\cot x})}{d(\cot x)}\cdot\dfrac{d(\cot x)}{dx}$

$$=e^{\sqrt{\cot x}}\cdot\frac{1}{2\sqrt{\cot x}}\cdot(-\operatorname{cosec}^2 x).$$

**Ex. 3.** Let $y=(\sin x)^{\log x}\cot\{e^x(a+bx)\}$.

Taking logarithms $\log y=\log x\cdot\log\sin x+\log\cot\{e^x(a+bx)\}$.

The differential coefficient of $\log y$ is $\dfrac{1}{y}\dfrac{dy}{dx}$.

Again, log $x \cdot$ log sin $x$ is a product, and when differentiated becomes (Art. 31)

$$\frac{1}{x} \log \sin x + \log x \cdot \frac{1}{\sin x} \cdot \cos x.$$

Also, log cot $\{e^x (a+bx)\}$ becomes when differentiated

$$\frac{1}{\cot\{e^x \ (a+bx)^3\}} \cdot [-\text{cosec}^2 \ \{e^x (a+bx)\}] \cdot \{e^x \ (a+bx)+be^x\};$$

$$\therefore \frac{dy}{dx} = (\sin x)^{\log x} \cdot \cot\{e^x (a+bx)\} \left[ \frac{1}{x} \log \sin x + \cot x \cdot \log x - 2e^x \right.$$

$$\left. (a+b+bx) \text{cosec} 2(e^x \ \overline{a+bx}) \right].$$

**Ex. 4.** Let $y = \sqrt{a^2 - b^2 \cos^2(\log x)}$. Then

$$\frac{dy}{dx} = \frac{d\sqrt{a^2 - b^2 \cos^2 (\log x)}}{d\{a^2 - b^2 \cos^2 (\log x)\}} \times \frac{d\{a^2 - b^2 \cos^2 (\log x)\}}{d\{\cos (\log x)\}}$$

$$\times \frac{d\{\cos (\log x)\}}{d(\log x)} \times \frac{d(\log x)}{dx}$$

$$= \frac{1}{2} \{a^2 - b^2 \cos^2 (\log x)\}^{-\frac{1}{2}} \times \{-2b^2 \cos(\log x)\} \times$$

$$\{-\sin (\log x)\} \times \frac{1}{x}$$

$$= -\frac{b^2 \sin 2(\log x)}{2x\sqrt{a^2 - b^2 \cos^2(\log x)}}.$$

**Ex. 5.** Differentiate $x^5$ **with regard to** $x^2$.

Let $x^2 = z.$

Then $$\frac{dx^5}{dz} = \frac{dx^5}{dx} \cdot \frac{dx}{dz} = \frac{\frac{dx^5}{dx}}{\frac{dz}{dx}} = \frac{5x^4}{2x} = \frac{5}{2}x^3.$$

## 56. Implicit relation of $x$ and $y$.

**56. Implicit relation of $x$ and $y$.** So far we have been concerned with the case in which $y$ is expressed *explicitly*, i.e. directly in terms of $x$.

Cases however are of frequent occurrence in which $y$ is not expressed directly in terms of $x$, but its functionality is implied by an algebraic relation connecting $x$ and $y$.

In the case of such an *implicit* relation we proceed as follows:—

Suppose for instance

$$x^3 + y^3 = 3axy,$$

then $$3x^2 + 3y^2 \frac{dy}{dx} = 3a\left(y + x\frac{dy}{dx}\right),$$

i.e. $3(x^2 - ay) + 3(y^2 - ax)\dfrac{dy}{dx} = 0,$

giving $$\frac{dy}{dx} = -\frac{x^2 - ay}{y^2 - ax}.$$

## 57. Partial Differentiation.

It will be perceived in the foregoing example that the expressions $3(x^2 - ay)$ and $3(y^2 - ax)$ occurring are algebraically the same as would be given by differentiating the expression $x^3 + y^3 - 3axy$ first with regard to $x$, keeping $y$ a constant, and second with regard to $y$, keeping $x$ a constant.

When such processes are applied to a function $f(x, y)$ of two or more variables the results are denoted by the symbols $\dfrac{\partial f}{\partial x}, \dfrac{\partial f}{\partial y}$. Thus in the above example $\dfrac{\partial f}{\partial x} = 3(x^2 - ay)$, and $\dfrac{\partial f}{\partial y} = 3(y^2 - ax)$.

This is termed *partial* differentiation, and the results are called partial differential coefficients.

## 58. A general proposition.

It appears that in the preceding example

$$\frac{\partial f}{\partial x} + \frac{\partial f}{\partial y}\cdot\frac{dy}{dx} = 0, \quad \text{or} \quad \frac{dy}{dx} = -\frac{\dfrac{\partial f}{\partial x}}{\dfrac{\partial f}{\partial y}}.$$

This proposition is true for all implicit relations between two variables, such as $f(x, y) = 0$.

Suppose the function capable of expansion by any means in powers of $x$ and $y$, so that any general term may be denoted by $Ax^p y^q$.

Then $$f(x, y) \equiv \Sigma Ax^p y^q = 0.$$

Then differentiating $\Sigma\left(Apx^{p-1}y^q + Ax^p qy^{q-1}\dfrac{dy}{dx}\right) = 0,$

or $$\Sigma Apx^{p-1}y^q + (\Sigma Aqx^p y^{q-1})\frac{dy}{dx} = 0,$$

or $$\frac{\partial f}{\partial x} + \frac{\partial f}{\partial y}\cdot\frac{dy}{dx} = 0.$$

**Ex.** If $f(x, y) \equiv x^5 + x^4 y + y^3 = 0,$

we have $$\frac{\partial f}{\partial x} = 5x^4 + 4x^3 y, \quad \frac{\partial f}{\partial y} = x^4 + 3y^2;$$

$$\therefore \quad \frac{dy}{dx} = -\frac{5x^4 + 4x^3 y}{x^4 + 3y^2}.$$

## EXAMPLES

*Find* $\dfrac{dy}{dx}$ *in the following cases :*

**1.** $x^3 + y^3 = a^3$. **2.** $x^n + y^n = a^n$.

**3.** $e^y = xy$. **4.** $\log xy = x^2 + y^2$.

**5.** $x^y \cdot y^x = 1$. **6.** $x^y + y^x = 1$.

## 59. Euler's Theorem.

If $u = Ax^{\alpha}y^{\beta} + Bx^{\alpha'}y^{\beta'} + \ldots = \Sigma\, Ax^{\alpha}y^{\beta}$, *say, where*

$$\alpha + \beta = \alpha' + \beta' = \ldots = n,$$

*to show that*

$$x\frac{\partial u}{\partial x} + y\frac{\partial u}{\partial y} = nu.$$

By partial differentiation we obtain

$$\frac{\partial u}{\partial x} = \Sigma A\alpha x^{\alpha-1}y^{\beta}, \quad \frac{\partial u}{\partial y} = \Sigma A\beta x^{\alpha}y^{\beta-1},$$

then
$$x\frac{\partial u}{\partial x} + y\frac{\partial u}{\partial y} = \Sigma A\alpha x^{\alpha}y^{\beta} + \Sigma A\beta x^{\alpha}y^{\beta}$$

$$= \Sigma A(\alpha + \beta)\, x^{\alpha}y^{\beta}$$

$$= n\, \Sigma Ax^{\alpha}y^{\beta} = nu.$$

It is clear that this theorem can be extended to the case of three or of any number of independent variables, and that if, for example,

$$u = Ax^{\alpha}y^{\beta}z^{\gamma} + Bx^{\alpha'}y^{\beta'}z^{\gamma'} + \ldots,$$

where
$$\alpha + \beta + \gamma = \alpha' + \beta' + \gamma' = \ldots = n,$$

then will
$$x\frac{\partial u}{\partial x} + y\frac{\partial u}{\partial y} + z\frac{\partial u}{\partial z} = nu.$$

The functions thus described are called *homogeneous functions of the* $n^{\text{th}}$ *degree*, and the above result is known as Euler's Theorem on homogeneous functions.

## EXAMPLES

Verify Euler's theorem for the expressions:

$$\left(x^{\frac{1}{2}} + y^{\frac{1}{2}}\right)(x^n + y^n),\ \frac{1}{x^2 + xy + y^2},\ x^n \sin\frac{y}{x}.$$

## EXAMPLES

*Find* $\dfrac{dy}{dx}$ *in the following cases:*

**1.** $y=\dfrac{2+x^2}{1+x}$.

**2.** $y=\sqrt[n]{a+x}$.

**3.** $y=\sqrt[n]{a^2+x^2}$.

**4.** $y=\sqrt{\dfrac{1-x}{1+x}}$.

**5.** $y=\dfrac{1-x^2}{\sqrt{1+x^2}}$.

**6.** $y=\dfrac{x\sqrt{x^2-4a^2}}{\sqrt{x^2-a^2}}$.

**7.** $y=\sqrt{\dfrac{1-x}{1+x+x^2}}$.

**8.** $y=\log\dfrac{x^2+x+1}{x^2-x+1}$.

**9.** $y=\tan^{-1}(\log x)$.

**10.** $y=\sin x^{\circ}$.

**11.** $y=\sin(e^x)\log x$.

**12.** $y=\tan^{-1}(e^x)\log\cot x$.

**13.** $y=\log\cosh x$.

**14.** $y=\text{vers}^{-1}\log(\cot x)$.

**15.** $y=\cot^{-1}(\text{cosec}\, x)$.

**16.** $y=\sin^{-1}\dfrac{1}{\sqrt{1+x^2}}$.

**17.** $y=\tan^{-1}\dfrac{1}{\sqrt{x^2-1}}$.

**18.** $y=(\sin^{-1}x)^m(\cos^{-1}x)^n$.

**19.** $y=\sin(e^x\log x)\cdot\sqrt{1-(\log x)^2}$.

**20.** $y=\left(\dfrac{x}{n}\right)^{nx}\left(1+\log\dfrac{x}{n}\right)$.

**21.** $y=b\tan^{-1}\left(\dfrac{x}{a}\tan^{-1}\dfrac{x}{a}\right)$.

**22.** $y=\dfrac{x\cos^{-1}x}{\sqrt{1-x^2}}$.

**23.** $y=\cos\left(a\sin^{-1}\dfrac{1}{x}\right)$.

**24.** $y=\sin^{-1}\dfrac{a+b\cos x}{b+a\cos x}$.

**25.** $y=e^{\tan^{-1}x}\log(\sec^2x^3)$.

**26.** $y=e^{ax}\cos(b\tan^{-1}x)$.

**27.** $y=\tan^{-1}(a^{ax}\cdot x^2)$.

**28.** $y=\sec(\log_a\sqrt{a^2+x^2})$.

**29.** $y=\tan^{-1}x+\dfrac{1}{2}\log\dfrac{1+x}{1-x}$.

**30.** $y=\log(\log x)$.

**31.** $y=\log^n(x)$, where $\log^n$ means log log log..., (repeated $n$ times).

**32.** $y=\dfrac{1}{\sqrt{b^2-a^2}}\log\dfrac{\sqrt{b+a}+\sqrt{b-a}\tan\frac{x}{2}}{\sqrt{b+a}-\sqrt{b-a}\tan\frac{x}{2}}$.

**33.** $y=\sin^{-1}(x\sqrt{1-x}-\sqrt{x}\sqrt{1-x^2})$.

**34.** $y=10^{10^x}$.

**35.** $y=e^{e^{x}}$.

36. $y = e^{x^x}$.

37. $y = x^{e^x}$.

38. $y = x^{x^x}$.

39. $y = x^x + x^{\frac{1}{x}}$.

40. $y = (\cot x)^{\cot x} + (\cosh x)^{\cosh x}$.

41. $y = \tan^{-1}(a^{ex}\ x^{\sin x})\dfrac{\sqrt{x}}{1 + x^{\frac{3}{2}}}$.

42. $y = \sin^{-1}(e^{\tan^{-1}x})$.

43. $y = \sqrt{\left(1 + \cos\dfrac{m}{x}\right)\left(1 - \sin\dfrac{m}{x}\right)}$.

44. $y = \tan^{-1}\sqrt{\sqrt{x} + \cos^{-1} x}$.

45. $y = \left(\dfrac{1 + \sqrt{x}}{1 + 2\sqrt{x}}\right)^{\sin e^{x^2}}$.

46. $y = (\cos x)^{\cot^2 x}$.

47. $y = (\cot^{-1} x)^{\frac{1}{x}}$.

48. $y = \left(1 + \dfrac{1}{x}\right)^x + x^{1 + \frac{1}{x}}$.

49. $y = b\tan^{-1}\left(\dfrac{x}{a} + \tan^{-1}\dfrac{y}{x}\right)$.

50. $\tan y = e^{\cos^2 x}\sin x$.

51. $ax^2 + 2hxy + by^2 = 1$.

52. $e^y = \dfrac{(a + bx^n)^{\frac{1}{2}} - a^{\frac{1}{2}}}{(bx^n)^{\frac{1}{2}}}$.

53. $(\cos x)^y = (\sin y)^x$.

54. $x = e^{\tan^{-1}\frac{y - x^2}{x^2}}$.

55. $x = y \log xy$.

56. $y = x^y$.

57. $y = x^{y^x}$.

58. $y = x \log \dfrac{y}{a + bx}$.

59. $ax^2 + 2hxy + by^2 + 2gx + 2fy + c = 0$.

60. $x^m y^n = (x + y)^{m+n}$.

61. $y = e \tan^{-1} y \log \sec^2 x^3$.

62. If $y = \dfrac{1}{2}\dfrac{a^2 - b^2}{a^2 + b^2}\,x\left\{\dfrac{p\sqrt[p]{x}}{p+1} + \dfrac{q\sqrt[q]{x}}{q+1}\right\}$, shew that when

$$x = \left(\frac{a+b}{a-b}\right)^{\frac{2pq}{q-p}} \text{ then will } \frac{dy}{dx} = \left(\frac{a+b}{a-b}\right)^{\frac{q+p}{q-p}}.$$

63. Differentiate $\log_{10} x$ with regard to $x^2$.

64. Differentiate $(x^2 + ax + a^2)^n \log \cot \dfrac{x}{2}$ with regard to $\tan^{-1}(a \cos bx)$.

65. Differentiate $x^{\sin^{-1} x}$ with regard to $\sin^{-1} x$.

**66.** Differentiate $\tan^{-1}\dfrac{\sqrt{1+x^2}-1}{x}$ with regard to $\tan^{-1}x$.

**67.** Differentiate $\dfrac{\sqrt{1+x^2}+\sqrt{1-x^2}}{\sqrt{1+x^2}-\sqrt{1-x^2}}$ with regard to $\sqrt{1-x^4}$.

**68.** Differentiate $\sec^{-1}\dfrac{1}{2x^2-1}$ with regard to $\sqrt{1-x^2}$.

**69.** Differentiate $\tan^{-1}\dfrac{x}{\sqrt{1-x^2}}$ with regard to $\sec^{-1}\dfrac{1}{2x^2-1}$.

**70.** Differentiate $\tan^{-1}\dfrac{2x}{1-x^2}$ with regard to $\sin^{-1}\dfrac{2x}{1+x^2}$.

**71.** Differentiate $x^n\log\tan^{-1}x$ with regard to $\dfrac{\sin\sqrt{x}}{x^{\frac{3}{2}}}$.

**72.** If $y=x^{x^{x\cdots\text{ to }\infty}}$ prove $x\dfrac{dy}{dx}=\dfrac{y^2}{1-y\log x}$.

**73.** If $y=\cfrac{x}{1}+\cfrac{x}{1+\cfrac{x}{1}+\dots\text{ to }\infty}$, prove $\dfrac{dy}{dx}=\cfrac{1}{1+\cfrac{2x}{1+\cfrac{x}{1+\cfrac{x}{1+\cfrac{x}{1+\dots}}}}}$

**74.** If $y=x+\cfrac{1}{x+\cfrac{1}{x+\cfrac{1}{x+\cfrac{1}{x+\dots\text{ to }\infty}}}}$, prove that $\dfrac{dy}{dx}=\cfrac{1}{2-\cfrac{x}{x+\cfrac{1}{x+\cfrac{1}{x+\dots}}}}$

**75.** If $y=\sqrt{\sin x+\sqrt{\sin x+\sqrt{\sin x+\sqrt{\text{etc. to }\infty}}}}$, $y_1=\cos x/(2y-1)$.

**76.** If $S_n$ = the sum of a G.P. to $n$ terms of which $r$ is the common ratio, prove that $(r-1)\dfrac{dS_n}{dr}=(n-1)S_n-nS_{n-1}$.

**77.** If $\dfrac{P}{Q}=a+\cfrac{1}{a_1+\cfrac{1}{a_2+\cfrac{1}{a_3+\dots+\cfrac{1}{x}}}}$, prove $\dfrac{d}{dx}\left(\dfrac{P}{Q}\right)=\pm\dfrac{1}{Q^2}$.

**78.** Given $C=1+r\cos\theta+\dfrac{r^2\cos 2\theta}{2!}+\dfrac{r^3\cos 3\theta}{3!}+\dots$

and $S=r\sin\theta+\dfrac{r^2\sin 2\theta}{2!}+\dfrac{r^3\sin 3\theta}{3!}+\dots$

shew that $C\dfrac{dC}{dr}+S\dfrac{dS}{dr}=(C^2+S^2)\cos\theta$;

$$C\frac{dS}{dr}-S\frac{dC}{dr}=(C^2+S^2)\sin\theta.$$

79. If $y = \sec 4x$, prove that $\dfrac{dy}{dt} = \dfrac{16t(1-t^4)}{(1-6t^2+t^4)^2}$, where $t = \tan x$.

80. If $y = e^{-xz} \sec^{-1}(x\sqrt{z})$ and $z^4 + x^2 z = x^5$, find $\dfrac{dy}{dx}$ in terms of x and z.

81. Prove that if x be less than unity $\dfrac{1}{1+x} + \dfrac{2x}{1+x^2} + \dfrac{4x^3}{1+x^4} + \dfrac{8x^7}{1+x^8} +$ .... and inf. $= \dfrac{1}{1-x}$.

82. Prove that if x be less than unity

$$\frac{1-2x}{1-x+x^2} + \frac{2x-4x^3}{1-x^2+x^4} + \frac{4x^3-8x^7}{1-x^4+x^8} + \text{... ad inf.} = \frac{1+2x}{1+x+x^2}.$$

83. Given Euler's Theorem that

$$Lt_{n=\infty} \cos\frac{x}{2} \cos\frac{x}{2^2} \cos\frac{x}{2^3} \dots \cos\frac{x}{2^n} = \frac{\sin x}{x},$$

prove $\dfrac{1}{2}\tan\dfrac{x}{2} + \dfrac{1}{2^2}\tan\dfrac{x}{2^2} + \dfrac{1}{2^3}\tan\dfrac{x}{2^3} + \text{... ad inf.} = \dfrac{1}{x} - \cot x,$

and $\dfrac{1}{2^2}\sec^2\dfrac{x}{2} + \dfrac{1}{2^4}\sec^2\dfrac{x}{2^2} + \dfrac{1}{2^6}\sec^2\dfrac{x}{2^3} + \text{.... ad inf.} = \operatorname{cosec}^2 x - \dfrac{1}{x^2}.$

84. Differentiate logarithmically the expressions for $\sin\theta$ and $\cos\theta$ in factors, and deduce the sums to infinity of the following series

(a) $\dfrac{1}{\theta^2-\pi^2} + \dfrac{1}{\theta^2-2^2\pi^2} + \dfrac{1}{\theta^2-3^2\pi^2} + \dfrac{1}{\theta^2-4^2\pi^2} + \dots$

(b) $\dfrac{1}{1^2+x^2} + \dfrac{1}{2^2+x^2} + \dfrac{1}{3^2+x^2} + \dfrac{1}{4^2+x^2} + \dots$

(c) $\dfrac{1}{1^2+x^2} + \dfrac{1}{3^2+x^2} + \dfrac{1}{5^2+x^2} + \dfrac{1}{7^2+x^2} + \dots$

(d) $1 + \dfrac{2}{1+1^2} + \dfrac{2}{1+2^2} + \dfrac{2}{1+3^2} + \dots$

85. Sum to infinity the series

$$\frac{1}{1+x} + \frac{1}{2}\,\frac{1}{1+x^{\frac{1}{2}}} + \frac{1}{4}\,\frac{1}{1+x^{\frac{1}{4}}} + \frac{1}{8}\,\frac{1}{1+x^{\frac{1}{8}}} + \dots$$

86. If $H_n$ represent the sum of the homogeneous products of $n$ dimensions of x, y, z, prove

(a) $x\dfrac{\partial H_n}{\partial x} + y\dfrac{\partial H_n}{\partial y} + z\dfrac{\partial H_n}{\partial z} = nH_n;$

(b) $\dfrac{\partial H_n}{\partial x} + \dfrac{\partial H_n}{\partial y} + \dfrac{\partial H_n}{\partial z} = (n+2)H_{n-1}.$

# CHAPTER V.

# SUCCESSIVE DIFFERENTIATION.

**60.** WHEN $y$ is a given function of $x$, and $\frac{dy}{dx}$ has been found, we may proceed to differentiate a second time obtaining $\frac{d}{dx}\left(\frac{dy}{dx}\right)$.

This expression is called the *second differential coefficient* of $y$ with respect to x. We may then differentiate again and obtain the *third* differential coefficient and so on.

The expression $\frac{d}{dx}\left(\frac{dy}{dx}\right)$ is abbreviated into $\left(\frac{d}{dx}\right)^2 y$ or $\frac{d^2y}{dx^2}$; $\frac{d}{dx}\left(\frac{d^2y}{dx^2}\right)$ is written $\frac{d^3y}{dx^3}$; and so on.

Thus the several differential coefficients of $y$ are written

$$\frac{dy}{dx}, \frac{d^2y}{dx^2}, \frac{d^3y}{dx^n}, \ldots \frac{d^ny}{dx^n} \ldots$$

They are often further abbreviated into

$$y_1, y_2, y_3, \ldots y_n \ldots$$

**Ex. 1.** Thus if $y = x^n$, we have

$$y_1 = nx^{n-1},$$

$$y_2 = n(n-1)x^{n-2},\ y_3 = n(n-1)(n-2)x^{n-3},$$

and generally $y_r = n(n-1)\ldots(n-r+1)x^{n-r}$,

$$\ldots\ldots\ y_n = n!$$

$$y_{n+1} = y_{n+2} = y_{n+3} = \ldots = 0.$$

**Ex. 2.** If $y = \tan x$,

$$y_1 = \sec^2 x = 1 + y^2,\ y_2 = 2yy_1 = 2(y + y^3),$$

$$y_3 = 2(1 + 3y^2)\, y_1 = 2(1 + 4y^2 + 3y^4),$$

$$y_4 = 2(8y + 12y^3)\, y_1 = 8(2y + 5y^3 + 3y^5), \&c.$$

**Ex. 3.** If $y = (\sin^{-1} x)^2$,

$$y_1 = 2(\sin^{-1} x)/\sqrt{1-x^2},$$

$\therefore$ squaring, $(1 - x^2)\, y_1^2 = 4y$.

Hence differentiating, $(1 - x^2)\, 2y_1 y_2 - 2xy_1^2 = 4y_1$,

and dividing by $2y_1$, $(1 - x^2)\, y_2 - xy_1 = 2$.

## 61. Standard results and processes.

The $n^{th}$ differential coefficient of some functions are easy to find.

**Ex. 1.** If $y = e^{ax}$ we have $y_1 = ae^{ax}$, $y_2 = a^2e^{ax}$, .......

$$y_n = a^n e^{ax}.$$

COR. i. If $a = 1$, $y = e^x$, $y_1 = e^x$, $y_2 = e^x$,.... $y_n = e^x$.

COR. ii. $y = a^x = e^{x \log_e a}$;

$$y_1 = (\log_e a) e^{x \log_e a} = (\log_e a) a^x;$$

$$y_2 = (\log_e a)^2 e^{x \log_e a} = (\log_e a)^2 a^x;$$

etc. = etc.

$$y_n = (\log_e a)^n e^{x \log_e a} = (\log_e a)^n a^x.$$

**Ex. 2.** If $y = \log_e (x + a)$;

$$y_1 = \frac{1}{x+a}; y_2 = -\frac{1}{(x+a)^2}; y_3 = \frac{(-1)(-2)}{(x+a)^3};......$$

$$y_n = \frac{(-1)(-2)(-3).....(-n+1)}{(x+a)^n}$$

$$= \frac{(-1)^{n-1}(n-1)!}{(x+a)^n}.$$

COR. If $y = \dfrac{1}{x+a}$, $y_n = \dfrac{(-1)^n n!}{(x+a)^{n+1}}$

**Ex. 3.** If $y = \sin(ax + b)$;

$$y_1 = a\cos(ax+b) = a\sin\left(ax+b+\frac{\pi}{2}\right);$$

$$y_2 = a^2 \sin\left(ax+b+\frac{2\pi}{2}\right);$$

$$y_3 = a^3 \sin\left(ax+b+\frac{3\pi}{2}\right);$$

..............................................

$$y_n = a^n \sin\left(ax+b+\frac{n\pi}{2}\right).$$

Similarly, if $y = \cos(ax+b)$,

$$y_n = a^n \cos\left(ax+b+\frac{n\pi}{2}\right).$$

COR. If $a = 1$ and $b = 0$;

then, when $y = \sin x$, $y_n = \sin\left(x+\dfrac{n\pi}{2}\right)$;

and, when $y = \cos x$, $y_n = \cos\left(x+\dfrac{n\pi}{2}\right)$.

**Ex. 4.** If $y = e^{ax} \sin(bx + c)$;

$y_1 = ae^{ax} \sin(bx + c) + be^{ax} \cos(bx + c)$.

Let $a = r \cos \phi$ and $b = r \sin \phi$,

so that $r^2 = a^2 + b^2$ and $\tan \phi = \dfrac{b}{a}$;

and therefore $y_1 = re^{ax} \sin(bx + c + \phi)$.

Thus the operation of differentiating this expression is equivalent to multiplying by $r$ and adding $\phi$ to the angle.

Thus $y_2 = r^2 e^{ax} \sin(bx + c + 2\phi)$,

and generally $y_n = r^n e^{ax} \sin(bx + c + n\phi)$.

Similarly, if $y = e^{ax} \cos(bx + c)$,

$$y_n = r^n e^{ax} \cos(bx + c + n\phi).$$

These results are often wanted and the student should be able to obtain them immediately.

**Ex. 5.** Find the $n^{th}$ differential coefficient of $\sin^3 x$.

We have $y = \sin^3 x = \dfrac{1}{4}(3 \sin x - \sin 3x)$.

Hence $y_n = \dfrac{1}{4}\left\{3 \sin\left(x + \dfrac{n\pi}{2}\right) - 3^n \sin\left(3x + \dfrac{n\pi}{2}\right)\right\}$.

**Ex. 6.** If $y = \sin^2 x \cos^3 x$, find $y_n$.

Here, $y = \dfrac{1}{4} \sin^2 2x \cos x = \dfrac{1}{8}(1 - \cos 4x) \cos x$

$$= \frac{1}{16}(2 \cos x - \cos 3x - \cos 5x),$$

and $y_n = \dfrac{1}{16}\left\{2 \cos\left(x + \dfrac{n\pi}{2}\right) - 3^n \cos\left(3x + \dfrac{n\pi}{2}\right) - 5^n \cos\left(5x + \dfrac{n\pi}{2}\right)\right\}$.

## EXAMPLES

*Find $y_n$ in the following cases :*

1. $\dfrac{1}{ax + b}$.
2. $\dfrac{1}{a - x}$.
3. $\dfrac{1}{a - bx}$.
4. $\dfrac{x}{a + bx}$.
5. $\dfrac{ax + b}{cx + d}$.
6. $\dfrac{x^2}{x - a}$.
7. $\dfrac{1}{(x + a)^4}$.
8. $\sqrt{x + a}$.

9. $(x+a)^{\frac{-3}{5}}$.

10. $\log(ax+b)^p$.

11. $y=\sin x \sin 2x$.

12. $y=e^x \sin x \sin 2x$.

13. $y=e^x \sin^2 x$.

14. $y=e^{ax} \cos^2 bx$.

15. $y=\sin x \sin 2x \sin 3x$.

16. $y=e^{3x} \sin^2 x \cos^3 x$.

17. $y=\sin^2 x \sin 2x$.

18. $y=e^x \sin^2 x \sin 2x$.

## 62. Use of Partial Fractions.

Fractional expressions whose numerators and denominators are both rational algebraic expressions are differentiated $n$ times by first putting them into partial fractions.

**Ex. 1.** $y=\dfrac{x^2}{(x-a)(x-b)(x-c)}=\dfrac{a^2}{(a-b)(a-c)}\dfrac{1}{x-a}$

$$+\frac{b^2}{(b-c)(b-a)}\frac{1}{x-b}+\frac{c^2}{(c-a)(c-b)}\frac{1}{x-c}$$

(see note on partial fractions Art. 66);

therefore $y_n=\dfrac{a^2}{(a-b)(a-c)}\dfrac{(-1)^n n!}{(x-a)^{n+1}}+\dfrac{b^2}{(b-c)(b-a)}\dfrac{(-1)^n n!}{(x-b)^{n+1}}$

$$+\frac{c^2}{(c-a)(c-b)}\frac{(-1)^n n!}{(x-c)^{n+1}}.$$

**Ex. 2.** $y=\dfrac{x^2}{(x-1)^2(x+2)}$.

To put this into Partial Fractions let $x=1+z$;

then $y=\dfrac{1}{z^2}\cdot\dfrac{1+2z+z^2}{3+z}$

$$=\frac{1}{z^2}\left(\frac{1}{3}+\frac{5z}{9}+\frac{4}{9}\frac{z^2}{3+z}\right)\text{ by division}$$

$$=\frac{1}{3z^2}+\frac{5}{9z}+\frac{4}{9}\frac{1}{3+z}$$

$$=\frac{1}{3(x-1)^2}+\frac{5}{9(x-1)}+\frac{4}{9(x+2)},$$

whence $y_n=\dfrac{(n+1)!(-1)^n}{3(x-1)^{n+2}}+\dfrac{5n!(-1)^n}{9(x-1)^{n+1}}+\dfrac{4n!(-1)^n}{9(x+2)^{n+1}}$.

## ■ 63. Application of Demoivre's Theorem.

When quadratic factors which are not resolvable into real linear factors occur in the denominator, it is often convenient to make use of Demoivre's Theorem as in the following example.

Let $$y = \frac{1}{x^2 + a^2} = \frac{1}{(x + ia)(x - ia)}$$

$$= \frac{1}{2ia}\left\{\frac{1}{x - ia} - \frac{1}{x + ia}\right\}.$$

Then $$y_n = \frac{1}{2ia}(-1)^n n!\left\{\frac{1}{(x - ia)^{n+1}} - \frac{1}{(x + ia)^{n+1}}\right\}$$

Let $x = r\cos\theta$ and $a = r\sin\theta$,

whence $r^2 = x^2 + a^2$ and $\tan\theta = \dfrac{a}{x}$.

Hence $$y_n = \frac{(-1)^n n!}{2iar^{n+1}}\{(\cos\theta - i\sin\theta)^{-n-1} - (\cos\theta + i\sin\theta)^{-n-1}\}$$

$$= \frac{(-1)^n n!}{2iar^{n+1}}.2i\sin(n+1)\theta$$

$$= \frac{(-1)^n n!}{a^{n+2}}\sin(n+1)\theta\sin^{n+1}\theta,$$

where $\theta = \tan^{-1}\dfrac{a}{x}$.

COR. 1. Similarly if $y = \dfrac{1}{(x + b)^2 + a^2}$,

$$y_n = \frac{(-1)^n n!}{a^{n+2}}\sin(n+1)\theta\sin^{n+1}\theta,$$

where $\theta = \tan^{-1}\dfrac{a}{b + x}$.

COR. 2. If $y = \tan^{-1}\dfrac{x}{a}$, $y_1 = \dfrac{a}{x^2 + a^2}$,

and $$y_n = \frac{(-1)^{n-1}(n-1)!}{a^n}\sin n\theta\sin^n\theta,$$

where $\tan\theta = \dfrac{a}{x} = \cot y$.

## EXAMPLES

Find the $n^{th}$ differential coefficients of $y$ with respect to $x$ in the following cases :

**1.** $y = \dfrac{1}{4x^2 - 1}$. **2.** $y = \dfrac{1}{4x^2 + 1}$.

**3.** $y = \dfrac{1}{2} \log \dfrac{x+a}{x-a}$. **4.** $y = \dfrac{1}{x^4 - a^4}$.

**5.** $y = \dfrac{1}{(x^2 - a^2)(x^2 - b^2)}$. **6.** $y = \dfrac{1}{(x^2 + a^2)(x^2 + b^2)}$.

**7.** $y = \tan^{-1} \dfrac{2x}{1 - x^2}$. **8.** $y = \dfrac{1}{x^2 + x + 1}$.

**9.** $y = \dfrac{x}{x^4 + x^2 + 1}$. **10.** $y = \dfrac{x}{x^4 + x^3 + 2x^2 + x + 1}$.

## 64. Leibnitz's Theorem.

[Lemma. If ${}_nC_r$ denote the number of combinations of $n$ things $r$ at a time then will

$${}_nC_r + {}_nC_{r+1} = {}_{n+1}C_{r+1}.$$

For $$\frac{\lfloor n}{\lfloor r \, \lfloor n-r} + \frac{\lfloor n}{\lfloor r+1 \, \lfloor n-r-1} = \frac{\lfloor n}{\lfloor r \, \lfloor n-r-1} \left\{ \frac{1}{n-r} + \frac{1}{r+1} \right\}$$

$$= \frac{\lfloor n+1}{\lfloor r+1 \, \lfloor n-r} = {}_{n+1}C_{r+1}.]$$

Let $y = uv$, and let suffixes denote differentiations with regard to $x$. Then

$$y_1 = u_1 v + u v_1,\ y_2 = u_2 v + 2\, u_1 v_1 + u v_2, \text{ by differentiation.}$$

Assume generally that

$$y_n = u_n v + {}_nC_1 u_{n-1} v_1 + {}_nC_2 u_{n-2} v_2 + \dots$$
$$+ {}_nC_r u_{n-r} v_r + {}_nC_{r+1} u_{n-r-1} v_{r+1} + \dots + u v_n \dots (\alpha).$$

Therefore differentiating

$$y_{n+1} = u_{n+1} v + u_n v_1 \begin{Bmatrix} {}_nC_1 \\ +1 \end{Bmatrix} + u_{n-1} v_2 \begin{Bmatrix} {}_nC_2 \\ + {}_nC_1 \end{Bmatrix} + \dots$$
$$+ u_{n-r} v_{r+1} \begin{Bmatrix} {}_nC_{r+1} \\ + {}_nC_r \end{Bmatrix} + \dots + u v_{n+1}$$

$$= u_{n+1} v + {}_{n+1}C_1 u_n v_1 + {}_{n+1}C_2 u_{n-1} v_2 + {}_{n+1}C_3 u_{n-2} v_3 + \dots$$
$$+ {}_{n+1}C_{r+1} u_{n-r} v_{r+1} + \dots + u v_{n+1}, \text{ by the Lemma;}$$

therefore if the law ($\alpha$) hold for $n$ differentiations it holds for $n + 1$.

But it was proved to hold for two differentiations, and therefore it holds for three; therefore for four; and so on; and therefore it is generally true, *i.e.*,

$$(uv)_n = u_n v + {}_nC_1 u_{n-1} v_1 + {}_nC_2 u_{n-2} v_2 + \dots + {}_nC_r u_{n-r} v_r + \dots + u v_n.$$

## 65. Applications.

**Ex. 1.** $y = x^3 \sin ax$.

Here we take $\sin ax$ as $u$ and $x^3$ as $v$.

Now $v_1 = 3x^2$, $v_2 = 3.2x$, $v_3 = 3 \cdot 2$, and $v_4$ . & c. are all zero.

Also $\quad u_n = a^n \sin\left(ax + \frac{n\pi}{2}\right)$, etc.

Hence by Leibnitz's Theorem we have

$$y_n = x^3 a^n \sin\left(ax + \frac{n\pi}{2}\right) + n3x^2 a^{n-1} \sin\left(ax + \frac{n-1}{2}\pi\right)$$

$$+ \frac{n(n-1)}{2!} 3 \,.\, 2xa^{n-2} \sin\left(ax + \frac{n-2}{2}\pi\right)$$

$$+ \frac{n(n-1)(n-2)}{3!} 3.2.\, 1a^{n-3} \sin\left(ax + \frac{n-3}{2}\pi\right).$$

The student will note that if one of the factors be a power of $x$ it will be advisable to take that factor as $v$.

**Ex. 2.** Let $y = x^4 \cdot e^{ax}$; find $y_5$.

Here $v = x^4, u = e^{ax}$,

so that $v_1 = 4x^3$, $v_2 = 12x^2$, $v_3 = 24x$, $v_4 = 24$, and $v_5$ etc. all vanish.

Also $u_n = a^n e^{ax}$, etc.

whence $y_5 = a^5 e^{ax} x^4 + 5a^4 e^{ax} \cdot 4x^3 + 10 \cdot a^3 e^{ax} \cdot 12x^2$

$$+ 10a^2 e^{ax} \cdot 24x + 5ae^{ax} \cdot 24$$

$$= ae^{ax} \{a^4 x^4 + 20a^3 x^3 + 120a^2 x^2 + 240ax + 120\}.$$

**Ex. 3.** Differentiate $n$ times the equation

$$x^2 \frac{d^2y}{dx^2} + x\frac{dy}{dx} + y = 0.$$

$$\frac{d^n}{dx^n}(x^2 y_2) = x^2 y_{n+2} + n \cdot 2x \cdot y_{n+1} + \frac{n(n-1)}{2!} 2y_n,$$

$$\frac{d^n}{dx^n}(xy_1) = x \qquad y_{n+1} \quad ny_n,$$

$$\frac{d^n y}{dx^n} = \qquad\qquad y_n;$$

therefore by addition

$$x^2 y_{n+2} + (2n+1)\, xy_{n+1} + (n^2+1)\, y_n = 0,$$

or $$x^2 \frac{d^{n+2}y}{dx^{n+2}} + (2n+1)\, x\frac{d^{n+1}y}{dx^{n+1}} + (n^2+1)\frac{d^n y}{dx^n} = 0.$$

**Ex. 4.** Even when the general value of $y_n$ cannot be obtained we may sometimes find its value for $x = 0$ as follows.

Suppose $y = [\log (x + \sqrt{1 + x^2})]^2$,

then $y_1 = 2 \log (x + \sqrt{1 + x^2}) / \sqrt{1 + x^2}$ ...(1),

and $(1 + x^2) y_1^2 = 4y$,

Whence differentiating and dividing by $2y_1$,

$$(1 + x^2) y_2 + xy_1 = 2 \quad ....(2).$$

Differentiating $n$ times by Leibnitz's Theorem

$$(1 + x^2) y_{n+2} + 2nxy_{n+1} + n(n-1) y_n + xy_{n+1} + ny_n = 0$$

or $$(1 + x^2) y_{n+2} + (2n + 1) xy_{n+1} + n^2 y_n = 0.$$

Putting $x = 0$ we have

$$(y_{n+2})_0 = -n^2 (y_n)_0 \quad ...(3),$$

indicating by suffix zero the value attained upon the vanishing of $x$.

Now, when $x = 0$ we have from the value of $y$ and equations (1) and (2)

$$(y)_0 = 0, (y_1)_0 = 0, (y_2)_0 = 2.$$

Hence equation (3) gives

$$(y_3)_0 = (y_5)_0 = (y_7)_0 = \ldots\ldots = (y_{2k+1})_0 = 0$$

and $$(y_4)_0 = -2^2 \cdot 2, (y_6)_0 = 4^2 \cdot 2^2 \cdot 2,$$

$$(y_8)_0 = -6^2 \cdot 4^2 \cdot 2^2 \cdot 2, \text{etc.},$$

etc $$(y_{2k})_0 = (-1)^{k-1}\, 2 \cdot 2^2 \cdot 4^2 \cdot 6^2 \ldots\ldots (2k-2)^2$$

$$= (-1)^{k-1}\, 2^{2k-1} \{(k-1)!\}^2.$$

## EXAMPLES

*Apply Leibnitz's Theorem to find $y_n$ in the following cases :*

1. $y = xe^x$.
2. $y = x^2 e^{ax}$.
3. $y = x^2 \log x$.
4. $y = x^2 \sin x$.
5. $y = e^{ax} \cdot \sin bx$.
6. $y = \dfrac{x^n}{1 + x}$.
7. $y = x \tan^{-1} x$.
8. $y = x^2 \tan^{-1} x$.

## 66. Note On Partial Fractions.

Since a number of examples on successive differentiation and on integration depend on the ability of the student to put certain fractional forms into partial fractions, we give the methods to be pursued in a short note.

Let $\dfrac{f(x)}{\phi(x)}$ be the fraction which is to be resolved into its partial fractions.

**1.** If $f(x)$ be not already of lower degree than the denominator, *we can divide out until the numerator of the remaining fraction is of lower degree*: *e.g.*

$$\frac{x^2}{(x-1)(x-2)}=1+\frac{3x-2}{(x-1)(x-2)}.$$

Hence we shall consider only the case in which $f(x)$ is of lower degree than $\phi(x)$.

**2.** If $\phi(x)$ contain a single factor $(x-a)$, not repeated, we proceed thus : suppose $\phi(x)=(x-a)\,\psi(x)$,

and let $$\frac{f(x)}{(x-a)\,\psi(x)}\equiv\frac{A}{x-a}+\frac{\chi(x)}{\psi(x)},$$

$A$ being independent of $x$.

Hence $$\frac{f(x)}{\psi(x)}\equiv A+(x-a)\frac{\chi(x)}{\psi(x)}.$$

This is an identity and therefore true for all values of the variable $x$; put $x=a$. Then, since $\psi(x)$ does not vanish when $x=a$ (for by hypothesis $\psi(x)$ does not contain $x-a$ as a factor), we have $A=\dfrac{f(a)}{\psi(a)}$.

Hence the rule to find $A$ is, "Put $x=a$ in every portion of the fraction except in the factor $x-a$ itself."

**Ex.** (i) $$\frac{x-c}{(x-a)(x-b)}=\frac{a-c}{a-b}\cdot\frac{1}{x-a}+\frac{b-c}{b-a}\cdot\frac{1}{x-b}.$$

**Ex.** (ii) $$\frac{x^2+px+q}{(x-a)(x-b)(x-c)}=\frac{a^2+pa+q}{(a-b)(a-c)}\frac{1}{x-a}+\frac{b^2+pb+q}{(b-c)(b-a)}\frac{1}{x-b}+\frac{c^2+pc+q}{(c-a)(c-b)}\frac{1}{x-c}.$$

**Ex.** (iii) $$\frac{x}{(x-1)(x-2)(x-3)}=\frac{1}{2(x-1)}-\frac{2}{x-2}+\frac{3}{2(x-3)}.$$

**Ex.** (iv) $$\frac{x^2}{(x-a)(x-b)}.$$

Here the numerator not being of *lower degree than the denominator*, we divide the numerator by the denominator. The result will then be expressible in the form $1+\dfrac{A}{x-a}+\dfrac{B}{x-b}$, where $A$ and $B$ are found as before and are respectively $\dfrac{a^2}{a-b}$ and $\dfrac{b^2}{b-a}$.

3. Suppose the factor $(x-a)$ in the denominator to be repeated $r$ times so that

$$\phi(x) = (x-a)^r \, \psi(x).$$

Put $$x - a = y.$$

Then $$\frac{f(x)}{\phi(x)} = \frac{f(a+y)}{y^r \, \psi(a+y)},$$

or expanding each function by any means in ascending powers of $y$,

$$= \frac{A_0 + A_1 y + A_2 y^2 + \ldots}{y^r (B_0 + B_1 y + b_2 y^2 + \ldots}$$

Divide out thus:—

$$B_0 + B_1 y + \ldots \; A_0 + A_1 \, y + \ldots \; C_0 + C_1 y + C_2 y^2 + \ldots,$$

etc.,

and let the division be continued until $y^r$ is a factor of the remainder.

Let the remainder be $y^r \chi(y)$.

$$\text{Hence the fraction} = \frac{C_0}{y^r} + \frac{C_1}{y^{r-1}} + \frac{C_2}{y^{r-2}} + \ldots + \frac{C_{r-1}}{y} + \frac{\chi(y)}{\psi(a+y)}$$

$$= \frac{C_0}{(x-a)^r} + \frac{C_1}{(x-a)^{r-1}} + \frac{C_2}{(x-a)^{r-2}} + \ldots + \frac{C_{r-1}}{x-a} + \frac{\chi(x-a)}{\psi(x)}.$$

Hence the partial fractions corresponding to the factor $(x-a)^r$ are determined by a long division sum.

**Ex.** Take $$\frac{x^2}{(x-1)^3 (x+1)}.$$

Put $$x - 1 = y.$$

Hence the fraction $$= \frac{(1+y)^2}{y^3 (2+y)}.$$

$$\begin{array}{r|l}
2+y & 1 + 2y + y^2 \left( \frac{1}{2} + \frac{3}{4} y + \frac{1}{8} y^2 - \frac{1}{8} \frac{y^3}{2+y} \right. \\
 & \underline{1 + \frac{1}{2} y} \\
 & \quad \frac{3}{2} y + y^2 \\
 & \quad \underline{\frac{3}{2} y + \frac{3}{4} y^2} \\
 & \qquad \frac{1}{4} y^2 \\
 & \qquad \underline{\frac{1}{4} y^2 + \frac{1}{8} y^3} \\
 & \qquad\quad -\frac{1}{8} y^3
\end{array}$$

Therefore the fraction

$$=\frac{1}{2y^3}+\frac{3}{4y^2}+\frac{1}{8y}-\frac{1}{8(2+y)}$$

$$=\frac{1}{2(x-1)^3}+\frac{3}{4(x-1)^2}+\frac{1}{8(x-1)}-\frac{1}{8(x+1)}.$$

**4.** If a factor, such as $x^2+ax+b$, which is not resolvable into real linear factors occur in the denominator, the form of the corresponding partial fraction is $\frac{Ax+B}{x^2+ax+b}$. For instance, if the expression be

$$\frac{1}{(x-a)(x-b)^2(x^2+a^2)(x^2+b^2)^2}$$

the proper assumption for the form in partial fractions would be

$$\frac{A}{x-a}+\frac{B}{x-b}+\frac{C}{(x-b)^2}+\frac{Dx+E}{x^2+a^2}+\frac{Fx+G}{x^2+b^2}+\frac{Hx+K}{(x^2+b^2)^2},$$

where $A, B,$ and $C$ can be found according to the preceding methods, and on reduction to a common denominator we can, by equation coefficients of like powers in the two numerators, find the remaining letters $D, E, F, G, H, K$. Variations upon these methods will suggest themselves to the student.

## EXAMPLES

**1.** Given $y=\sin x^2$, find $y_2, y_3, y_4$.

**2.** Given $y=x\sin x$, find $y_2, y_3, y_4$.

**3.** Given $y=e^x \sin x$, find $y_2, \ldots\ldots, y_6$.

**4.** Given $y=x^3 e^{ax}$, find $y_3$ and $y_n$.

**5.** If $y=Ae^{mx}+Be^{-mx}$, prove $y_2=m^2y$.

**6.** If $y=A\sin mx+B\cos mx$, prove $y_2=-m^2y$.

**7.** If $y=a\sin\log x$, prove $x^2y_2+xy_1+y=0$.

**8.** If $y=\log\left(\frac{x}{a+bx}\right)^x$, prove $x^3y_2=(y-xy_1)^2$.

**9.** If $y=A(x+\sqrt{x^2-1})^n+B(x-\sqrt{x^2-1})^n$,

prove $(x^2-1)y_2+xy_1-n^2y=0$.

**10.** If $y=\frac{(x-a)(x-b)}{(x-c)(x-d)}$, find $y_n$.

**11.** If $y=\frac{1}{(x-1)^3(x-2)}$, find $y_n$.

12. If $y = x^n \log x$, find $y_2, y_3, y_n, y_{n+1}$.

13. If $x = \cosh\left(\frac{1}{m}\log y\right)$,

prove $(x^2 - 1)y_2 + xy_1 - m^2 y = 0$,

and $(x^2 - 1)\, y_{n+2} + (2n + 1)\, xy_{n+1} + (n^2 - m^2)\, y_n = 0$.

14. Find $y_n$ if $y = \frac{1}{x^3 + 1}$.

15. Find $y_n$ if $y = \frac{1}{(x+1)(x^2+1)}$.

16. Find $y_n$ if $y = \frac{x^2}{(x-1)^3 (x+1)}$.

17. Prove that if $y = \sin(m \sin^{-1} x)$,

$$(1 - x^2)\, y_2 = xy_1 - m^2 y,$$

and $(1 - x^2)\, y_{n+2} = (2n + 1)\, xy_{n+1} + (n^2 - m^2)\, y_n$.

Hence shew that

$$Lt_{x=0} \frac{y_{n+2}}{y_n} = n^2 - m^2.$$

18. If $y = e^{\tan^{-1} x}$, prove that

$$(1 + x^2)\, y_{n+2} + \{2(n+1)\, x - 1\} y_{n+1} + n(n+1)\, y_n = 0.$$

19. If $y = e^{a \sin^{-1} x}$, prove that

$$(1 - x^2)\, y_{n+2} - (2n + 1)\, xy_{n+1} - (n^2 + a^2)\, y_n = 0,$$

and $$Lt_{x=0} \frac{y_{n+2}}{y_n} = n^2 + a^2.$$

20. If $u = \sin nx + \cos nx$, $u_r = n^r \{1 + (-1)^r \sin 2nx\}^{\frac{1}{2}}$.

21. If $y = e^{ax} \{a^2 x^2 - 2nax + n(n+1)\}$,

$$y_n = a^{n+2}\, x^2 e^{ax}.$$

22. If $x \cos\theta + y \sin\theta = a$, and $x \sin\theta - y \cos\theta = b$,

prove that $\frac{d^p x}{d\theta^p} \cdot \frac{d^q y}{d\theta^q} - \frac{d^q x}{d\theta^q} \cdot \frac{d^p y}{d\theta^p}$ is constant.

**23.** Prove that

$$\frac{d^n}{dx^n}\left(\frac{\sin x}{x}\right)=\left[P\sin\left(x+\frac{n\pi}{2}\right)+Q\cos\left(x+\frac{n\pi}{2}\right)\right]/x^{n+1},$$

where

$$P=x^n-n(n-1)x^{n-2}+n(n-1)(n-2)(n-3)x^{n-4}-\ldots,$$

and $Q=nx^{n-1}-n(n-1)(n-2)x^{n-3}+\ldots$

**24.** Prove $\dfrac{d^n}{dx^n}\left(\dfrac{\cos x}{x}\right)=\left[P\cos\left(x+\dfrac{n\pi}{2}\right)-Q\sin\left(x+\dfrac{n\pi}{2}\right)\right]/x^{n+1},$

where $P$ and $Q$ have the same values as in 23.

**25.** Prove that

$$\frac{d^n}{dx^n}\left(\frac{e^{ax}\sin bx}{x}\right)=e^{ax}\{P\sin(bx+n\phi)+Q\cos(bx+n\phi)\}/x^{n+1},$$

where

$$P=(rx)^n-n(rx)^{n-1}\cos\phi+n(n-1)(rx)^{n-2}\cos 2\phi-\ldots,$$

$$Q=n(rx)^{n-1}\sin\phi-n(n-1)(rx)^{n-2}\sin 2\phi+\ldots,$$

$r^2=a^2+b^2$, and $\tan\phi=b/a$.

**26.** Prove that

$$\frac{d^n}{dx^n}(x^n\sin x)=n!(P\sin x+Q\cos x),$$

where

$$P=1-{}^nC_2\frac{x^2}{2!}+{}^nC_4\frac{x^4}{4!}-\ldots$$

and $$Q={}^nC_1\,x-{}^nC_3\frac{x^3}{3!}+{}^nC_5\frac{x^5}{5!}-\ldots$$

**27.** Shew that

$$\frac{d^n}{dx^n}\left(\frac{\log x}{x^m}\right)$$

$$=\frac{(-1)^n n!}{(m-1)!\,x^{m+n}}\left[\frac{(m+n-1)!}{n!}\log x-\sum_{r=0}^{r=n-1}\left\{\frac{(m+r-1)!}{r!(n-r)}\right\}\right].$$

[I.C.S., 1892.]

# CHAPTER VI.

# EXPANSIONS.

**67.** THE student will have already met with several expansions of given explicit functions in ascending integral powers of the independent variable; for example, those tabulated on pages 10 and 11, which occur in ordinary Algebra and Trigonometry.

The principal methods of development in common use may be briefly classified as follows:

**I.** By purely Algebraical or Trigonometrical processes.
**II.** By Taylor's or Maclaurin's Theorems.
**III.** By the use of a differential equation.
**IV.** By Differentiation of a known series, or a converse process.

These methods we proceed to explain and exemplify.

## 68. METHOD I. Algebraic and Trigonometrical Methods.

**Ex. 1.** Find the first three terms of the expansion of log sec $x$ in ascending powers of $x$.

By Trigonometry

$$\cos x = 1 - \frac{x^2}{2!} + \frac{x^4}{4!} - \frac{x^6}{6!} + \ldots$$

Hence $\log \sec x = -\log \cos x = -\log(1-z),$

where $z = \frac{x^2}{2!} - \frac{x^4}{4!} + \frac{x^6}{6!} - \ldots;$

and expanding $\log(1-z)$ by the logarithmic theorem we obtain

$$\log \sec x = z + \frac{z^2}{2} + \frac{z^3}{3} + \ldots$$

$$= \left[\frac{x^2}{2!} - \frac{x^4}{4!} + \frac{x^6}{6!} - \ldots\right] + \frac{1}{2}\left[\frac{x^2}{2!} - \frac{x^4}{4!} + \ldots\right]^2 + \frac{1}{3}\left[\frac{x^2}{2!} - \ldots\right]^3 \ldots$$

$$= \frac{x^2}{2} - \frac{x^4}{24} + \frac{x^6}{720} - \ldots$$

$$+ \frac{x^4}{8} - \frac{x^6}{48} + \ldots$$

$$+ \frac{x^6}{24} - \ldots;$$

hence $\log \sec x = \frac{x^2}{2} + \frac{x^4}{12} + \frac{x^6}{45} \ldots$

**Ex. 2.** Expand $\cos^3 x$ in powers of $x$.

Since $4\cos^3 x = \cos 3x + 3\cos x = 1 - \dfrac{3^2 x^2}{2!} + \dfrac{3^4 x^4}{4!} - \ldots$

$$+ (-1)^n \frac{3^{2n} x^{2n}}{(2n)!} + \ldots + 3\left[1 - \frac{x^2}{2!} + \frac{x^4}{4!} - \ldots + (-1)^n \frac{x^{2n}}{(2n)!} + \ldots\right],$$

we obtain $\cos^3 x = \dfrac{1}{4}\left\{(1+3) - (3^2+3)\dfrac{x^2}{2!} + (3^4+3)\dfrac{x^4}{4!} - \ldots\right.$

$$\left. + (-1)^n (3^{2n}+3)\frac{x^{2n}}{(2n)!} + \ldots\right\}.$$

Similarly $\sin^3 x = \dfrac{1}{4}\left\{(3^3-3)\dfrac{x^3}{3!} - (3^5-3)\dfrac{x^5}{5!} + (3^7-3)\dfrac{x^7}{7!} - \ldots\right.$

$$\left. + (-1)^n \frac{3^{2n-1}-3}{(2n-1)!} x^{2n-1} - \ldots\right\}.$$

**Ex. 3.** Expand $\tan x$ in powers of $x$ as far as the term involving $x^5$.

Since $\tan x = \dfrac{x - \dfrac{x^3}{3!} + \dfrac{x^5}{5!} - \ldots}{1 - \dfrac{x^2}{2!} + \dfrac{x^4}{4!} - \ldots}$

may by actual division show that

$$\tan x = x + \frac{x^3}{3} + \frac{2}{15}x^5 + \ldots$$

**Ex. 4.** Expand $\dfrac{1}{2}\{\log(1+x)\}^2$ in powers of $x$.

Since $(1+x)^y \equiv e^{y\log(1+x)}$,

we have, by expanding each side of this identity,

$$1 + yx + \frac{y(y-1)}{2!}x^2 + \frac{y(y-1)(y-2)}{3!}x^3 + \frac{y(y-1)(y-2)(y-3)}{4!}x^4 + \ldots$$

$$\equiv 1 + y\log(1+x) + \frac{y^2}{2!}\{\log(1+x)\}^2 + \ldots$$

Hence, equation coefficients of $y^2$,

$$\frac{1}{2}\{\log(1+x)\}^2 = \frac{x^2}{2!} - \frac{1+2}{3!}x^3 + \frac{1\cdot 2 + 2\cdot 3 + 3\cdot 1}{4!}x^4 - \text{etc.},$$

a series which may be written in the form

$$\frac{x^2}{2} - \left(1 + \frac{1}{2}\right)\frac{x^3}{3} + \left(1 + \frac{1}{2} + \frac{1}{3}\right)\frac{x^4}{4} - \left(1 + \frac{1}{2} + \frac{1}{3} + \frac{1}{4}\right)\frac{x^5}{5} + \ldots$$

## EXAMPLES

**1.** Prove $e^{x \sin x} = 1 + x^2 + \frac{1}{3}x^4 + \frac{1}{120}x^6 \ldots..$

**2.** Prove $\cos h^n x = 1 + \frac{nx^2}{2!} + n(3n-2)\frac{x^4}{4!} \ldots..$

**3.** Prove $\log \frac{\sin x}{x} = -\frac{x^2}{6} - \frac{x^4}{180} \ldots..$

**4.** Prove $\log \frac{\sin h\, x}{x} = \frac{x^2}{6} - \frac{x^4}{180} \ldots..$

**5.** Prove $\log x \cot x = -\frac{x^2}{3} - \frac{7}{90}x^4 \ldots..$

**6.** Prove $\log \frac{\tan^{-1} x}{x} = -\frac{x^2}{3} + \frac{13}{90}x^4 - \frac{251}{5 \cdot 7 \cdot 9^2}x^6 \ldots..$

**7.** Prove $\log(1 - x + x^2) = -x + \frac{x^2}{2} + \frac{2x^3}{3} + \frac{x^4}{4} - \frac{x^5}{5} - \frac{x^6}{3} - \frac{x^7}{7} + \frac{x^8}{8} \ldots..$

**8.** Expand $\log(1 + x^3 e^x)$ as far as the term containing $x^5$.

**9.** Expand in powers of $x$,

(*a*) $\tan^{-1} \frac{p - qx}{q + px}$. (*b*) $\tan^{-1} \frac{3x - x^3}{1 - 3x^2}$.

(*c*) $\sin^{-1} \frac{2x}{1 + x^2}$. (*d*) $\cos^{-1} \frac{x - x^{-1}}{x + x^{-1}}$.

## ■ 69. METHOD II. Taylor's and Maclaurin's Theorems.

It has been discovered that the Binomial, Exponential, and other well-known expansions are all particular cases of one general theorem, which has for its object the *expansion of $f(x + h)$ in ascending integral positive powers of h, $f(x)$* being a function of $x$ *of any form whatever*. It is found that such an expansion is not always possible, but the student is referred to a later chapter for a rigorous discussion of the limitations of the Theorem.

## ■ 70. Taylor's Theorem.

The theorem referred to is that *under certain circumstances*

$$f(x + h) = f(x) + hf'(x) + \frac{h^2}{2!}f''(x) + \frac{h^3}{3!}f'''(x) + \ldots$$

$$+ \frac{h^n}{n!}f^n(x) + \ldots \text{to infinity},$$

an expansion of $f(x + h)$ in powers of $h$.

This is known as Taylor's Theorem.

*Assuming the possibility* of expanding $f(x+h)$ in a *convergent* series of *positive integral* powers of $h$, let

$$f(x+h)=A_0+A_1h+A_2\frac{h^2}{2!}+A_3\frac{h^3}{3!}+ \qquad ...(1)$$

where $A_0, A_1, A_2, ...$ are functions of $x$ alone which are to be determined.

Now $$\frac{df(x+h)}{dh}=\frac{df(x+h)}{d(x+h)}\cdot\frac{d(x+h)}{dh}=f'(x+h),$$

for $x$ and $h$ are independent quantities and therefore $x$ may be considered constant in differentiating with regard to $h$, so that $\frac{d(x+h)}{dh}=1$.

Similarly $$\frac{d^2f(x+h)}{dh^2}=f''(x+h);\text{ and so on.}$$

Differentiating (1) then with regard to $h$, we have

$$f'(x+h)=\frac{df(x+h)}{dh}=A_1+A_2h+A_3\frac{h^2}{2!}+A_4\frac{h^3}{3!}+ \qquad ...(2)$$

$$f''(x+h)=\frac{df'(x+h)}{dh}=A_2+A_3h+A_4\frac{h^2}{2!}+ \qquad ...(3)$$

$$f'''(x+h)=\frac{df''(x+h)}{dh}=A_3+A_4h+ \qquad ...(4)$$

etc. = etc.

Putting $h=0$, we have at once from (1), (2), etc. $A_0=f(x)$, $A_1=f'(x)$, $A_2=f''(x)$, $A_3=f'''(x)$, etc., where $f'(x), f''(x), f'''(x)...$ are the several differential coefficients of $f(x)$ with respect to $x$. Substituting these values in (1),

$$f(x+h)=f(x)+hf'(x)+\frac{h^2}{2!}f''(x)+\frac{h^3}{3!}f'''(x)+....$$

**Ex. 1.** Let $f(x)=x^n$.

Then $f'(x)=nx^{n-1}$, $f''(x)=n(n-1)x^{n-2}$, etc., and $f(x+h)=(x+h)^n$.

Thus Taylor's Theorem gives the Binomial expansion

$$(x+h)^n=x^n+nhx^{n-1}+\frac{n(n-1)}{2!}h^2x^{n-2}+....$$

**Ex. 2.** Let $f(x)=\sin x$.

Then $f'(x)=\cos x$, $f''(x)=-\sin x$, $f'''(x)=-\cos x$, etc.,

and $f(x+h)=\sin(x+h)$.

Thus we obtain

$$\sin(x+h)=\sin x+h\cos x-\frac{h^2}{2!}\sin x-\frac{h^3}{3!}\cos x+...$$

# EXAMPLES

*Prove the following results:*

**1.** $e^{x+h} = e^x + he^x + \frac{h^2}{2!}e^x + \frac{h^3}{3!}e^x + \ldots\ldots$

**2.** $\tan^{-1}(x+h) = \tan^{-1} x + \frac{h}{1+x^2} - \frac{xh^2}{(1+x^2)^2} - \frac{1-3x^2}{(1+x^2)^3} \cdot \frac{h^3}{3} + \ldots\ldots$

**3.** $\sin^{-1}(x+h) = \sin^{-1} x + \frac{h}{\sqrt{1-x^2}} + \frac{x}{(1-x^2)^{3/2}} \frac{h^2}{2!} + \frac{1+2x^2}{(1-x^2)^{5/2}} \frac{h^3}{3!} + \ldots\ldots$

**4.** $\sec^{-1}(x+h) = \sec^{-1} x + \frac{h}{x\sqrt{x^2-1}} - \frac{2x^2-1}{x^2(x^2-1)^{3/2}} \frac{h^2}{2!} + \ldots\ldots$

**5.** $\log \sin (x+h) = \log \sin x + h \cot x - \frac{h^2}{2} \operatorname{cosec}^2 x + \frac{h^3}{3} \frac{\cos x}{\sin^3 x} + \ldots\ldots$

## 71. Stirling's or Maclaurin's Theorem.

If in Taylor's expansion

$$f(x+h) = f(x) + hf'(x) + \frac{h^2}{2!} f''(x) + \frac{h^3}{3!} f'''(x) + \ldots$$

we put 0 for $x$, and $x$ for $h$, we arrive at the result

$$f(x) = f(0) + xf'(0) + \frac{x^2}{2!} f''(0) + \frac{x^3}{3!} f'''(0) + \ldots + \frac{x^n}{n!} f^n(0) + \ldots,$$

the meaning of $f^r(0)$ being that $f(x)$ is to be differentiated $r$ times with respect to $x$, and then $x$ is to be put zero in the result.

This result is generally known as Maclaurin's Theorem. Being a form of Taylor's Theorem it is subject to similar limitations.

**Ex. 1.** Expand $\sin x$ in powers of $x$.

$$\begin{aligned} &\text{Here } f(x) = \sin x, && \text{Hence } f(0) = 0, \\ &f'(x) = \cos x, && f'(0) = 1, \\ &f''(x) = -\sin x, && f''(0) = 0, \\ &f'''(x) = -\cos x, && f'''(0) = -1. \\ &\&\text{c.} && \&\text{c.} \end{aligned}$$

$$f^n(x) = \sin\left(x + \frac{n\pi}{2}\right). \quad f^n(0) = \sin \frac{n\pi}{2}.$$

$$\text{Thus } \sin x = x - \frac{x^3}{3!} + \frac{x^5}{5!} - \ldots + \frac{x^n \sin \frac{n\pi}{2}}{n!} + \ldots$$

**Ex. 2.** Expand log cos $x$ in powers of $x$.

Here $f(x) = \log \cos x,$

$$f'(x) = -\tan x = -t, \text{ say},$$

$$f''(x) = -\sec^2 x = -(1+t^2),$$

$$f'''(x) = -2 \tan x \sec^2 x = -2t(1+t^2),$$

$$f^{(4)}(x) = -2(1+3t^2)(1+t^2) = -2(1+4t^2+3t^4),$$

$$f^{(5)}(x) = -2(8t+12t^3)(1+t^2) = -2(8t+20t^3+12t^5),$$

$$f^{(6)}(x) = -2(8+60t^2+60t^4)(1+t^2)$$

$$= -2(8+68t^2+120t^4+60t^6),$$

etc.

Whence $f(0) = \log \cos 0 = \log 1 = 0,$

and $f'(0) = f^{(3)}(0) = f^{(5)}(0) = \dots = 0,$

also $f''(0) = -1, f^{(4)}(0) = -2, f^{(6)}(0) = -16,$ etc.

Hence $\log \cos x = -\dfrac{x^2}{2!} - 2\dfrac{x^4}{4!} - 16\dfrac{x^6}{6!} - \text{etc.}$

# EXAMPLES

*Apply Maclaurin's Theorem to prove*

**1.** $\cos x = 1 - \dfrac{x^2}{2!} + \dfrac{x^4}{4!} - \dots + \dfrac{x^n \cos \dfrac{n\pi}{2}}{n!} + \dots.$

**2.** $\log(1+x) = x - \dfrac{x^2}{2} + \dfrac{x^3}{3} - \dfrac{x^4}{4} + \dots + (-1)^{n-1}\dfrac{x^n}{n} + \dots.$

**3.** $\tan^{-1} x = x - \dfrac{x^3}{3} + \dfrac{x^5}{5} - \dots + (-1)^{n-1}\dfrac{x^{2n-1}}{2n-1} + \dots.$

**4.** $e^{\sin x} = 1 + x + \dfrac{1}{2}x^2 - \dfrac{1}{8}x^4 - \dots.$

**5.** $\log(1+e^x) = \log 2 + \dfrac{1}{2}x + \dfrac{1}{8}x^2 - \dfrac{x^4}{192} \dots.$

**6.** $e^{ax} \cos bx = 1 + ax + \dfrac{a^2-b^2}{2!}x^2 + \dfrac{a(a^2-3b^2)}{3!}x^3 + \dots$

$$+ \frac{(a^2+b^2)^{\frac{n}{2}}}{n!} x^n \cos\left(n \tan^{-1} \frac{b}{a}\right) + \dots.$$

## 72. METHOD III. By the formation of a Differential Equation.

First form a differential equation as in Ex. 3, Art. 60, etc., and assume the series

$$a_0 + a_1x + a_2x^2 + \ldots$$

for the expansion.

Substitute the series for $y$ in the differential equation and equate coefficients of like powers of $x$ in the resulting identity. We thus obtain sufficient equations to find all the coefficients except one or two of the first which may easily be obtained from the values of $f(0)$, $f'(0)$, etc.

**Ex. 1.** To apply this method to the expansion of $(1 + x)^n$.

Let $\qquad y = (1 + x)^n = a_0 + a_1x + a_2x^2 + a_3x^3 + \ldots \qquad \ldots(1).$

Then $\qquad y_1 = n(1 + x)^{n-1}$ or $(1 + x)y_1 = ny\ldots \qquad \ldots(2).$

But $\qquad y_1 = a_1 + 2a_2x + 3a_3x^2 + \ldots \qquad \ldots(3).$

Therefore substituting from (1) and (3) in the differential equation (2)

$$(1 + x)(a_1 + 2a_2x + 3a_3x^2 + \ldots) \equiv n(a_0 + a_1x + a_2x^2 + \ldots).$$

Hence, comparing coefficients

$$a_1 = na_0,\ 2a_2 + a_1 = na_1,$$

$$3a_3 + 2a_2 = na_2, \text{ etc.,}$$

and $\quad$ by putting $x = 0$ in equation (1),

$$a_0 = 1,$$

giving

$$a_1 = n,$$

$$a_2 = \frac{n-1}{2}a_1 = \frac{n(n-1)}{2!},$$

$$a_3 = \frac{n-2}{3}a_2 = \frac{n(n-1)(n-2)}{3!}, \text{ etc.,}$$

$$a_r = \frac{n-r+1}{r}a_{r-1} = \frac{n(n-1)\ldots(n-r+1)}{r!},$$

whence $\qquad (1 + x)^n = 1 + nx + \dfrac{n(n-1)}{2!}x^2 + \ldots.$

**Ex. 2.** Let $y = f(x) = (\sin^{-1} x)^2$.

$$y_1 = 2\sin^{-1} x \cdot \frac{1}{\sqrt{1-x^2}},$$

$\therefore \quad (1 - x^2)\,y_1^2 = 4y.$

Differentiating, and dividing by $2y_1$, we have

$$(1 - x^2)\,y_2 = xy_1 + 2 \qquad \ldots(1).$$

Now, let $y = a_0 + a_1x + a_2x^2 + \ldots + a_nx^n + a_{n+1}x^{n+1} + a_{n+2}x^{n+2} + \ldots,$

therefore

$$y_1 = a_1 + 2a_2x + \ldots + na_nx^{n-1} + (n+1)\,a_{n+1}x^n + (n+2)\,a_{n+2}x^{n+1} + \ldots,.$$

and $y_2 = 2a_2 + \ldots + n(n-1)\, a_n x^{n-2} + (n+1)\, na_{n+1} x^{n-1}$

$$+ (n+2)(n+1)\, a_{n+2} x^n + \ldots$$

Picking out the coefficient of $x^n$ in the equation (*which may be done without actual substitution*) we have

$$(n+2)(n+1)\, a_{n+2} - n(n-1)\, a_n = na_n;$$

therefore $$a_{n+2} = \frac{n^2}{(n+1)(n+2)}\, a_n \qquad \ldots (2).$$

Now, $a_0 = f(0) = (\sin^{-1} 0)^2$,

and if we consider $\sin^{-1} x$ to be the *smallest positive angle* whose sine is $x$, $\quad \sin^{-1} 0 = 0.$

Hence $\quad a_0 = 0.$

Again, $\quad a_1 = f'(0) = 2 \sin^{-1} 0 \,.\, \dfrac{1}{\sqrt{1-0}} = 0,$

and $\quad a_2 = \dfrac{1}{2} f''(0) = \dfrac{1}{2}\left(\dfrac{2}{1-0} + 0\right) = 1.$

Hence, from equation (2), $a_3, a_5, a_7, \ldots$, are each $= 0$,

and $$a_4 = \frac{2^2}{3 \cdot 4} \,.\, a_2 = \frac{2^2}{3 \cdot 4} = \frac{2^2}{4!}\, 2,$$

$$a_6 = \frac{4^2}{5 \cdot 6} \,.\, a_4 = \frac{2^2 \cdot 4^2}{3 \cdot 4 \cdot 5 \cdot 6} = \frac{2^2 \cdot 4^2}{6!} \,.\, 2, \text{ etc.} = \text{etc.};$$

therefore $$(\sin^{-1} x)^2 = \frac{2x^2}{2!} + \frac{2^2}{4!}\, 2x^4 + \frac{2^2 \cdot 4^2}{6!}\, 2x^6 + \frac{2^2 \cdot 4^2 \cdot 6^2}{8!}\, 2x^8 + \ldots.$$

A different method of proceeding is indicated in the following example:—

**Ex. 3.** Let

$$y = \sin (m \sin^{-1} x) = a_0 + a_1 x + a_2 \frac{x^2}{2!} + a_3 \frac{x^3}{3!} + \ldots. \qquad \ldots(1).$$

Then $y_1 = \cos (m \sin^{-1} x) \dfrac{m}{\sqrt{1-x^2}}$,

whence $(1-x^2)\, y_1^2 = m^2 (1-y^2)$.

Differentiating again, and dividing by $2y_1$, we have

$$(1-x^2)\, y_2 - xy_1 + m^2 y = 0 \qquad \ldots(2).$$

Differentiating this $n$ times by Leibnitz's Theorem

$$(1-x^2)\, y_{n+2} - (2n+1)\, xy_{n+1} + (m^2 - n^2)\, y_n = 0 \qquad \ldots(3).$$

Now $a_0 = (y)_{x=0} = \sin (m \sin^{-1} 0) = 0,$

(assuming that $\sin^{-1} x$ is the smallest positive angle whose sine is $x$)

$$a_1 = (y_1)_{x=0} = m, \quad a_2 = (y_2)_{x=0} = 0,$$

etc.

$$a_n = (y_n)_{x=0}.$$

Hence, putting $x = 0$ in equation (3),

$$a_{n+2} = -(m^2 - n^2)\,a_n.$$

Hence $a_4, a_6, a_8, \ldots$, each $= 0$,

and $$a_3 = -(m^2 - 1^2)\,a_1 = -m(m^2 - 1^2),$$

$$a_5 = -(m^2 - 3^2)\,a_3 = m(m^2 - 1^2)(m^2 - 3^2),$$

$$a_7 = -(m^2 - 5^2)\,a_5 = -m(m^2 - 1^2)(m^2 - 3^2)(m^2 - 5^2),$$

etc.

Whence

$$\sin(m\sin^{-1} x) = mx - \frac{m(m^2 - 1^2)}{3!}x^3 + \frac{m(m^2 - 1^2)(m^2 - 3^2)}{5!}x^5 - \frac{m(m^2 - 1^2)(m^2 - 3^2)(m^2 - 5^2)x^7}{7!} + \ldots.$$

The corresponding series for $\cos(m\sin^{-1} x)$ is

$$\cos(m\sin^{-1} x) = 1 - \frac{m^2x^2}{2!} + \frac{m^2(m^2 - 2^2)}{4!}x^4 - \frac{m^2(m^2 - 2^2)(m^2 - 4^2)}{6!}x^6 + \ldots$$

If we write $x = \sin\theta$ these series become

$$\sin m\theta = m\sin\theta - \frac{m(m^2 - 1^2)}{3!}\sin^3\theta + \frac{m(m^2 - 1^2)(m^2 - 3^2)}{5!}\sin^5\theta - \text{etc.},$$

$$\cos m\theta = 1 - \frac{m^2}{2!}\sin^2\theta + \frac{m^2(m^2 - 2^2)}{4!}\sin^4\theta - \frac{m^2(m^2 - 2^2)(m^2 - 4^2)}{6!}\sin^6\theta + \text{etc.}$$

## EXAMPLES

**1.** Apply this method to find the known expansions of $a^x$, $\log(1 + x)$, $\sin x$, $\tan^{-1} x$.

**2.** If $y = \sin^{-1} x = a_0 + a_1x + a_2x^2 + a_3x^3 + \ldots$,

prove (1) $(1 - x^2)\,y_2 = xy_1$,

(2) $(n + 1)(n + 2)\,a_{n+2} = n^2 a_n$,

(3) $\sin^{-1} x = x + \frac{1}{2}\frac{x^3}{3} + \frac{1\cdot 3}{2\cdot 4}\cdot\frac{x^5}{5} + \ldots.$

**3.** If $y = e^{a \sin^{-1} x} = a_0 + a_1 x + a_2 x^2 + a_3 x^3 + \ldots,$

prove (1) $(1 - x^2)\, y_2 = xy_1 + a^2 y,$

(2) $(n + 1)(n + 2)\, a_{n+2} = (n^2 + a^2)\, a_n,$

(3) $$e^{a \sin^{-1} x} = 1 + ax + \frac{a^2 x^2}{2!} + \frac{a(a^2+1)}{3!} x^3 + \frac{a^2(a^2+2^2)}{4!} x^4 + \frac{a(a^2+1)(a^2+3^2)}{5!} x^5 + \ldots,$$

(4) Deduce from (3) by expanding the left side by the exponential theorem and equating coefficients of $a, a^2, a^3 \ldots$ the series for $\sin^{-1} x, (\sin^{-1} x)^2, (\sin^{-1} x)^3$.

**4.** Prove that $$\frac{(\tan^{-1} x)^2}{2!} = \frac{x^2}{2} - \left(1 + \frac{1}{3}\right)\frac{x^4}{4} + \left(1 + \frac{1}{3} + \frac{1}{5}\right)\frac{x^6}{6} - \left(1 + \frac{1}{3} + \frac{1}{5} + \frac{1}{7}\right)\frac{x^8}{8} + \ldots.$$

**5.** Prove that

(a) $$\frac{1}{2}[\log(x + \sqrt{1 + x^2})]^2 = \frac{x^2}{2} - \frac{2}{3} \cdot \frac{x^4}{4} + \frac{2 \cdot 4}{3 \cdot 5} \cdot \frac{x^6}{6} - \ldots,$$

(b) $$\frac{\log(x + \sqrt{1 + x^2})}{\sqrt{1 + x^2}} = x - \frac{2}{3} x^3 + \frac{2 \cdot 4}{3 \cdot 5} \cdot x^5 - \ldots.$$

## 73. METHOD IV. **Differentiation or integration of a known series.**

The method of treatment is best indicated by examples.

**Ex. 1.** If we differentiate the series

$$\sin^{-1} x = x + \frac{1}{2}\frac{x^3}{3} + \frac{1 \cdot 3}{2 \cdot 4}\frac{x^5}{5} + \frac{1 \cdot 3 \cdot 5}{2 \cdot 4 \cdot 6}\frac{x^7}{7} + \ldots$$

we obtain the binomial expansion

$$\frac{1}{\sqrt{1 - x^2}} = 1 + \frac{1}{2} x^2 + \frac{1 \cdot 3}{2 \cdot 4} x^4 + \frac{1 \cdot 3 \cdot 5}{2 \cdot 4 \cdot 5} x^6 + \ldots,$$

and it is clear that we must be able by a reverse process (integration) to infer the first series from the second.

The student unacquainted with integration may obtain the expansion of $\sin^{-1} x$ from that of $(1 - x^2)^{-\frac{1}{2}}$ as follows:

Let $\sin^{-1} x = a_0 + a_1 x + a_2 x^2 + a_3 x^3 + \ldots\ldots,$

then differentiating $\dfrac{1}{\sqrt{1 - x^2}} = a_1 + 2a_2 x + 3a_3 x^2 + 4a_4 x^3 + \ldots\ldots.$

But $$\frac{1}{\sqrt{1-x^2}} = 1 + \frac{1}{2}x^2 + \frac{1\cdot 3}{2\cdot 4}x^2 + \ldots.$$

Hence $a_1 = 1, 2a_2 = 0, 3a_3 = \frac{1}{2}, 4a_4 = 0, 5a_5 = \frac{1\cdot 3}{2\cdot 4}$, etc.

Also $a_0 = \sin^{-1} 0 = 0$

(if we take the smallest positive value of the inverse function).

Hence substituting the values of these coefficients

$$\sin^{-1} x = x + \frac{1}{2}\frac{x^3}{3} + \frac{1\cdot 3}{2\cdot 4}\frac{x^5}{5} + \ldots\ldots.$$

**Ex. 2.** We have proved in Ex. 2 Art. 72 that

$$\frac{(\sin^{-1} x)^2}{2!} = \frac{x^2}{2!} + \frac{2^2 x^4}{4!} + \frac{2^2\cdot 4^2}{6!}x^6 + \frac{2^2\cdot 4^2\cdot 6^2}{8!}x^8 + \ldots.$$

Hence differentiating we arrive at a new series

$$\frac{\sin^{-1} x}{\sqrt{1-x^2}} = x + \frac{2^2}{3!}x^3 + \frac{2^2\cdot 4^2}{5!}x^5 + \frac{2^2\cdot 4^2\cdot 6^2}{7!}x^7 + \ldots.$$

If we put $x = \sin\theta$ we may write this as

$$\frac{2\theta}{\sin 2\theta} = 1 + \frac{2^2}{3!}\sin^2\theta + \frac{2^2.4^2}{5!}\sin^4\theta + \frac{2^2.4^2\cdot 6^2}{7!}\sin^6\theta + \ldots,$$

or $$= 1 + \frac{2}{3}\sin^2\theta + \frac{2\cdot 4}{3\cdot 5}\sin^4\theta + \frac{2\cdot 4\cdot 6}{3\cdot 5\cdot 7}\sin^6\theta + \ldots.$$

# EXAMPLES

**1.** Obtain in this manner the expansion of

$$\log(1+x),\ \tan^{-1} x,\ \log\frac{1+x}{1-x}.$$

**2.** Prove $\log(x + \sqrt{1+x^2}) = x - \frac{1}{2}\frac{x^3}{3} + \frac{1\cdot 3}{2\cdot 4}\frac{x^5}{5} - \ldots$

**3.** Expand $\sin^{-1}\frac{2x}{1+x^2}$, $\tan^{-1}\frac{x}{\sqrt{1-x^2}}$, $\tan^{-1}\frac{\sqrt{1+x^2}-\sqrt{1-x^2}}{\sqrt{1+x^2}+\sqrt{1-x^2}}$ in powers of $x$.

**4.** Prove $$\left(\frac{\theta}{\sin\theta}\right)^2 = 1 + \frac{2^2}{3\cdot 4}\sin^2\theta + \frac{2^2\,4^2}{3\cdot 4\cdot 5\cdot 6}\sin^4\theta + \frac{2^2\cdot 4^2\cdot 6^2}{3\cdot 4\cdot 5\cdot 6\cdot 7\cdot 8}\sin^6\theta + \ldots.$$

**5.** Prove that

(1) $\dfrac{e^{a\sin^{-1}x}}{\sqrt{1-x^2}}=1+\dfrac{ax}{1!}+\dfrac{(a^2+1^2)x^2}{2!}+\dfrac{a(a^2+2^2)x^3}{3!}+\dfrac{(a^2+1^2)(a^2+3^2)x^4}{4!}+\ldots,$

(2) $\dfrac{e^{\theta}}{\cos\theta}=1+\dfrac{\sin\theta}{1!}+\dfrac{(1+1^2)\sin^2\theta}{2!}+\dfrac{(1+2^2)\sin^3\theta}{3!}+\dfrac{(1+1^2)(1+3^2)\sin^4\theta}{4!}+\ldots$

# EXAMPLES

**1.** Prove $\log(1+\tan x)=x-\dfrac{1}{2}x^2+\dfrac{2}{3}x^3+\ldots.$

**2.** Prove $e^{x\cos x}=1+x+\dfrac{x^2}{2}-\dfrac{x^3}{3}-\dfrac{11x^4}{24}-\dfrac{x^5}{5}\ldots.$

**3.** Prove $\log\left\{\dfrac{1}{x}e^{\frac{x}{2}}\log(1+x)\right\}=\dfrac{5x^2}{24}-\dfrac{x^3}{8}+\dfrac{251}{2880}x^4\ldots.$

**4.** Prove $\log(1-x+x^2)=-x+\dfrac{x^2}{2}+\dfrac{2x^3}{3}+\dfrac{x^4}{4}-\dfrac{x^5}{5}+\dfrac{x^6}{6}-\dfrac{x^7}{7}+\dfrac{x^8}{8}\ldots.$

**5.** Prove $\cosh(x\cos x)=1+\dfrac{x^2}{2}-\dfrac{11x^4}{24}\ldots,$

$\sinh(x\cos x)=x-\dfrac{x^3}{3}-\dfrac{x^5}{5}\ldots.$

**6.** Prove $\log\dfrac{\tan x}{x}=\dfrac{x^2}{3}+\dfrac{7}{90}x^4\ldots.$

**7.** Prove $\cos^{-1}(\tanh\log x)=\pi-2\left\{x-\dfrac{x^3}{3}+\dfrac{x^5}{5}-\ldots\right\}.$

**8.** Prove $\tan^{-1}\dfrac{\sqrt{1+x^2}-1}{x}=\dfrac{x}{2}-\dfrac{x^3}{6}+\dfrac{x^5}{10}-\dfrac{x^7}{14}+\ldots.$

**9.** Prove $\log(3x+4x^3+\sqrt{1+9x^2+24x^4+16x^6})$

$$=3\left\{x-\frac{1}{2}\frac{x^3}{3}+\frac{1\cdot3}{2\cdot4}\cdot\frac{x^5}{5}-\ldots\right\}.$$

**10.** Prove that

(*a*) $(1-x^2)^{\frac{1}{2}}\sin^{-1}x=x-\dfrac{x^3}{3}-\dfrac{2}{3}\dfrac{x^5}{5}-\dfrac{2\cdot4}{3\cdot5}\dfrac{x^7}{7}-\ldots,$

(*b*) $\theta\cot\theta=1-\dfrac{\sin^2\theta}{3}-\dfrac{2}{3}\dfrac{\sin^4\theta}{5}-\dfrac{2\cdot4}{3\cdot5}\dfrac{\sin^6\theta}{7}-\ldots,$

(*c*) $\dfrac{\pi}{4}=1-\dfrac{1}{3}\left(\dfrac{1}{2}\right)-\dfrac{2}{3}\cdot\dfrac{1}{5}\left(\dfrac{1}{2}\right)^2-\dfrac{2\cdot4}{3\cdot5}\cdot\dfrac{1}{7}\left(\dfrac{1}{2}\right)^3-\ldots.$

**11.** Prove that $(x+\sqrt{1+x^2})^n = 1 + nx + \frac{n^2x^2}{2\,!} + \frac{n(n^2-1^2)}{3\,!}x^3$

$$+\frac{n^2(n^2-2^2)}{4\,!}x^4 + \frac{n(n^2-1^2)(n^2-3^2)}{5\,!}x^5 + \ldots,$$

and deduce the expansions of

$$\log(x+\sqrt{1+x^2}),\ \frac{1}{2\,!}\{\log(x+\sqrt{1+x^2})\}^2,\ \frac{1}{3\,!}\{\log(x+\sqrt{1+x^2})\}^3.$$

**12.** If $y = e^{ax}\cos bx$, prove that $y_2 - 2ay_1 + (a^2+b^2)\,y = 0$,

and hence that

$$e^{ax}\cos bx = 1 + ax + \frac{a^2-b^2}{2\,!}x^2 + \frac{a(a^2-3b^2)}{3\,!}x^3 + \ldots.$$

**13.** Prove

(a) $\sin(m\tan^{-1}x)(1+x^2)^{\frac{m}{2}} = mx - \frac{m(m-1)(m-2)}{3\,!}x^3 + \frac{m(m-1)(m-2)(m-3)(m-4)}{5\,!}x^5 - \ldots,$

(b) $\cos(m\tan^{-1}x)(1+x^2)^{\frac{m}{2}}$

$$= 1 - \frac{m(m-1)}{2\,!}x^2 + \frac{m(m-1)(m-2)(m-3)}{4!}x^4 - \ldots$$

**14.** Deduce from 13 (a) $\tan^{-1}x\log\sqrt{1+x^2}$

$$= \left(\frac{1}{1}+\frac{1}{2}\right)\frac{x^3}{3} - \left(\frac{1}{1}+\frac{1}{2}+\frac{1}{3}+\frac{1}{4}\right)\frac{x^5}{5} + \left(\frac{1}{1}+\frac{1}{2}+\ldots+\frac{1}{6}\right)\frac{x^7}{7} - \ldots.$$

**15.** Prove

(a) $\frac{\cosh\theta}{\cos\theta} = 1 + \frac{1^2+1^2}{2\,!}\sin^2\theta + \frac{(1^2+1^2)(1^2+3^2)}{4!}\sin^4\theta + \ldots,$

(b) $\frac{\sinh\theta}{\cos\theta} = \frac{1^2}{1\,!}\sin\theta + \frac{(1^2+2^2)}{3\,!}\sin^3\theta + \frac{(1^2+2^2)(1^2+4^2)}{5\,!}\sin^5\theta + \ldots.$

**16.** Prove $\tan^{-1}(x+h) = \tan^{-1}x + (h\sin\theta)\sin\theta - \frac{(h\sin\theta)^2}{2}\sin 2\theta$

$$+\frac{(h\sin\theta)^3}{3}\sin 3\theta - \frac{(h\sin\theta)^4}{4}\sin 4\theta + \text{etc., where } x = \cot\theta.$$

**17.** Deduce from Ex. 16

(a) $\frac{\pi}{2} = \theta + \cos\theta\sin\theta + \frac{\cos^2\theta}{2}\sin 2\theta + \frac{\cos^3\theta}{3}\sin 3\theta + \ldots,$

by putting $h = -x = -\cot\theta$.

(b) $\frac{\pi-\theta}{2} = \sin\theta + \frac{1}{2}\sin 2\theta + \frac{1}{3}\sin 3\theta + \frac{1}{4}\sin 4\theta + \ldots,$

by putting $h = -\sqrt{1+x^2}$.

(c) $\dfrac{\pi}{2} = \dfrac{\sin\theta}{\cos\theta} + \dfrac{1}{2}\dfrac{\sin 2\theta}{\cos^2\theta} + \dfrac{1}{3}\dfrac{\sin 3\theta}{\cos^3\theta} + \dfrac{1}{4}\dfrac{\sin 4\theta}{\cos^4\theta} + \ldots,$

by putting $h = -x - x^{-1}$.

**18.** Show that

(a) $$\frac{1}{2!}\frac{(\sin^{-1} x)^2}{\sqrt{1-x^2}} = \frac{x^2}{2!} + 1^2 \cdot 3^2\left(\frac{1}{1^2} + \frac{1}{3^2}\right)\frac{x^4}{4!} + 1^2 \cdot 3^2 \cdot 5^2\left(\frac{1}{1^2} + \frac{1}{3^2} + \frac{1}{5^2}\right)\frac{x^6}{6!} + \ldots,$$

(b) $$\frac{\theta^2}{\sin 2\theta} = \frac{\sin\theta}{2!} + 1^2 \cdot 3^2\left(\frac{1}{1^2} + \frac{1}{3^2}\right)\frac{\sin^3\theta}{4!} + 1^2 \cdot 3^2 \cdot 5^2\left(\frac{1}{1^2} + \frac{1}{3^2} + \frac{1}{5^2}\right)\frac{\sin^5\theta}{6!} + \ldots.$$

**19.** Prove $$\frac{(\tan^{-1} x)^3}{3!} = \frac{1}{2}\frac{x^3}{3} - \left\{\frac{1}{2} + \frac{1}{4}\left(1 + \frac{1}{3}\right)\right\}\frac{x^5}{5} + \left\{\frac{1}{2} + \frac{1}{4}\left(1 + \frac{1}{3}\right) + \frac{1}{6}\left(1 + \frac{1}{3} + \frac{1}{5}\right)\right\}\frac{x^7}{7} - \ldots.$$

**20.** Prove

(a) $$\frac{\text{vers}^{-1} x}{\sqrt{2x}} = 1 + \frac{1}{3 \cdot 4}x + \frac{1 \cdot 3}{5 \cdot 4^2}\frac{x^2}{2!} + \frac{1 \cdot 3 \cdot 5}{7 \cdot 4^3}\frac{x^3}{3!} + \ldots,$$

(b) $$\frac{(\text{vers}^{-1} x)^2}{2} = x + \frac{1}{3}\frac{x^2}{2} + \frac{1 \cdot 2}{3 \cdot 5}\frac{x^3}{3} + \frac{1 \cdot 2 \cdot 3}{3 \cdot 5 \cdot 7}\frac{x^4}{4} + \ldots.$$

**21.** Prove that $$\frac{f(x+h) + f(x-h)}{2} = f(x) + \frac{h^2}{2!}f''(x) + \frac{h^4}{4!}f''''(x) + \ldots.$$

**22.** Prove that

(a) $f(mx)$
$$= f(x) + (m-1)\,x f'(x) + (m-1)^2\frac{x^2}{2!}f''(x) + (m-1)^3\frac{x^3}{3!}f'''(x) + \ldots,$$

(b) $f\left(\dfrac{x^2}{1+x}\right)$
$$= f(x) - \frac{x}{1+x}f'(x) + \frac{x^2}{(1+x)^2}\frac{1}{2!}f''(x) - \frac{x^3}{(1+x)^3}\frac{1}{3!}f'''(x) + \ldots,$$

(c) $f(x) = f(0) + xf'(x) - \dfrac{x^2}{2!}f''(x) + \dfrac{x^3}{3!}f'''(x) - \text{etc.}$

# CHAPTER VII.

# INFINITESIMALS.

## 74. Orders of Smallness.

If we conceive any magnitude $A$ divided into any large number of equal parts, say a billion ($10^{12}$), then each part $\frac{A}{10^{12}}$ is extremely small, and for all practical purposes negligible, in comparison with $A$. If this part be again subdivided into a billion equal parts, each $= \frac{A}{10^{24}}$, each of these last is extremely small in comparison with $\frac{A}{10^{12}}$, and so on. We thus obtain a series of magnitudes, $A, \frac{A}{10^{12}}, \frac{A}{10^{24}}, \frac{A}{10^{36}}, \ldots$, each of which is excessively small in comparison with the one which precedes it, but very large compared with the one which follows it. This furnishes us with what we may designate *a scale of smallness.*

## 75. More generally, if we agree to consider any given fraction $f$ as being small in comparison with unity, then $fA$ will be small in comparison with $A$, and we may term the expressions $fA, f^2A, f^3A, \ldots$, *small quantities of the first, second, third, etc., orders*; and the numerical quantities $f, f^2, f^3, \ldots$, may be called *small fractions* of the first, second, third, etc., orders.

Thus, supposing $A$ to be any given finite magnitude, any given fraction of $A$ is at our choice to designate a small quantity of the first order in comparison with $A$. When this is chosen, any quantity which has to this small quantity of the first order a ratio which is a small fraction of the first order, is itself a small quantity of the second order. Similarly, any quantity whose ratio to a small quantity of the second order is a small fraction of the first order is a small quantity of the third order, and so on. So that generally, if a small quantity be such that its ratio to a small quantity of the $p^{\text{th}}$ order be a small fraction of the $q^{\text{th}}$ order, it is itself termed a small quantity of the $(p+q)^{\text{th}}$ order.

## 76. Infinitesimals.

If these small quantities $Af, Af^2, Af^3, \ldots$, be all quantities whose limits are zero, then supposing $f$ *made smaller than any assignable quantity* by sufficiently increasing its denominator, these small quantities of the first, second, third, etc., orders are termed *infinitesimals of the first, second, third, etc., orders*. From the nature of an infinitesimal it is clear that, *if any equation contain finite quantities and infinitesimals, the infinitesimals may be rejected.*

**77.** PROP. *In any equation between infinitesimals of different orders, none but those of the lowest order need be retained.*

Suppose, for instance the equation to be

$$A_1 + B_1 + C_1 + D_2 + E_2 + F_3 + \dots = 0 \qquad \dots\text{(i)},$$

each letter denoting an infinitesimal of the order indicated by the suffix.

Then, dividing by $A_1$,

$$1 + \frac{B_1}{A_1} + \frac{C_1}{A_1} + \frac{D_2}{A_1} + \frac{E_2}{A_1} + \frac{F_3}{A_1} + \dots = 0 \qquad \dots\text{(ii)},$$

the limiting ratios $\frac{B_1}{A_1}$ and $\frac{C_1}{A_1}$ are finite, while $\frac{D_2}{A_1}, \frac{E_2}{A_1}$, are infinitesimals of the first order, $\frac{F_3}{A_1}$ is an infinitesimal of the second order, and so on. Hence, by Art. 76, equation (ii) may be replaced by

$$1 + \frac{B_1}{A_1} + \frac{C_1}{A_1} = 0,$$

and therefore equation (i) by $A_1 + B_1 + C_1 = 0_1$,

which proves the statements.

**78.** PROP. *In any equation connecting infinitesimals we may substitute for any one of the quantities involved any other which differs from it by a quantity of higher order.*

For if $\qquad A_1 + B_1 + C_1 + D_2 + \dots = 0$

be the equation, and if $A_1 = F_1 + f_2$,

$f_2$ denoting an infinitesimal of higher order than $F_1$, we have

$$F_1 + B_1 + C_1 + f_2 + D_2 + \dots = 0,$$

*i.e.* by the last proposition we may write

$$F_1 + B_1 + C_1 = 0,$$

which may therefore, if desirable, replace the equation

$$A_1 + B_1 + C_1 = 0.$$

**79. Illustrations.**

(1) Since $\qquad \sin\theta = \theta - \frac{\theta^3}{3!} + \frac{\theta^5}{5!} - \dots$

and $\qquad \cos\theta = 1 - \frac{\theta^2}{2!} + \frac{\theta^4}{4!} - \dots$

$\sin\theta, 1 - \cos\theta, \theta - \sin\theta$ are respectively of the first, second, and third orders of small quantities, when $\theta$ is of the first order; also, 1 may be written instead of $\cos\theta$ if second order quantities are to be rejected, and $\theta$ for $\sin\theta$ when cubes and higher powers are rejected.

(2) Again, suppose $AP$ the arc of a circle of centre $O$ and radius $a$. Suppose the angle $AOP$ $(=\theta)$ to be a small quantity of the first order. Let $PN$ be the perpendicular from $P$ upon $OA$ and $AQ$ the tangent at $A$, meeting $OP$ produced in $Q$. Join $P$, $A$.

Then arc $AP = a\theta$ and is of the first order,

$NP = a\sin\theta$ do. do.,

$AQ = a\tan\theta$ do. do.,

chord $AP = 2a\sin\frac{\theta}{2}$ do. do.,

$NA = a(1-\cos\theta)$ and is of the second order.

So that $OP - ON$ is a small quantity of the second order.

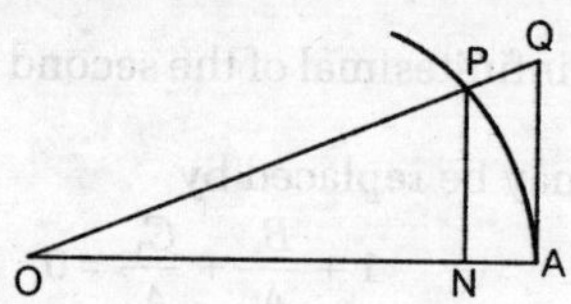


Again, arc $AP$ − chord $AP = a\theta - 2a\sin\frac{\theta}{2}$

$$= a\theta - 2a\left(\frac{\theta}{2} - \frac{\theta^3}{8\cdot 3!} + \ldots\right) = \frac{a\theta^3}{4\cdot 3!} - \text{etc.},$$

and is of the third order.

$$PQ - NA = NA(\sec\theta - 1) = NA \cdot \frac{2\sin^2\frac{\theta}{2}}{\cos\theta}$$

= (second order) (second order)

= fourth order of small quantities,

and similarly for others.

**80.** *The base angles of a triangle being given to be small quantities of the first order, to find the order of the difference between the base and the sum of the sides.*

By what has gone before, (Art. 79 (2)), if $APB$ be the triangle and $PM$ the perpendicular on $AB$, $AP - AM$

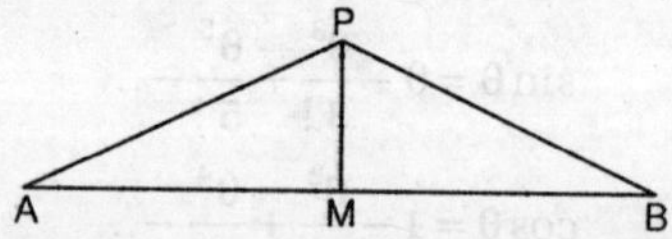


and $BP - BM$ are both small quantities of the second order as compared with $AB$.

Hence $AP + PB - AB$ is of the second order compared with $AB$.

If $AB$ itself be of the first order of small quantities, then $AP + PB - AB$ is *of the third order.*

**81.** *Degree of approximation in taking a small chord for a small arc in any curve.*

Let $AB$ be an arc of a curve supposed continuous between $A$ and $B$, and so small as to be concave at each point throughout its length to

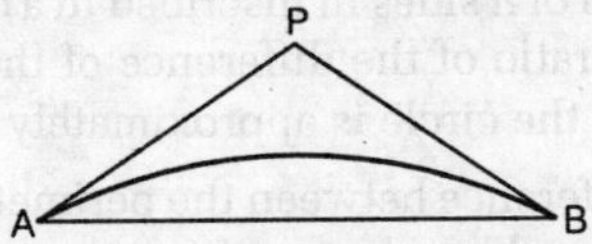

the foot of the perpendicular from that point upon the chord. Let $AP$, $BP$ be the tangents at $A$ and $B$. Then, when $A$ and $B$ are taken sufficiently near together, the chord $AB$ and the angles at $A$ and $B$ may each be considered small quantities of at least the first order, and therefore, by what has gone before, $AP + PB - AB$ will be at least of the third order. Now we may take *as an axiom* that the *length of the arc AB is intermediate between the length of the chord AB and the sum of the tangents AP, BP.* Hence the difference of the arc $AB$ and the chord $AB$, which is less than that between $AP + PB$ and the chord $AB$, must be at least *of the third order.*

## EXAMPLES

**1.** In the figure on page 70 suppose $PM$ drawn at right angles to $AQ$, and prove

(*a*) Segment cut off by $AP$ is of the third order of small quantities,

(*b*) Triangle $PNA$ is of the third order,

(*c*) Triangle $PQM$ is of the fifth order.

**2.** $OA_1B$ is a triangle right-angled at $A_1$ and of which the angle at $O$ is small and of the first order. $A_1B_1$ is drawn perpendicular to $OB$, $B_1A_2$ to $A_1B$, $A_2B_2$ to $OB$, and so on.

Prove

(*a*) $A_nB_n$ is a small quantity of the $(2n-1)^{\text{th}}$ order,

(*b*) $B_nA_{n+1}$ is of the $2n^{\text{th}}$ order,

(*c*) $B_nB$ is of the $2n^{\text{th}}$ order,

(*d*) triangle $BA_mB_n$ is of the $(2m+2n-1)^{\text{th}}$ order.

**3.** A straight line of constant length slides between two straight lines at right angles, viz. $CAa$, $CbB$; $AB$, $ab$ are two positions of the line, and $P$ their point of intersection. Show that, in the limit, when the two positions coincide, we have $\dfrac{Aa}{Bb} = \dfrac{CB}{CA}$ and $\dfrac{PA}{PB} = \dfrac{CB^2}{CA^2}$.

**4.** From a point $T$ in a radius of a circle, produced, a tangent $TP$ is drawn to the circle touching it in $P$. $PN$ is drawn perpendicular to the radius $OA$. Show that, in the limit when $P$ moves up to $A$,

$$NA = AT.$$

5. Tangents are drawn to a circular arc at its middle point and at its extremities; show that the area of the triangle formed by the chord of the arc and the two tangents at the extremities is ultimately four times that of the triangle formed by the three tangents.

6. A regular polygon of $n$ sides in inscribed in a circle. Show that when $n$ is very great the ratio of the difference of the circumferences to the circumference of the circle is approximately $\pi^2 / 6n^2$.

7. Show that the difference between the perimeters of the earth and that of an inscribed regular polygon of ten thousand sides is less than a yard (rad. of Earth = 4000 miles).

8. The sides of a triangle are 5 and 6 feet and the included angle exceeds 60° by 10′′. Calculating the third side for an angle of 60°, find the correction to be applied for the extra 10′′.

9. A person at a distance $q$ from a tower of height $p$ observes that a flag-pole upon the top of it subtends an angle $\theta$ at his eye. Neglecting his height, show that if the observed angle be subject to a small error $a$, the corresponding error in the length of the pole has to the calculated length the ratio

$$qa \operatorname{cosec}\theta /(q \cos\theta - p\sin\theta).$$

10. If in the equation $\sin(\omega - \theta) = \sin\omega \cos a, \theta$ be small, show that its approximate value is

$$2 \tan\omega \sin^2 \frac{a}{2}\left(1 - \tan^2 \omega \sin^2 \frac{a}{2}\right).$$ [I.C.S.]

11. A small error $x$ is made in measuring the side $a$ of a triangle, a small error $y$ in measuring $b$, and a small error $n''$ in measuring $C$. Prove that the consequent errors in $A$ and $B$ are each $\frac{1}{2}n''$, provided the relation

$$2\frac{bx - ay}{a^2 - b^2}\sin C = n \sin 1''$$

be satisfied. [I.C.S., 1892.]

# CHAPTER VIII.

# TANGENTS AND NORMALS.

## 82. Equation of TANGENT.

It was shown in Art. 18 that the equation of the tangent at the point $(x, y)$ on the curve $y = f(x)$ is

$$Y - y = \frac{dy}{dx}(X - x) \qquad ...(1),$$

$X$ and $Y$ being the current co-ordinates of any point on the tangent.

Suppose the equation of the curve to be given in the form $f(x, y) = 0$.

It is shown in Art. 58 that $\frac{dy}{dx} = -\frac{\frac{\partial f}{\partial x}}{\frac{\partial f}{\partial y}}$.

Substituting this expression for $\frac{dy}{dx}$ in (1) we obtain

$$Y - y = -\frac{\frac{\partial f}{\partial x}}{\frac{\partial f}{\partial y}}(X - x),$$

or

$$(X - x)\frac{\partial f}{\partial x} + (Y - y)\frac{\partial f}{\partial y} = 0 \qquad ...(2)$$

for the equation of the tangent.

If the partial differential coefficients $\frac{\partial u}{\partial x}, \frac{\partial u}{\partial y}$, etc. be denoted by $f_x, f_y$, etc., equation (2) may then be written

$$(X - x) f_x + (Y - y) f_y = 0.$$

## 83. Simplification for Algebraic Curves.

If $f(x, y)$ be an algebraic function of $x$ and $y$ of degree $n$, suppose it made *homogeneous in x, y and z by the introduction of a proper power of the linear unit z* wherever necessary. Call the function thus altered $f(x, y, z)$. Then $f(x, y, z)$ is a homogeneous algebraic function of the $n^{\text{th}}$ degree; hence we have by Euler's Theorem (Art. 59)

$$xf_x + yf_y + zf_z = nf(x, y, z) = 0,$$

by virtue of the equation to the curve.

Adding this to equation (2), the equation of the tangent takes the form

$$Xf_x + Yf_y + zf_z = 0 \qquad ...(3),$$

where the $z$ is to be put $=1$ after the differentiations have been performed.

We often for the sake of symmetry write $Z$ instead of $z$ in this equation and write the tangent in the form $Xf_x + Yf_y + Zf_z = 0$.

**Ex.** $f(x, y) \equiv x^4 + a^2xy + b^3y + c^4 = 0$.

The equation, when made *homogeneous* in $x, y, z$ *by the introduction of a proper power of z*, is

$$f(x, y, z) \equiv x^4 + a^2xyz^2 + b^3yz^3 + c^4z^4 = 0$$

and
$$f_x = 4x^3 + a^2yz^2,$$
$$f_y = a^2xz^2 + b^3z^3,$$
$$f_z = 2a^2xyz + 3b^3yz^2 + 4c^4z^3.$$

Substituting these in Equation 3, and putting $Z = z = 1$, we have for the equation of the tangent to the curve at the point $(x, y)$

$$X(4x^3 + a^2y) + Y(a^2x + b^3) + 2a^2xy + 3b^3y + 4c^4 = 0.$$

With very little practice the introduction of the $z$ can be performed *mentally*. It is generally *more advantageous* to use equation (3) than equation (2), because (3) gives the result *in its simplest form*, whereas if (2) be used it is often necessary to reduce by substitutions from the equation of the curve.

## 84. NORMAL.

DEF. *The normal at any point of a curve is a straight line through that point and perpendicular to the tangent to the curve at that point.*

Let the axes be assumed rectangular. The equation of the normal may then be at once written down. For if he equation of the curve be $y = f(x)$,

the tangent at $(x, y)$ is $Y - y = \dfrac{dy}{dx}(X - x)$,

and the normal is therefore $(X - x) + (Y - y)\dfrac{dy}{dx} = 0$.

If the equation of the curve be given in the form $f(x, y) = 0$,

the equation of the tangent is $(X - x)f_x + (Y - y)f_y = 0$,

and therefore that of the normal is $\dfrac{X - x}{f_x} = \dfrac{Y - y}{f_y}$.

**Ex. 1.** Consider the ellipse $\dfrac{x^2}{a^2} + \dfrac{y^2}{b^2} = 1$.

This requires $z^2$ in the last term to make a homogeneous equation in $x$, $y$, and $z$. We have then $\dfrac{x^2}{a^2} + \dfrac{y^2}{b^2} - z^2 = 0$.

Hence the equation of the tangent is $X \cdot \dfrac{2x}{a^2} + Y \cdot \dfrac{2y}{b^2} - z \cdot 2z = 0$, where $z$ is to be put = 1. Hence we get $\frac{Xx}{a^2} + \frac{Yy}{b^2} = 1$ for the tangent,

and therefore $\frac{X - x}{\frac{x}{a^2}} = \frac{Y - y}{\frac{y}{b^2}}$ for the normal.

**Ex. 2.** Take the general equation of a conic

$$ax^2 + 2hxy + by^2 + 2gx + 2fy + c = 0.$$

When made homogeneous this becomes

$$ax^2 + 2hxy + by^2 + 2gxz + 2fyz + cz^2 = 0,$$

The equation of the tangent is therefore

$$X(ax + hy + g) + Y(hx + by + f) + gx + fy + c = 0,$$

and that of the normal is $\frac{X - x}{ax + hy + g} = \frac{Y - y}{hx + by + f}$.

**Ex. 3.** Consider the curve $\frac{y}{a} = \log \sec \frac{x}{a}$.

Then $$\frac{dy}{dx} = \tan\frac{x}{a},$$

and the equation of the tangent is $Y - y = \tan\frac{x}{a}(X - x)$,

and of the normal $(Y - y)\tan\frac{x}{a} + (X - x) = 0$.

**85.** If $f(x, y) = 0$ and $F(x, y) = 0$ be two curves intersecting at the point $x, y$, their respective tangents at that point are

$$Xf_x + Yf_y + Zf_z = 0,$$

and $$XF_x + YF_y + ZF_z = 0,$$

The angle at which these lines cut is $\tan^{-1}\frac{f_xF_y - f_yF_x}{f_xF_x + f_yF_y}$.

Hence if the curves touch $f_x / F_x = f_y / F_y$;
and if they cut orthogonally, $f_xF_x + f_yF_y = 0$.

**Ex.** Find the angle of intersection of the curves

$$x^3 - 3xy^2 = a$$
$$3x^2y - y^3 = l$$

Calling the left-hand members $f$ and $F$ respectively, we have

$$f_x = 3(x^2 - y^2) = F_y,$$
$$f_y = -6xy = -F_x.$$

Hence clearly $f_xF_x + f_yF_y = 0$,
and the curves cut orthogonally.

**86.** If the form of a curve be given by the equations

$$x = \phi\ (t),\ y = \psi\ (t)$$

the tangent at the point determined by the third variable $t$ is by equation 1, Art. 82,

$$Y - \psi\ (t) = \frac{\psi'\ (t)}{\phi'\ (t)}\ \{X - \phi(t)\},$$

or $$X\ \psi'\ (t) - Y\ \phi'\ (t) = \phi\ (t)\ \psi'\ (t) - \psi\ (t)\ \phi'\ (t).$$

Similarly by Art. 84 the corresponding normal is

$$X\ \phi'\ (t) + Y\ \psi'\ (t) = \phi\ (t)\ \phi'\ (t) + \psi\ (t)\ \psi'\ (t).$$

## EXAMPLES

**1.** Find the equations of the tangents and normals at the point $(x, y)$ on each of the following curves:—

(1) $x^2 + y^2 = c^2$. (2) $y^2 = 4ax$.

(3) $xy = k^2$. (4) $y = c \cosh \dfrac{x}{c}$.

(5) $x^2 y + xy^2 = a^3$. (6) $e^y = \sin x$.

(7) $x^3 - 3axy + y^3 = 0$. (8) $(x^2 + y^2)^2 = a^2\ (x^2 - y^2)$.

**2.** Write down the equations of the tangents and normals to the curve $y\ (x^2 + a^2) = ax^2$ at the points where $y = \dfrac{a}{4}$.

**3.** Prove that $\dfrac{x}{a} + \dfrac{y}{b} = 1$ touches the curve $y = be^{\frac{-x}{a}}$ at the point where the curve crosses the axis of $y$.

**4.** Find where the tangent is parallel to the axis of $x$ and where it is perpendicular to that axis for the following curves:—

(α) $ax^2 + 2hxy + by^2 = 1$. (β) $y = \dfrac{x^3 - a^3}{ax}$.

(γ) $y^3 = x^2\ (2a - x)$.

**5.** Find the tangent and normal at the point determined by θ on

(α) The ellipse $\left.\begin{aligned} x &= a \cos \theta \\ y &= b \sin \theta \end{aligned}\right\}$.

(β) The cycloid $\left.\begin{aligned} x &= a\ (\theta + \sin \theta) \\ y &= a\ (1 - \cos \theta) \end{aligned}\right\}$

(γ) The epicycloid $\left.\begin{aligned} x &= A \cos \theta - B \cos \frac{A}{B} \theta \\ y &= A \sin \theta - B \sin \frac{A}{B} \theta \end{aligned}\right\}$

6. If $p = x\cos a + y\sin a$ touch the curve $\dfrac{x^m}{a^m} + \dfrac{y^m}{b^m} = 1$,

prove that $p^{\frac{m}{m-1}} = (a\cos a)^{\frac{m}{m-1}} + (b\sin a)^{\frac{m}{m-1}}$.

Hence write down the polar equation of the locus of the foot of the perpendicular from the origin on the tangent to this curve.

Examine the cases of an ellipse and of a rectangular hyperbola.

7. Find the condition that the conics

$$ax^2 + by^2 = 1, a'x^2 + b'y^2 = 1$$

shall cut orthogonally.

8. Prove that, if the axes be oblique and inclined at an angle ω, the equation of the normal to $y = f(x)$ at $(x, y)$ is

$$(Y - y)\left(\cos\omega + \frac{dy}{dx}\right) + (X - x)\left(1 + \cos\omega\frac{dy}{dx}\right) = 0.$$

9. Show that the parabolas $x^2 = ay$ and $y^2 = 2ax$ intersect upon the Folium of Descartes $x^3 + y^3 = 3axy$; and find the angles between each pair at the points of intersection.

## 87. Tangents at the Origin.

It will be shown in a subsequent article (124) that in the case in which a curve, whose equation is given in the rational algebraic form, passes through the origin, the equation of the tangent or tangents at that point can be at once written down by inspection; the rule being to *equate to zero the terms of lowest degree* in the equation of the curve.

**Ex. 1.** In the curve $x^2 + y^2 + ax + by = 0$, $ax + by = 0$ is the equation of the tangent at the origin; and in the curve $(x^2 + y^2)^2 = a^2(x^2 - y^2)$, $x^2 - y^2 = 0$ is the equation of a pair of tangents at the origin.

**Ex. 2.** Write down the equations of the tangents at the origin in the following curves:—

(α) $(x^2 + y^2)^2 = a^2x^2 - b^2y^2$.

(β) $x^5 + y^5 = 5ax^2y^2$.

(γ) $(y - a)^2\dfrac{x^2 + y^2}{y^2} = b^2$.

# GEOMETRICAL RESULTS.

## 88. Cartesians. Intercepts.

From the equations $Y - y = \frac{dy}{dx}(X - x)$ it is clear that the *intercepts* which the tangent cuts off from the axes of $x$ and $y$ are respectively

$$x - \frac{y}{\frac{dy}{dx}} \quad \text{and } y - x\frac{dy}{dx},$$

for these are respectively the values of $X$ when $Y = 0$ and of $Y$ when $X = 0$.

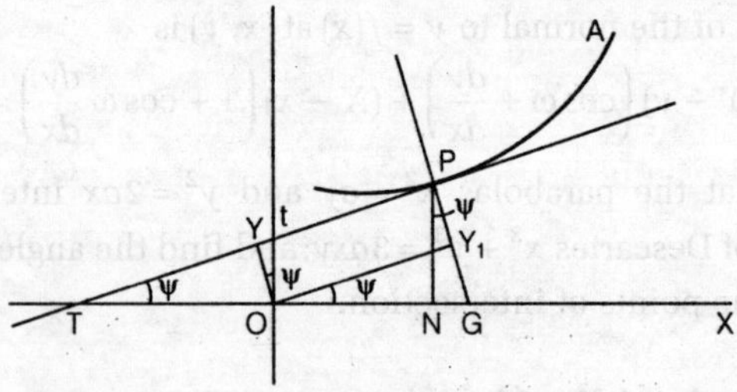


Let $PN$, $PT$, $PG$ be the ordinate, tangent, and normal to the curve, and let $PT$ make an angle $\psi$ with the axis of $x$; then $\tan\psi = \frac{dy}{dx}$. Let the tangent cut the axis of $y$ in $t$, and let $OY$, $OY_1$ be perpendiculars from $O$, the origin, on the tangent and normal. Then the above values of the intercepts are also obvious from the figure.

## 89. Subtangent, etc.

DEF. The line $TN$ is called the *subtangent* and the line $NG$ is called the *subnormal*.

From the figure

$$\textit{Subtangent} = TN = y\cot\psi = \frac{y}{\frac{dy}{dx}}.$$

$$\textit{Subnormal} = NG = y\tan\psi = y\frac{dy}{dx}.$$

$$\textit{Normal} = PG = y\sec\psi = y\sqrt{1+\tan^2\psi} = y\sqrt{1+\left(\frac{dy}{dx}\right)^2}$$

$$\textit{Tangent} = TP = y\,\mathrm{cosec}\,\psi = y\frac{\sqrt{1+\tan^2\psi}}{\tan\psi} = y\frac{\sqrt{1+\left(\frac{dy}{dx}\right)^2}}{\frac{dy}{dx}}.$$

$$OY = Ot \cos\psi = \frac{y - x\dfrac{dy}{dx}}{\sqrt{1+\tan^2\psi}} = \frac{y - x\dfrac{dy}{dx}}{\sqrt{1+\left(\dfrac{dy}{dx}\right)^2}}.$$

$$OY_1 = OG \cos\psi = \frac{ON + NG}{\sqrt{1+\tan^2\psi}} = \frac{x + y\dfrac{dy}{dx}}{\sqrt{1+\left(\dfrac{dy}{dx}\right)^2}}.$$

These and other results may of course also be obtained analytically from the equation of the tangent.

Thus if the equation of the curve be given in the form $f(x, y) = 0$, the tangent $Xf_x + Yf_y + Zf_z = 0$ makes intercepts $-f_z / f_x$ and $-f_z / f_y$ upon the co-ordinate axes, and the perpendicular from the origin upon the tangent is $f_z / \sqrt{f_x^2 + f_y^2}$;

and indeed, any lengths or angles desired may be written down by the ordinary methods and formulae of analytical geometry.

**Ex. 1.** For the "chainette"

$$y = \frac{c}{2}\left(e^{\frac{x}{c}} + e^{-\frac{x}{c}}\right)$$

we have $\quad y_1 = \frac{1}{2}\left(e^{\frac{x}{c}} - e^{-\frac{x}{c}}\right).$

Hence Subtangent $\quad = \dfrac{y}{y_1} = c\,\dfrac{e^{\frac{x}{c}} + e^{-\frac{x}{c}}}{e^{\frac{x}{c}} - e^{-\frac{x}{c}}}.$

Subnormal $\quad = yy_1 = \dfrac{c}{4}\left(e^{\frac{2x}{c}} - e^{-\frac{2x}{e}}\right).$

Normal $\quad = y\sqrt{1 + y_1^2} = \dfrac{y^2}{c}$, etc.

**Ex. 2.** Find that curve of the class $y = \dfrac{x^n}{a^{n-1}}$ whose subnormal is constant.

Here $\quad y_1 = n\,\dfrac{x^{n-1}}{a^{n-1}},$

and $\quad$ subnormal $= yy_1 = n\,\dfrac{x^{2n-1}}{a^{2n-2}}.$

Thus if $2n = 1$ the $x$ disappears and leaves subnormal $= \dfrac{a}{2}$, and the curve is the ordinary parabola

$$y^2 = ax.$$

## 90. Values of $\frac{ds}{dx}, \frac{dx}{ds}$, etc.

Let $P, Q$ be contiguous points on a curve. Let the co-ordinates of $P$ be $(x, y)$ and of $Q$ $(x + \delta x, y + \delta y)$.

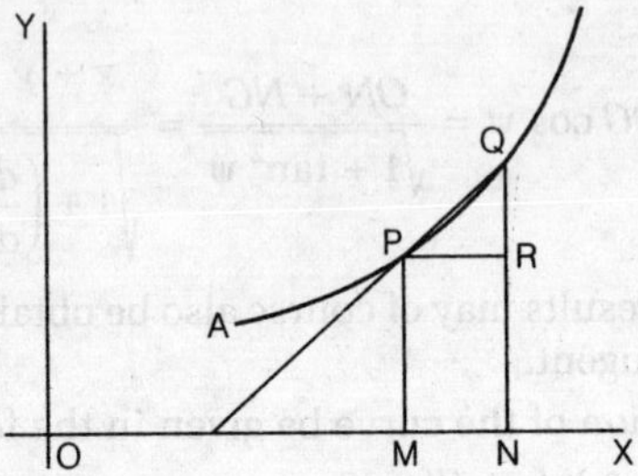


Then the perpendicular $PR = \delta x$, and $RQ = \delta y$. Let the arc $AP$ measured from some fixed point $A$ on the curve be called $s$ and the arc $AQ = s + \delta s$. Then arc $PQ = \delta s$. When $Q$ travels along the curve so as to come indefinitely near to $P$, the arc $PQ$ and the chord $PQ$ differ ultimately by a quantity of higher order of smallness than the arc $PQ$ itself. (Art. 81.)

Hence, rejecting infinitesimals of order higher than the second, we have

$$\delta s^2 = (\text{chord } PQ)^2 = (\delta x^2 + \delta y^2),$$

or

$$1 = Lt\left(\frac{\delta x^2}{\delta s^2} + \frac{\delta y^2}{\delta s^2}\right) = \left(\frac{dx}{ds}\right)^2 + \left(\frac{dy}{ds}\right)^2.$$

Similarly

$$Lt\,\frac{\delta s^2}{\delta x^2} = Lt\left(1 + \frac{\delta y^2}{\delta x^2}\right),$$

or

$$\left(\frac{ds}{dx}\right)^2 = 1 + \left(\frac{dy}{dx}\right)^2;$$

and in the same manner

$$\left(\frac{ds}{dy}\right)^2 = 1 + \left(\frac{dx}{dy}\right)^2$$

If $\psi$ be the angle which the tangent makes with the axis of $x$ we have as in Art. 18,

$$\tan\psi = Lt\,\frac{RQ}{PR} = Lt\,\frac{\delta y}{\delta x} = \frac{dy}{dx},$$

and also

$$\cos\psi = Lt\,\frac{PR}{\text{chord } PQ} = Lt\,\frac{PR}{\text{arc } PQ} = Lt\,\frac{\delta x}{\delta s} = \frac{dx}{ds},$$

and

$$\sin\psi = Lt\,\frac{RQ}{\text{chord } PQ} = Lt\,\frac{RQ}{\text{arc } PQ} = Lt\,\frac{\delta y}{\delta s} = \frac{dy}{ds}.$$

# EXAMPLES

**1.** Find the length of the perpendicular from the origin on the tangent at the point $x, y$ of the curve

$$x^4 + y^4 = c^4.$$

**2.** Show that in the curve $y = be^{\frac{x}{a}}$ the subtangent is of constant length.

**3.** Show that in the curve $by^2 = (x + a)^3$ the square of the subtangent varies as the subnormal.

**4.** For the parabola $y^2 = 4ax$, prove $\dfrac{ds}{dx} = \sqrt{\dfrac{a + x}{x}}$.

**5.** Prove that for the ellipse $\dfrac{x^2}{a^2} + \dfrac{y^2}{b^2} = 1$, if $x = a \sin \phi$,

$$\frac{ds}{d\phi} = a\sqrt{1 - e^2 \sin^2 \phi}.$$

**6.** For the cycloid $\left.\begin{array}{l} x = a \text{ vers } \theta \\ y = a(\theta + \sin \theta) \end{array}\right\}$,

prove $$\frac{ds}{dx} = \sqrt{\frac{2a}{x}}.$$

**7.** In the curve $y = a \log \sec \dfrac{x}{a}$,

prove $$\frac{d\varepsilon}{dx} = \sec \frac{x}{a}, \frac{ds}{dy} = \operatorname{cosec} \frac{x}{a}, \text{ and } x = a\psi.$$

**8.** Show that the portion of the tangent to the curve

$$x^{\frac{2}{3}} + y^{\frac{2}{3}} = a^{\frac{2}{3}},$$

which is intercepted between the axes, is of constant length.

Find the area of the portion included between the axes and the tangent.

**9.** Find for what value of $n$ the length of the subnormal of the curve $xy^n = a^{n+1}$ is constant. Also for what value of $n$ the area of the triangle included between the axes and any tangent in constant.

**10.** Prove that for the catenary $y = c \cosh \dfrac{x}{c}$, the length of the perpendicular from the foot of the ordinate on the tangent is of constant length.

**11.** In the tractory $x = \sqrt{c^2 - y^2} + \dfrac{c}{2} \log \dfrac{c - \sqrt{c^2 - y^2}}{c + \sqrt{c^2 - y^2}}$,

prove that the portion of the tangent intercepted between the point of contact and the axis of $x$ is of constant length.

## 91. Polar Co-ordinates.

If the equation of the curve be referred to polar co-ordinates, suppose $O$ to be the pole and $P, Q$ two contiguous points on the curve. Let the co-ordinates of $P$ and $Q$ be $(r, \theta)$ and $(r + \delta r, \theta + \delta\theta)$ respectively. Let $PN$ be the perpendicular on $OQ$, then $NQ$ differs from

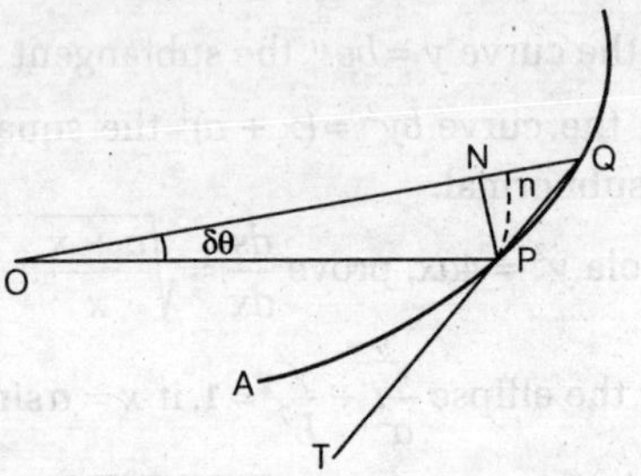


$\delta r$ and $NP$ from $r\delta\theta$ *by a quantity of higher order of smallness than* $\delta\theta$. (Art. 79).

Let the arc measured from some fixed point $A$ to $P$ be called $s$ and from $A$ to $Q$, $s + \delta s$. Then arc $PQ = \delta s$. Hence, rejecting infinitesimals of order higher than the second, we have $\delta s^2 = (\text{chord } PQ)^2 = (NQ^2 + PN^2) = (\delta r^2 + r^2\delta\theta^2)$,

and therefore

$$\left(\frac{dr}{ds}\right)^2 + r^2\left(\frac{d\theta}{ds}\right)^2 = 1, \text{ or } \left(\frac{ds}{dr}\right)^2 = 1 + r^2\left(\frac{d\theta}{dr}\right)^2,$$

or

$$\left(\frac{ds}{d\theta}\right)^2 = r^2 + \left(\frac{dr}{d\theta}\right)^2,$$

according as we divide by $\delta s^2, \delta r^2$, or $\delta\theta^2$ before proceeding to the limit.

## 92. Inclination of the Radius Vector to the Tangent.

Next, let $\phi$ be the angle which the tangent at any point $P$ makes with the radius vector, then

$$\tan\phi = r\frac{d\theta}{dr}, \cos\phi = \frac{dr}{ds}, \sin\phi = \frac{rd\theta}{ds}.$$

For, with the figure of the preceeding article, since, when $Q$ has moved along the curve so near to $P$ that $Q$ and $P$ may be considered as ultimately coincident, $QP$ becomes the tangent at $P$ and the angles $OQT$ and $OPT$ are each of them ultimately equal to $\phi$, and

$$\tan\phi = Lt \tan NQP = Lt\frac{NP}{QN} = Lt\frac{r\delta\theta}{\delta r} = r\frac{d\theta}{dr};$$

$$\cos\phi = Lt\cos NQP = Lt\frac{NQ}{\text{chord } QP}$$

$$= Lt\frac{NQ}{\text{arc } QP} = Lt\frac{\delta r}{\delta s} = \frac{dr}{ds};$$

$$\sin\phi = Lt \sin NQP = Lt \frac{NP}{\text{chord } QP}$$

$$= Lt \frac{NP}{\text{arc } QP} = Lt \frac{r\delta\theta}{\delta s} = \frac{rd\theta}{ds}.$$

**Ex.** Find the angle $\phi$ in the case of the curve

$$r^n = a^n \sec(n\theta + \alpha),$$

and prove that this curve is intersected by the curve

$$r^n = b^n \sec(n\theta + \beta)$$

at an angle which is independent of $a$ and $b$. [I.C.S, 1886.]

Taking the logarithmic differential,

$$\frac{1}{r}\frac{dr}{d\theta} = \tan(n\theta + \alpha),$$

whence $\frac{\pi}{2} - \phi = n\theta + \alpha.$

In a similar manner for the second curve

$$\frac{\pi}{2} - \phi' = n\theta + \beta,$$

$\phi'$ being the angle which the radius vector makes with the tangent to the second curve. Hence the angle between the tangents at the point of intersection is $\alpha \sim \beta$.

## 93. Polar Subtangent, Subnormal.

Let $OY$ be the perpendicular from the origin on the tangent at $P$. Let $TOt$ be drawn through $O$ perpendicular to $OP$ and cutting the

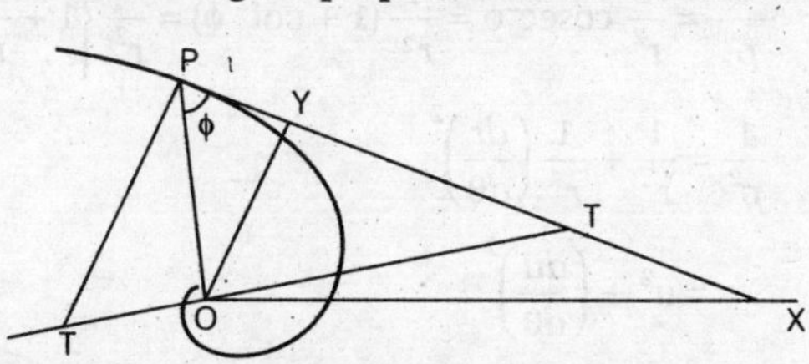


tangent in $T$ and the normal in $t$. Then $OT$ is called the "*Polar Subtangent*" and $Ot$ is called the "*Polar Subnormal*".

It is clear that

$$OT = OP\tan\phi = r^2\frac{d\theta}{dr} \qquad \text{...(1)},$$

and that $$Ot = OP\cot\phi = \frac{dr}{d\theta} \qquad \text{...(2)},$$

**94.** It is often found convenient when using polar co-ordinates to write $\frac{1}{u}$ for $r$, and therefore $-\frac{1}{u^2}\frac{du}{d\theta}$ for $\frac{dr}{d\theta}$. With this notation,

$$\text{Polar Subtangent} = r^2\frac{d\theta}{dr} = -\frac{d\theta}{du}.$$

**Ex.** In the conic $lu = 1 + e\cos\theta$

$$\text{we have } l = -e\sin\theta\frac{d\theta}{du}.$$

Thus the length of the polar subtangent is $l/e\sin\theta$.

Also, from the figure, the angular co-ordinate of its extremity is

$$\theta - \frac{\pi}{2}.$$

Hence the co-ordinates of $T\ (r_1, \theta_1)$ satisfy the equation

$$r_1 = l/e\sin\left(\frac{\pi}{2} + \theta_1\right).$$

The locus of the extremity is therefore $lu = e\cos\theta$;

that is, the directrix corresponding to that focus which is taken as origin.

## 95. Perpendicular from Pole on Tangent.

Let $OY = p.$

Then $p = r\sin\phi,$

and therefore

$$\frac{1}{p^2} = \frac{1}{r^2}\operatorname{cosec}^2\phi = \frac{1}{r^2}(1 + \cot^2\phi) = \frac{1}{r^2}\left\{1 + \frac{1}{r^2}\left(\frac{dr}{d\theta}\right)^2\right\};$$

therefore
$$\frac{1}{p^2} = \frac{1}{r^2} + \frac{1}{r^4}\left(\frac{dr}{d\theta}\right)^2 \qquad \text{...(1)}$$

$$= u^2 + \left(\frac{du}{d\theta}\right)^2 \qquad \text{...(2).}$$

**Ex.** In the spiral $r = a\frac{\theta^2}{\theta^2 - 1}$

we have $au = 1 - \theta^{-2},$

whence $a\frac{du}{d\theta} = 2\theta^{-3};$

and therefore, squaring and adding, $\frac{a^2}{p^2} = 1 - 2\theta^{-2} + \theta^{-4} + 4\theta^{-6}.$

Thus, corresponding to $\theta = \pm 1$, we have $\frac{a^2}{p^2} = 4$ and $p = \pm\frac{a}{2}.$

## 96. The Pedal Equation.

The relation between $p$ and $r$ often forms a very convenient equation to the curve. It is called the Pedal equation.

(1) If the curve be given in Cartesians,

say $$F(x, y) = 0 \quad \ldots(1),$$
the tangent is $$XF_x + YF_y + ZF_z = 0$$
and $$p^2 = \frac{F_z^2}{F_x^2 + F_y^2} \quad \ldots(2).$$

If $x, y$ be eliminated between equations (1), (2) and $x^2 + y^2 = r^2 \ldots$ (3), the required equation will result.

**Ex.** If $x^2 + y^2 = 2ax$, $X(x - a) + Yy = ax$

is the equation of the tangent, and

$$p^2 = \frac{a^2 x^2}{(x-a)^2 + y^2} = \frac{1}{4}\frac{r^4}{a^2},$$

or $$r^2 = 2ap.$$

This result will also be evident geometrically.

(2) If the curve be given in Polars we may first obtain $p$ in terms of $r$ and $\theta$ by Art. 95, and then eliminate $\theta$ between this result and the equation to the curve.

**Ex.** Required the pedal equation of $r^m = a^m \sin m\theta$.

By logarithmic differentiation,

$$\frac{m}{r}\frac{dr}{d\theta} = m \cot m\theta,$$

$$\therefore \quad \cot\phi = \cot m\theta \text{ or } \phi = m\theta,$$

whence $$p = r\sin\phi = r\sin m\theta = r\frac{r^m}{a^m},$$

or $$pa^m = r^{m+1}.$$

# EXAMPLES

**1.** In the equiangular spiral $r = ae^{\theta\cot\alpha}$, prove $\dfrac{dr}{ds} = \cos\alpha$ and $p = r\sin\alpha$.

**2.** For the involute of a circle, viz,

$$\theta = \frac{\sqrt{r^2 - a^2}}{a} - \cos^{-1}\frac{a}{r},$$

prove $\cos\phi = \dfrac{a}{r}$.

**3.** In the parabola $\frac{2a}{r} = 1 - \cos\theta$, prove the following results:—

($\alpha$) $\phi = \pi - \frac{\theta}{2}$. ($\beta$) $p = \frac{a}{\sin\frac{\theta}{2}}$.

($\gamma$) $p^2 = ar$. ($\delta$) Polar subtangent $= 2a \operatorname{cosec}\theta$.

**4.** For the cardioide $r = a(1 - \cos\theta)$, prove

($\alpha$) $\phi = \frac{\theta}{2}$. ($\beta$) $p = 2a\sin^3\frac{\theta}{2}$.

($\gamma$) $p^2 = \frac{r^3}{2a}$. ($\delta$) Polar subtangent $= 2a\frac{\sin^3\frac{\theta}{2}}{\cos\frac{\theta}{2}}$.

## 97. Maximum number of tangents from a point to a curve of the $n^{th}$ degree.

Let the equation of the curve be $f(x, y) = 0$. The equation of the tangent at the point $(x, y)$ is

$$Xf_x + Yf_y + Zf_z = 0,$$

where $z$ is to be put equal to unity after the differentiation is performed. If this pass through the point $h, k$ we have $hf_x + kf_y + f_z = 0$.

This is an equation of the $(n-1)^{th}$ degree in $x$ and $y$ and represents a curve of the $(n-1)^{th}$ degree *passing through the points of contact* of the tangents drawn from the point $(h, k)$ to the curve $f(x, y) = 0$. These two curves have $n(n-1)$ points of intersection, and therefore there are $n(n-1)$ *points of contact* corresponding to $n(n-1)$ *tangents, real or imaginary*, which can be drawn from a given point to a curve of the $n^{th}$ degree.

Thus for a conic, a cubic, a quartic, the maximum number of tangents which can be drawn from a given point is 2, 6, 12 respectively.

## 98. Number of Normals which can be drawn to a Curve to pass through a given point.

Let $h, k$ be the point through which the normals arc to pass.

The equation of the normal to the curve $f(x, y) = 0$ at the point $(x, y)$ is

$$\frac{X - x}{f_x} = \frac{Y - y}{f_y}.$$

If this pass through $h, k$,

$$(h - x) f_y = (k - y) f_x.$$

This equation is of the $n^{th}$ degree in $x$ and $y$ and represents a curve which goes *through the feet of all normals* which can be drawn from the point

$h, k$ to the curve. Combining this with $f(x, y) = 0$, which is also of the $n^{th}$ degree, it appears that there are $n^2$ points of intersection, and that therefore there can be $n^2$ *normals, real or imaginary*, drawn to a given curve to pass through a given point.

For example, if the curve be an ellipse, $n = 2$, and the number of normals is 4. Let $\frac{x^2}{a^2} + \frac{y^2}{b^2} = 1$ be the equation of the curve, then

$$(h - x)\frac{y}{b^2} = (k - y)\frac{x}{a^2}$$

is the curve which, with the ellipse, determines the feet of the normals drawn from the point $(h, k)$. This is a rectangular hyperbola which passes through the origin and through the point $(h, k)$.

The student should consider how it is that an *infinite* number of normals can be drawn from the centre of a circle to the circumference.

**99.** The curves

$$(h - x) f_x + (k - y) f_y = 0 \qquad \ldots(1),$$

and

$$(h - x) f_y - (k - y) f_x = 0 \qquad \ldots(2),$$

on which lie the points of contact of tangents and the feet of the normals respectively, which can be drawn to the curve $f(x, y) = 0$ so as to pass through the point $(h, k)$ are the same for the curve $f(x, y) = a$. And, as equations (1) and (2) do not depend on $a$, they represent *the loci of the points of contact and of the feet of the normals* respectively for all values of $a$, that is, for all members of the family of curves obtained by varying $a$ in $f(x, y) = a$ in any manner.

# EXAMPLES

1. Through the point $h, k$ tangents are drawn to the curve $Ax^3 + By^3 = 1$; show that the points of contact lie on a conic.
2. If from any point $P$ normals be drawn to the curve whose equation is $y^m = max^n$, show that the feet of the normals lie on a conic of which the straight line joining $P$ to the origin is a diameter. Find the position of the axes of this conic.
3. The points of contact of tangents from the point $h, k$ to the curve $x^3 + y^3 = 3axy$ lie on a conic which passes through the origin.
4. Through a given point $h, k$ tangents are drawn to curves where the ordinate varies as the cube of the abscissa. Show that the locus of the points of contact is the rectangular hyperbola $2xy + kx - 3hy = 0$, and the locus of the remaining point in which each tangent cuts the curve is the rectangular hyperbola

$$xy - 4kx + 3hy = 0.$$

# EXAMPLES

1. Find the points on the curve, $y = (x-1)(x-2)(x-3)$ at which the tangent is parallel to the axis of $x$.

   Show also that the tangents at the first and third intersections with the $x$-axis are parallel, and at the middle intersection the tangent makes an angle 135° with that axis.

2. In any Cartesian curve the rectangle contained by the subtangent and the subnormal is equal to the square on the corresponding ordinate.

3. Show that the only Cartesian locus in which the ratio of the subtangent to the subnormal is constant is a straight line.

4. If the ratio of the subnormal to the subtangent vary as the square of the abscissa the curve is a parabola.

5. Show that in any curve $\dfrac{\text{Subnormal}}{\text{Subtangent}} = \left(\dfrac{\text{Normal}}{\text{Tangent}}\right)^2$.

6. Find that normal to $\sqrt{xy} = a + x$, which makes equal intercepts upon the co-ordinate axes.

7. Prove that the sum of the intercepts of the tangent to $\sqrt{x} + \sqrt{y} = \sqrt{a}$ upon the co-ordinate axes is constant.

8. Show that in the curve $y = a \log (x^2 - a^2)$, the sum of the tangent and the subtangent varies as the product of the co-ordinates of the point.

9. Show that in the curve $x^{m+n} = a^{m-n} y^{2n}$, the $m^{\text{th}}$ power of the subtangent varies as the $n^{\text{th}}$ power of the subnormal.

10. In the curve $y^n = a^{n-1} x$ the subnormal $\propto \dfrac{y^2}{x}$ and the subtangent $\propto x$.

11. Show that in the curve $y = be^{-\frac{\alpha}{x}}$ the subtangent varies as the square of the abscissa.

12. If in a curve the normal varies as the cube of the ordinate, find the subtangent and the subnormal.

13. Show that in the curve for which $s = c \log \dfrac{c}{y}$ the tangent is of constant length.

14. Show that in the curve for which $y^2 = c^2 + s^2$, The Catenary) the perpendicular from the foot of the ordinate upon the tangent is of constant length.

15. Show that the polar subtangent in the curve $r = a\theta$ (The Spiral of Archimedes) varies as the square of the radius vector, and the polar subnormal is constant.

16. Show that the polar subtangent is constant in the curve $r\,\theta = a$. (The Reciprocal Spiral.)

**17.** Show that in the curve $r = ae^{\theta \cot \alpha}$, (The Equiangular Spiral.)

(1) the tangent makes a constant angle with the radius vector;

(2) the Polar Subtangent $= r \tan \alpha$, the Polar Subnormal $= r \cot \alpha$;

(3) the loci of the extremities of the polar subtangent, the polar subnormal, the perpendicular upon the tangent from the pole are curves of the same species as the original.

**18.** Show that each of the several classes of curves (Cotes's Spirals) $r = ae^{m\theta}, r\theta = a, r \sin n\theta = a, r \sinh n\theta = a, r \cosh n\theta = a$, have pedal equations of the form $\dfrac{1}{P^2} = \dfrac{A}{r^2} + B$, where $A$ and $B$ are certain constants.

**19.** Find the angle of intersection of the Cardioides

$$r = a(1 + \cos\theta),\ r = b(1 - \cos\theta).$$

**20.** Find the angle of intersection of $\left.\begin{matrix} x^2 - y^2 = a^2 \\ x^2 + y^2 = a^2\sqrt{2} \end{matrix}\right\}$

**21.** Show that the condition of tangency of $x \cos\alpha + y \sin\alpha = p$, with $x^m y^n = a^{m+n}$, is $p^{m+n} \cdot m^m \cdot n^n = (m+n)^{m+n} a^{m+n} \cos^m \alpha \sin^n \alpha$. Hence write down the equation of the locus of the foot of the perpendicular from the origin upon a tangent.

**22.** Show that in the curve (the cycloid)

$$x = a(\theta + \sin\theta),\ y = a(1 - \cos\theta),\ \frac{ds}{d\theta} = 2a \cos\frac{\theta}{2} \text{ and } \frac{ds}{dy} = \sqrt{\frac{2a}{y}}.$$

**23.** Show that in the curve (an epicycloid)

$$x = (a+b)\cos\theta - b\cos\frac{a+b}{b}\theta,\ y = (a+b)\sin\theta - b\sin\frac{a+b}{b}\theta,$$

we have $p = (a+2b)\sin\dfrac{a}{2b}\theta;\ \psi = \dfrac{a+2b}{2b}\theta;\ p = (a+2b)\sin\dfrac{a\psi}{a+2b};$

and that the pedal equation is $r^2 = a^2 + 4\dfrac{(a+b)b}{(a+2b)^2}p^2$.

**24.** Show that the normal to $y^2 = 4ax$ touches the curve

$$27ay^2 = 4(x - 2a)^3.$$

**25.** Show that the locus of the extremity of the polar subtangent of the curve $u = f(\theta)$, is $u + f'\left(\dfrac{\pi}{2} + \theta\right) = 0$.

**26.** Show that the locus of the extremity of the polar subnormal of the curve $r = f(\theta)$, is $r = f'\left(\theta - \dfrac{\pi}{2}\right)$.

**27.** In the curve $r\left(m + n\tan\dfrac{\theta}{2}\right) = 1 + \tan\dfrac{\theta}{2}$, show that the locus of the extremity of the polar subtangent is $\dfrac{m-n}{2} r = 1 + \cos\theta$.

# CHAPTER IX.

# ASYMPTOTES.

**100.** DEF. If a straight line cut a curve in two points at an infinite distance from the origin and yet is not itself wholly at infinity, it is called an asymptote to the curve.

## 101. To obtain the Asymptotes.

If $$\phi(x, y) = 0 \qquad \ldots(1)$$

be the equation of any rational algebraic curve of the $n$th degree, and

$$y = mx + c \qquad \ldots(2)$$

that of any straight line, the equation

$$\phi(x, mx + c) = 0 \qquad \ldots(3)$$

obtained by substituting the expression $mx + c$ for $y$ gives the abscissae of the points of intersection.

This equation is in general of the $n^{\text{th}}$ degree, showing that a curve of the $n^{\text{th}}$ degree is in general cut in $n$ points real or imaginary by any straight line.

The two constants of the straight line, viz. $m$ and $c$, are at our choice. We are to choose them so as to make two of the roots of equation (3) infinite. We then have a line cutting the given curve so that two of the points of intersection are at an infinite distance from the origin.

Imagine equation (3) expanded out and expressed in descending powers of $x$ as

$$Ax^n + Bx^{n-1} + Cx^{n-2} + \ldots + K = 0 \qquad \ldots(4),$$

$A, B, C$ etc. being certain functions of $m$ and $c$.

The equation whose roots are the reciprocals of the roots of this equation is

$$A + Bz + Cz^2 + \ldots + Kz^n = 0 \qquad \left(\text{by putting } x = \frac{1}{z}\right);$$

and it is evident that if $A$ and $B$ be both zero two roots of this equation for $z$ will become evanescent, and therefore two roots of the equation for $x$ become infinite. If then we choose $m$ and $c$ to satisfy the equations.

$$A = 0, B = 0,$$

and substitute their values in the equation

$$y = mx + c,$$

we shall obtain the equation of an asymptote.

**102.** It will be found in examples (and it admits of general proof) that the equation $A=0$ contains $m$ only and in a degree not higher than $n$. Also that $B=0$ contains $c$ in the first degree. Hence a curve of the $n^{\text{th}}$ degree does not possess more than $n$ asymptotes.

**Ex.** Find the asymptotes of the curve

$$y^3 - x^2y + 2y^2 + 4y + x = 0.$$

Putting $$y = mx + c,$$

$$(mx+c)^3 - x^2(mx+c) + 2(mx+c)^2 + 4(mx+c) + x = 0,$$

or $$(m^3 - m)x^3 + (3m^2c - c + 2m^2)x^2 + \ldots \text{ etc.} = 0.$$

We now are to choose $m$ and $c$ so that

$$\left.\begin{aligned} m^3 - m &= 0 \\ \text{and} \quad 3m^2c - c + 2m^2 &= 0 \end{aligned}\right\}.$$

The first equation is a *cubic* for $m$ and gives $m = 0, 1$ or $-1$.

The second equation is of the *first degree* in $c$ and gives

$$c = \frac{2m^2}{1-3m^2}.$$

If $m = 0$ we have $c = 0$;

if $m = 1$ we have $c = -1$;

if $m = -1$ we have $c = -1$.

Hence we obtain *three* asymptotes, viz.

$$y = 0, \quad y = x - 1, \quad y = -x - 1.$$

# EXAMPLES

*Find the asymptotes of*

1. $y^3 - 6xy^2 + 11x^2y - 6x^3 + x + y = 0$.
2. $y^3 - 4x^2y - xy^2 + 4x^3 + 4xy - 4x^2 = 5$.
3. $y^3 - 3x^2y + xy^2 - 3x^3 + 2y^2 + 2xy + 4x + 5y + 6 = 0$.
4. $(y+x+1)(y+2x+2)(y+3x+3)(y-x) + x^2 + y^2 - 2 = 0$.
5. $(2x+3y)(3x+4y)(4x+5y) + 26x^2 + 70xy + 47y^2 + 2x + 3y = 1$.

## 103. The case of parallel Asymptotes.

After having formed equation (4) of Art. 101 by substitution of $mx + c$ for $y$ and rearrangement, it sometimes happens that one or more of the values of $m$, deduced from the equation $m = 0$ will make $B$ vanish *identically*, and therefore *any* value of $c$ will give a line cutting the curve in two points at infinity. In this case as the letter $c$ is still at our choice, it may be chosen so as to make the third coefficient $C$ vanish. It will be seen from examples that each such value of $m$ now gives rise to two values of $c$. This is the case of parallel asymptotes. The two lines thus obtained each cut the curve at three points at infinity.

**Ex.** Find the asymptotes of the cubic curve,

$y^3 - 5xy^2 + 8x^2y - 4x^3 - 3y^2 + 9xy - 6x^2 + 2y - 2x = 1$.

Putting $mx + c$ for $y$ and rearranging,

$$(m^3 - 5m^2 + 8m - 4)\,x^3 + (3m^2c - 10mc + 8c - 3m^2 + 9m - 6)x^2$$

$$+ (3mc^2 - 5c^2 - 6mc + 9c + 2m - 2)x + c^3 - 3c^2 + 2c - 1 = 0.$$

Choosing $\left.\begin{aligned} m^3 - 5m^2 + 8m - 4 &= 0 \\ 3m^2c - 10mc + 8c - 3m^2 + 9m - 6 &= 0 \end{aligned}\right]$ and

the first gives $(m-1)(m-2)^2 = 0$,

whence $m = 1, 2$ or $2$.

If $m = 1$ the second equation gives $c = 0$ and the corresponding asymptote is $y = x$.

If $m = 2$ we have $12c - 20c + 8c - 12 + 18 - 6$ which vanishes identically for all finite values of $c$. Thus *any* line parallel to $y = 2x$ will cut the curve in two points at infinity. We may however choose $c$ so that the next coefficient

$$3mc^2 - 5c^2 - 6mc + 9c + 2m - 2$$

vanishes for the value $m = 2$, giving $c^2 - 3c + 2 = 0$, *i.e.* $c = 1$ or $2$.

Thus each of the system of lines parallel to $y = 2x$ cuts the curve in *two* points at infinity. But of all this infinite system of parallel straight lines the two whose equations are

$$y = 2x + 1, \qquad \text{and} \qquad y = 2x + 2,$$

are the only ones which cut the curve in *three* points at infinity and therefore the name *asymptote* is confined to them.

The asymptotes are therefore

$$\left.\begin{aligned} y &= x \\ y &= 2x + 1 \\ y &= 2x + 2 \end{aligned}\right\}$$

## EXAMPLES

*Find the asymptotes of*

1. $y^3 - xy^2 - x^2y + x^3 + x^2 - y^2 = 1$.
2. $y^4 - 2xy^3 + 2x^3y - x^4 - 3x^3 + 3x^2y + 3xy^2 - 3y^3 - 2x^2 + 2y^2 = 1$.
3. $(y^2 - x^2)^2 - 2(x^2 + y^2) = 1$.

**104.** Those asymptotes which are parallel to the $y$-axis will not be discovered by the above processes for their equations are of the form $x = a$, and are not included in the form $y = mx + c$ for a finite value of $m$. We, therefore specially consider the case of those asymptotes which may be parallel to one or other of the co-ordinate axes.

## 105. Asymptotes Parallel to the Axes.

Let the equations of the curve be

$$\begin{aligned} a_0x^n &+ a_1x^{n-1}y + a_2x^{n-2}y^2 + \ldots + a_{n-1}xy^{n-1} + a_ny^n \\ &+ b_1x^{n-1} + b_2x^{n-2}y + \ldots\ldots\ldots\ldots + b_ny^{n-1} \\ &+ c_2x^{n-2} + \ldots \\ &+ \ldots = 0 \end{aligned} \quad \ldots (1)$$

If arranged in descending powers of $x$ this is

$$a_0x^n + (a_1y + b_1)x^{n-1} + \ldots = 0 \quad \ldots (2)$$

Hence, if $a_0$ vanish, and $y$ be so chosen that $a_1y + b_1 = 0$, the coefficients of the two highest powers of $x$ in equation (2) vanish, and therefore *two of its roots are infinite*. Hence the straight line $a_1y + b_1 = 0$ is an asymptote.

In the same way, if $a_n = 0$, $a_{n-1}x + b_n = 0$ is an asymptote.

Again, if $a_0 = 0$, $a_1 = 0$, $b_1 = 0$, and if $y$ be so chosen that

$$a_2y^2 + b_2y + c_2 = 0,$$

three roots of Equation (2) become infinite, and the lines represented by $\quad a_2y^2 + b_2y + c_2 = 0$

represent a pair of asymptotes, real or imaginary parallel to the axis of $x$.

Hence the rule to find those asymptotes which are parallel to the axes is, *"equate to zero the coefficients of the highest powers of x and y."*

**Ex. 1.** Find the asymptotes of the curve

$$x^2y^2 - x^2y - xy^2 + x + y + 1 = 0.$$

Here the coefficient of $x^2$ is $y^2 - y$ and the coefficient of $y^2$ is $x^2 - x$. Hence $x = 0$, $x = 1$, $y = 0$, and $y = 1$ are asymptotes. Also, since the curve is one of fourth degree, we have thus obtained all the asymptotes.

**Ex. 2.** Find the asymptotes of the cubic curve

$$x^3 + 2x^2y + xy^2 - x^2 - xy + 2 = 0.$$

Equating to zero the coefficient of $y^2$ we obtain $x = 0$, the only asymptote parallel to either axis.

Putting $mx + c$ for $y$,

$$x^2 + 2x^2(mx + c) + x(mx + c)^2 - x^2 - x(mx + c) + 2 = 0,$$

or rearranging, $x^3(1 + 2m + m^2) + x^2(2c + 2mc - 1 - m)$

$$+ x(c^2 - c) + 2 = 0,$$

$1 + 2m + m^2 = 0$ gives two roots $m = -1$. $2c + 2mc - 1 - m = 0$ is an identity if $m = -1$ and this fails to find $c$. Proceeding to the next coefficient $c^2 - c = 0$ gives $c = 0$ or 1.

Hence the three asymptotes are $x = 0$, and the pair of parallel lines

$$y + x = 0, \quad y + x = 1.$$

## EXAMPLES

1. The asymptotes of$y^2 (x^2 - a^2) = x$ are $\left.\begin{matrix} y = 0 \\ x = \pm a \end{matrix}\right\}$.

2. The co-ordinate axes are the asymptotes of
$$xy^3 + x^3y = a^4.$$

3. The asymptotes of the curve $x^2y^2 = c^2 (x^2 + y^2)$ are the sides of a square.

**106.** The methods given above will obtain all linear asymptotes. It is often more expeditious however to obtain the oblique asymptotes as an approximation of the curve to a linear from at infinity as described in the next article.

## 107. Form of the Curve at Infinity. Another Method for Oblique Asymptotes.

Let $P_r, F_r$ be used to denote rational algebraical expressions which contain terms of the $r^{\text{th}}$ and lower, but of no higher degrees.

Suppose the equation of a curve of the $n^{\text{th}}$ degree to be thrown into the form

$$(ax + by + c)\,P_{n-1} + F_{n-1} = 0 \qquad \text{... (1).}$$

Then *any* straight line parallel to $ax + by = 0$ obviously cuts the curve in *one* point at infinity; and to find the particular member of this family of parallel straight lines which cuts the curve in a second point at infinity, let us examine what is the ultimate linear form to which the curve gradually approximates as we travel to infinity in the above direction, thus obtaining the ultimate direction of the curve and forming the equation of the tangent at infinity. To do this we make the $x$ and $y$ of the curve become *large in the ratio given by*

$$x : y = -b : a,$$

and we obtain the equation

$$ax + by + c + \underset{y=-\frac{a}{b}x = \infty}{Lt} \left(\frac{F_{n-1}}{P_{n-1}}\right) = 0.$$

If this limit be finite we have arrived at the equation of a straight line which at infinity represents the limiting form of the curve, and which satisfies the definition of an asymptote.

To obtain the value of the limit it is advantageous to put $x = -\dfrac{b}{t}$ and $y = \dfrac{a}{t}$, and then after simplification make $t = 0$.

**Ex.** Find the asymptote of

$$x^3 + 3x^2y + 3xy^2 + 2y^3 = x^2 + y^2 + x.$$

We may write this curve as

$$(x + 2y)(x^2 + xy + y^2) = x^2 + y^2 + x,$$

whence the equation of the asymptote is given by

$$x + 2y = Lt_{x=-2\,y=\infty} \frac{x^2 + y^2 + x}{x^2 + xy + y^2},$$

and putting $x = \frac{-2}{t}$, $y = \frac{1}{t}$ we have

$$x + 2y = Lt_{t=0} \frac{\frac{4}{t^2} + \frac{1}{t^2} - \frac{2}{t}}{\frac{4}{t^2} - \frac{2}{t^2} + \frac{1}{t^2}} = Lt_{t=0} \frac{5 - 2t}{3} = \frac{5}{3},$$

*i.e.*, $$x + 2y = \frac{5}{3}.$$

**Ex.** Show that $x + y = \frac{a}{2}$ is the only real asymptote of the curve

$$(x + y)(x^4 + y^4) = a(x^4 + a^4).$$

**108.** Next, suppose the equation of a curve put into the form

$$(ax + by + c)F_{n-1} + F_{n-2} = 0,$$

then the line $ax + by + c = 0$ cuts the curve in two points at infinity, for no terms of the $n^{\text{th}}$ or $(n-1)^{\text{th}}$ degrees remain in the equation determining the points of intersection. Hence in general the line

$$ax + by + c = 0$$

is an asymptote. We say, *in general*, because if $F_{n-1}$ be of the form $(ax + by + c)P_{n-2}$, itself containing a factor $ax + by + c$, there will be a *pair of asymptotes* parallel to $ax + by + c = 0$, each cutting the curve in *three* points at infinity. The equation of the curve then becomes

$$(ax + by + c)^2 P_{n-2} + F_{n-2} = 0,$$

and the equations of the parallel asymptotes are

$$ax + by + c = \pm\sqrt{-Lt \frac{F_{n-2}}{P_{n-2}}},$$

where $x$ and $y$ in the limit on the right-hand side become infinite in the ratio $\frac{x}{y} = -\frac{b}{a}$.

Or, if the curve be written in the form

$$(ax + by)^2 P_{n-2} + (ax + by) F_{n-2} + f_{n-2} = 0,$$

in proceeding to infinity in the direction $ax + by = 0$, we have

$$(ax + by)^2 (ax + by) \cdot Lt \frac{F_{n-2}}{P_{n-2}} + Lt \frac{f_{n-2}}{P_{n-2}} = 0,$$

when the limits are to be obtained by putting $x = -\frac{b}{t}$, $y = \frac{a}{t}$, and then diminishing $t$ indefinitely. We thus obtain a pair of parallel asymptotes,

$$ax + by = \alpha \text{ and } ax + by = \beta.$$

where $\alpha$ and $\beta$ are the roots of $\rho^2 + \rho\, Lt \frac{F_{n-2}}{P_{n-2}} + Lt \frac{f_{n-2}}{P_{n-2}} = 0$.

And other particular forms which the equation of the curve may assume can be treated similarly.

**Ex. 1.** To find the pair of parallel asymptotes of the curve

$$(2x - 3y + 1)^2 (x + y) - 8x + 2y - 9 = 0.$$

Here $2x - 3y + 1 = \pm \sqrt{Lt \frac{8x - 2y + 9}{x + y}}$,

where $x$ and $y$ become infinite in the direction of the line $2x = 3y$.

Putting $x = \frac{3}{t}$, $y = \frac{2}{t}$, the right side becomes $\pm 2$. Hence the asymptotes required are $2x - 3y = 1$ and $2x - 3y + 3 = 0$.

**Ex. 2.** Find the asymptotes of

$$(x - y)^2 (x^2 + y^2) - 10 (x - y) x^2 + 12y^2 + 2x + y = 0.$$

Here, $$(x - y)^2 - 10(x - y) Lt_{x = y = \infty} \frac{x^2}{x^2 + y^2} + 12 Lt_{x = y = \infty} \frac{y^2}{x^2 + y^2} = 0,$$

or $$(x - y)^2 - 5(x - y) + 6 = 0,$$

giving the parallel asymptotes $x - y = 2$ and $x - y = -3$.

## 109. Asymptotes by Inspection.

It is now clear that if the equation $F_n = 0$ break up into linear factors so as to represent a system of $n$ straight lines, no two of which are parallel, they will be the asymptotes of any curve of the form

$$F_n + F_{n-2} = 0.$$

**Ex. 1.** $(x - y)(x + y)(x + 2y - 1) = 3x + 4x + 5$.

is a cubic curve whose asymptotes are obviously

$$x - y = 0,$$
$$x + y = 0,$$
$$x + 2y - 1 = 0.$$

**Ex. 2.** $(x-y)^2(x+2y-1)=3x+4y+5.$

Here $x+2y-1=0$ is one asymptote. The other two asymptotes are parallel to $y=x$. Their equations are

$$x-y=\pm\sqrt{Lt_{t=0}\frac{3+4+5t}{1+2-t}}=\pm\sqrt{\frac{7}{3}}.$$

## 110. Case in which all the Asymptotes pass through the Origin.

If then, when the equation of a curve is arranged in homogeneous sets of terms, as

$$u_n+u_{n-2}+u_{n-3}+\ldots=0,$$

it be found that there are no terms of degree $n-1$, and if also $u_n$ contain no repeated factor, the $n$ straight lines passing through the origin, and whose equation is $u_n=0$, are the $n$ asymptotes.

## EXAMPLES

*Find the asymptotes of the following curves:—*

**1.** $y^3=x^2(2a-x)$. **2.** $y^3=x(a^2-x^2)$.

**3.** $x^3+y^3=a^3$. **4.** $y(a^2+x^2)=a^2x$.

**5.** $axy=x^3-a^3$. **6.** $y^2(2a-x)=x^3$.

**7.** $x^3+y^3=3axy$. **8.** $x^2y+y^2x=a^3$.

**9.** $x^2y^2=(a+y)^2(b^2-y^2)$. **10.** $x^2y^2=a^2y^2-b^2x^2$.

**11.** $xy(x-y)-a(x^2-y^2)=b^3$. **12.** $(a^2-x^2)y^2=x^2(a^2+x^2)$.

**13.** $xy^2=4a^2(2a-x)$. **14.** $y^2(a-x)=x(b-x)^2$.

**15.** $x^2y=x^3+x+y$. **16.** $xy^2+a^2y=x^3+mx^2+nx+p$.

**17.** $x^3+2x^2y-xy^2-2y^3+4y^2+2xy+y-1=0$.

**18.** $x^3-2x^2y+xy^2+x^2-xy+2=0$.

**19.** $y(x-y)^3=y(x-y)+2$.

**20.** $x^3+2x^2y-4xy^2-8y^3-4x+8y=1$.

**21.** $(x+y)^2(x+2y+2)=x+9y-2$.

**22.** $3x^3+17x^2y+21xy^2-9y^3-2ax^2-12axy-18ay^2-3a^2x+a^2y=0$.

## 111. Intersections of a Curve with its Asymptotes.

If a curve of the $n^{th}$ degree have $n$ asymptotes, no two of which are parallel, we have seen in Art. 109 that the equations of the asymptotes and of the curve may be respectively written

$$F_n = 0,$$

and

$$F_n + F_{n-2} = 0.$$

The $n$ asymptotes therefore intersect the curve again at points lying upon the curve $F_{n-2} = 0$. Now each asymptote cuts its curve in two points at infinity, and therefore in $n - 2$ other points. Hence these $n(n-2)$ points lie on a certain curve of degree $n - 2$. For example,

1. The asymptotes of a *cubic* will cut the curve again in *three points lying in a straight line*;
2. The asymptotes of a *quartic* curve will cut the curve again in *eight points lying on a conic section*;

and so on with curves of higher degree.

# EXAMPLES

1. Find the equation of a cubic which has the same asymptotes as the curve $x^3 - 6x^2y + 11xy^2 - 6y^3 + x + y + 1 = 0$, and which touches the axis of $y$ at the origin, the goes through and point (3, 2).
2. Show that the asymptotes of the cubic $x^2y - xy^2 + xy + y^2 + x - y = 0$ cut the curve again in the three points which lie on the line $x + y = 0$.
3. Find the equation of the conic on which lie the eight points of intersection of the quartic curve
$$xy(x^2 - y^2) + a^2y^2 + b^2x^2 = a^2b^2$$
with its asymptotes.
4. Show that the four asymptotes of the curve
$$(x^2 - y^2)(y^2 - 4x^2) - 6x^3 + 5x^2y + 3xy^2 - 2y^3 - x^2 + 3xy - 1 = 0$$
cut the curve again in eight points which lie on a circle.

## 112. Polar co-ordinates.

When the equation of a curve is given in the form

$$rf_1(\theta) + f_0(\theta) = 0 \qquad ...(1),$$

it is clear that the directions given by

$$f_1(\theta) = 0 \qquad ...(2),$$

are those in which $r$ becomes infinite.

Let this equation be solved, and let the roots be $\alpha$, $\beta$, $\gamma$, etc.

Let $\widehat{XOP} = \alpha$. Then the radius $OP$, the curve, and the asymptote meet at infinity towards $P$. Let $OY = (= p)$ be the perpendicular upon the asymptote.

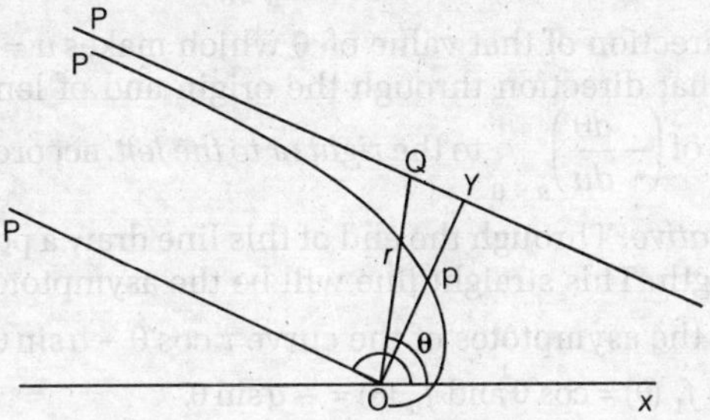


Since $OY$ is at right angles to $OP$ it is the polar subtangent, and $p = -\dfrac{d\theta}{du}$.

Let $\widehat{XOY} = \alpha'$, and let $Q$ be any point whose co-ordinates are $r$, $\theta$ upon the asymptote. Then the equation of the asymptote is

$$p = r\cos(\theta - \alpha') \qquad ...(3).$$

It is clear from the figure that $\alpha' = \alpha - \dfrac{\pi}{2}$.

To find the value of $-\dfrac{d\theta}{du}$ when $u = 0$, write $\dfrac{1}{u}$ for $r$ in equation (1), and we have

$$f_1(\theta) + u f_0(\theta) = 0.$$

whence differentiating

$$f_1'\,\theta + u f_0'(\theta) + \frac{du}{d\theta} f_0(\theta) = 0.$$

Putting $\theta = \alpha$, and therefore $u = 0$, we have (if $f_0'(\alpha)$ be finite)

$$\left(-\frac{d\theta}{du}\right)_{u=0} = \frac{f_0(\alpha)}{f_1'(\alpha)} \qquad ...(4).$$

Substitute this value of $\left(-\dfrac{d\theta}{du}\right)_{u=0}$ for $p$ in equation (3) and we obtain

$$\frac{f_0(\alpha)}{f_1'(\alpha)} = r\cos\left(\theta - \alpha + \frac{\pi}{2}\right) = r\sin(\alpha - \theta).$$

Hence the equations of the asymptotes are

$$r\sin(\alpha - \theta) = \frac{f_0(\alpha)}{f_1'(\alpha)},$$

$$r\sin(\beta - \theta) = \frac{f_0(\beta)}{f_1'(\beta)}$$

etc.

## 113. Rule for Drawing the Asymptote.

After having found the value of $\left(-\frac{d\theta}{du}\right)_{u=0}$ imagine we stand at the origin looking in the direction of that value of $\theta$ which makes $u = 0$. Draw a line at right angles to that direction through the origin and of length equal to the calculated value of $\left(-\frac{d\theta}{du}\right)_{u=0}$ to the *right or to the left*, according as that value is *positive or negative*. Through the end of this line draw a perpendicular to it of indefinite length. This straight line will be the asymptote.

**Ex.** Find the asymptotes of the curve $r \cos\theta - a \sin\theta = 0$.

Here $f_1(\theta) = \cos\theta$ and $f_0(\theta) = -a\sin\theta$,

$$\cos\theta = 0 \text{ gives } \alpha = \frac{\pi}{2}, \beta = \frac{3\pi}{2}, \text{ etc.}$$

and the length of the polar subtangent $= \frac{f_0(\alpha)}{f_1'(\alpha)} = \frac{-a\sin\alpha}{-\sin\alpha} = a.$

Hence the equations of the asymptotes are

$$r\sin\left(\frac{\pi}{2} - \theta\right) = a \quad \text{and} \quad r\sin\left(\frac{3\pi}{2} - \theta\right) = a,$$

*i.e.*, $r\cos\theta = a$ and $r\cos\theta = -a$.

These are perpendicular to the initial line and at distance $a$ respectively to right and left of the origin.

## EXAMPLES

*Find the asymptotes and draw their positions for the following curves:—*

**1.** $r\theta^{\frac{1}{2}} = a.$

**2.** $r\theta = a.$

**3.** $r\sin n\theta = a.$

**4.** $r = a \operatorname{cosec}\theta + b.$

**5.** $r = 2a\sin\theta\tan\theta.$

**6.** $r\sin 2\theta = a\cos 3\theta.$

**7.** $r = a + b\cot n\theta.$

**8.** $r^n \sin n\theta = a^n.$

## 114. Circular Asymptotes.

In many polar curves when $\theta$ is increased indefinitely it happens that the equation ultimately takes the form of an equation in $r$ which represents one or more concentric circles.

For example, in the curve $r = a\frac{\theta}{\theta - 1}$,

which may be written $r = a\frac{1}{1 - \frac{1}{\theta}}$,

it is clear that if $\theta$ becomes very large the curve approaches indefinitely near the limiting circle $r = a$.

Such a circle is called an *asymptotic circle* of the curve.

# EXAMPLES

*Find the asymptotes of the following curves:—*

**1.** $x^5 - y^5 = a^3 xy$.

**2.** $x^5 - y^5 = ax^4$.

**3.** $x^5 - y^5 = ay^4$.

**4.** $y = x \dfrac{x^2 + 1}{x^2 - 1}$.

**5.** $(x - a)\, y^2 = (2a - x)\, x^2$.

**6.** $y = \dfrac{x - 3}{(x - 1)(x - 2)}$.

**7.** $\dfrac{y^2}{y - 1} = \dfrac{x^2}{x - 2}$.

**8.** $(y - x)^4 = x^4 - a^4$.

**9.** $(x^2 - y^2)^2 = a^2 x^2 - b^2 y^2$.

**10.** $y^2 (a^2 - x^2) = (x^2 - 2a^2)^2$.

**11.** $\dfrac{y^2}{x^2} = \dfrac{(a - x)^2}{x^2 + a^2}$.

**12.** $y^3 = (x - 1)^2 (x - 4)$.

**13.** $(y - x)^2 x^2 = 4(y - x)^2 + 16$.

**14.** $(x^2 - 4y^2)^2 = 2(x^2 + y^2)$.

**15.** $xy^2 - y = ax^3 + bx^2 + cx + d$.

**16.** $(y - 2x)^2 (3x + 4y) + 3(y - 2x)(3x + 4y) = 5$.

**17.** $(y - 2x)^2 (3x + 4y) + 3(y - 2x)(3x + 4y) + 11y = 5$.

**18.** $y^4 - 4xy^3 + 3x^2y^2 + 4x^3y - 4x^4 + 3y^3 - 6xy^2 - 3x^2y + 6x^3 + 2y^2 - 2x^2 = x$.

**19.** $r = b \sec a\theta$.

**20.** $r(e^\theta - 1) = a(e^\theta + 1)$. Find also the circular asymptote.

**21.** $r(\theta^2 - 1) = a\theta^2$. Find also the circular asymptote.

**22.** $r \cos\theta = 2a \dfrac{\sin\theta}{1 + \sin\theta}$.

**23.** $r \cos 2\theta = a \sin 3\theta$.

**24.** Show that the asymptotes of $(x^2 - y^2)^2 = 2(x^2 + y^2)$ form a square.

**25.** Show that the asymptotes of $x^2y^2 - a^2(x^2 + y^2) - a^3(x + y) + a^4 = 0$ form a square, through two of whose angular points the curve passes.

**26.** Show that the asymptotes of

$$x^3 + 2x^2y - xy^2 - 2y^3 + x^2 - y^2 = 2x + 3y$$

cut the curve again in three points collinear with the origin.

**27.** Show that the asymptotes of the quartic
$$x^4 - 5x^2y^2 + 4y^4 + x^3 - xy^2 - 2x^2y + 2y^3 - xy = 1$$
cut the curve again in eight points lying upon a rectangular hyperbola.

**28.** Show that the asymptotes of the quartic
$$(x^2 - y^2)(x^2 - 4y^2) + 2x^3 - 2xy^2 + 2x^2 - 2xy = 2x + 2y - 1$$
cut the curve again in eight points lying upon a parabola which touches the co-ordinate axes.

**29.** Show that the three quartics

(a) $xy(x^2 - y^2) + 2x^2 + y^2 = 1,$

(b) $xy(x^2 - y^2) + x^2 + 2y^2 = 1,$

(c) $xy(x^2 - y^2) + 2x^2 + 2xy + 2y^2 = 1$

have the same asymptotes; and that each of the three conics on which lie the other eight points of intersection of each curve with its asymptotes have double contact with a certain circle.

**30.** Find the asymptotes of the sextic
$$xy(x^2 - y^2)(x^2 - 4y^2) + 2x^2y(x^2 - y^2) + 5x^2 + 5y^2 = 1.$$
Show that they cut the curve again in twenty-four points lying upon a certain quartic. Find the equation to this quartic and show that its own asymptotes are common with four asymptotes of the sextic and that they cut the quartic again in eight points lying upon a circle. Also that the remaining asymptotes of the sextic are tangents to this circle.

# CHAPTER X.

# CURVATURE.

## 115. Angle of Contingence.

Let $PQ$ be an arc of a curve. Suppose that between $P$ and $Q$ the bending is continuously in one direction. Let $LPR$ and $MQ$ be the tangents at $P$ and $Q$,

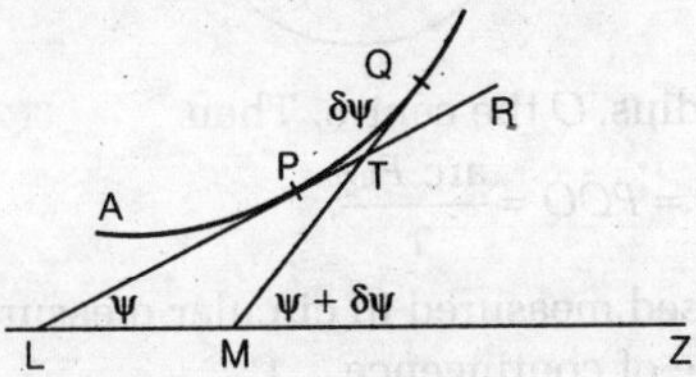


intersecting at $T$ and cutting a given fixed straight line $LZ$ in $L$ and $M$. Then the angle $RTQ$ is called the *angle of contingence* of the arc $PQ$.

The angle of contingence of any arc is therefore the difference of the angles which the tangents at its extremities make with any given fixed straight line. It is also obviously the angle *turned through* by a line which rolls along the curve from one extremity of the arc to the other.

## 116. Measure of Curvature.

It is clear that the *whole bending* or *curvature* which the curve undergoes between $P$ and $Q$ is greater or less according as the angle of contingence $RTQ$ is greater or less. The fraction $\frac{\text{angle of contingence}}{\text{length of arc}}$ is called the *average bending* or *average curvature* of the arc. We shall define the *curvature* of a curve in the immediate neighbourhood of a given point to be *the rate of deflection* from the tangent at that point. And we shall take as a measure of this rate of deflection at the given point the limit of the expression $\frac{\text{angle of contingence}}{\text{length of arc}}$ when the length of the arc measured from the given point, and therefore also the angle of contingence are indefinitely diminished.

## 117. Curvature of a Circle.

*In the case of the circle the curvature is the same at every point and is measured by the* RECIPROCAL OF THE RADIUS.

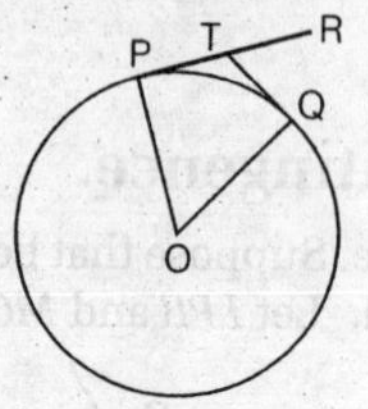


For let $r$ be the radius, $O$ the centre. Then

$$R\hat{T}Q = P\hat{O}Q = \frac{\text{arc } PQ}{r},$$

the angle being supposed measured in circular measure.

Hence $$\frac{\text{angle of contingence}}{\text{length of arc}} = \frac{1}{r},$$

and this is true whether the limit be taken or not. Hence the "curvature" of a circle at any point is measured by the reciprocal of the radius.

## 118. Circle of Curvature.

If three contiguous points $P, Q, R$ be taken on a curve, a circle may be drawn to pass through them. When the points are indefinitely close together, $PQ$ and $QR$ are ultimately tangents both to the curve and to the circle. Hence at the point of ultimate coincidence the curve and the circle have the *same angle of contingence*, viz. the angle $RQZ$ (see Fig.). Moreover, the *arcs PR* of the circle and the curve differ by a small quantity order higher than their own, and therefore *may be considered equal in the limit* (see Art. 81).

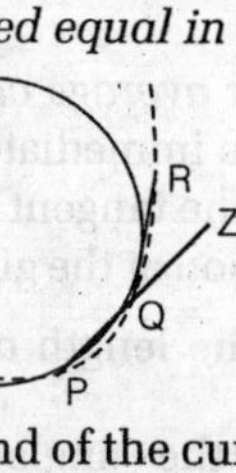


Hence the curvatures of this circle and of the curve at the point of contact are equal. It is therefore convenient to describe the curvature of a curve at a given point by reference to a circle thus drawn, the reciprocal of the radius being a correct measure of the *rate of bend*. We shall therefore consider such a circle to exist for each point of a curve and shall speak of it as the **circle of curvature** of that point. Its radius and centre will be called the **radius** and **centre of curvature** respectively, and a chord of this circle drawn through the point of contact in any direction will be referred to as the **chord of curvature** in that direction.

## 119. Formula for Radius of Curvature.

Let $PQ$ and $QR$ be considered equal chords, and therefore when we proceed to the limit the elementary arcs $PQ$ and $QR$ may be considered equal. Call each $\delta s$, and the angle $RQZ = \delta\psi$.

Now the radius of the circum-circle of the triangle $PQR$ is

$$\frac{PR}{2 \sin PQR}.$$

Hence if $\rho$ be the radius of curvature, we have

$$\rho = Lt \frac{PR}{2 \sin PQR} = Lt \frac{2\delta s}{2 \sin \delta\psi}$$

$$= Lt \frac{\delta s}{\delta\psi} \cdot \frac{\delta\psi}{\sin \delta\psi} = \frac{ds}{d\psi} \qquad \text{... (A).}$$

Also, it is clear that the lines which bisect at right angles the chords $PQ$, $QR$ intersect at the circum-centre of $PQR$, *i.e.* in the limit the centre of curvature of any point on a curve may be considered as the *point of intersection of the normal at that point with the normal at a contiguous and ultimately coincident point.*

## 120.

The formula (A) is useful in the case in which the equation of the curve is given in its intrinsic form, *i.e.* when the equation is given as a relation between $s$ and $\psi$. For example, that relation for a catenary is $s = c \tan \psi$, whence

$$\rho = \frac{ds}{d\psi} = c \sec^2 \psi,$$

and the rate of its deflection at any point is measured by

$$\frac{1}{\rho} = \frac{\cos^2 \psi}{c} = \frac{c}{s^2 + c^2}.$$

## 121. Transformations.

This formula must be transformed so as to suit each of the systems of co-ordinates in which it is usual to express the equation of a curve. These transformations we proceed to perform.

We have the equations

$$\cos \psi = \frac{dx}{ds}, \sin \psi = \frac{dy}{ds}.$$

Hence, differentiating each of these with respect to $s$,

$$-\sin \psi \frac{d\psi}{ds} = \frac{d^2 x}{ds^2}, \quad \cos \psi \frac{d\psi}{ds} = \frac{d^2 y}{ds^2},$$

whence
$$\frac{1}{\rho} = \frac{-\dfrac{d^2x}{ds^2}}{\dfrac{dy}{ds}} = \frac{\dfrac{d^2y}{ds^2}}{\dfrac{dx}{ds}} \qquad \text{...(B)},$$

and by squaring and adding

$$\frac{1}{\rho^2} = \left(\frac{d^2x}{ds^2}\right)^2 + \left(\frac{d^2y}{ds^2}\right)^2 \qquad \text{...(C)}.$$

These formulae (B) and (C) are only suitable for the case in which both $x$ and $y$ are known functions of $s$.

## 122. Cartesian Formula. Explicit Functions.

Again, since $\tan\psi = \dfrac{dy}{dx}$,

we have $\sec^2\psi\,\dfrac{d\psi}{dx} = \dfrac{d^2y}{dx^2}$,

by differentiating with regard to $x$.

Now
$$\frac{d\psi}{dx} = \frac{d\psi}{ds}\cdot\frac{ds}{dx} = \frac{1}{\rho\cos\psi};$$

therefore $\sec^3\psi\cdot\dfrac{1}{\rho} = \dfrac{d^2y}{dx^2}$,

and
$$\sec^2\psi = 1 + \tan^2\psi = 1 + \left(\frac{dy}{dx}\right)^2;$$

therefore
$$\rho = \pm\frac{\left[1 + \left(\dfrac{dy}{dx}\right)^2\right]^{\frac{3}{2}}}{\dfrac{d^2y}{dx^2}} \qquad \text{...(D)}.$$

This important form of the result is adapted to the evaluation of the radius of curvature when the equation of the curve is given in Cartesian co-ordinates, $y$ being an explicit function of $x$.

**Ex.** In the curve $y = \log\sin x$,

we have $y_1 = \cot x$,

$y_2 = -\operatorname{cosec}^2 x$.

Hence
$$\rho = \pm\frac{(1 + y_1^2)^{\frac{3}{2}}}{y_2} = \frac{(1 + \cot^2 x)^{\frac{3}{2}}}{\operatorname{cosec}^2 x} = \operatorname{cosec} x.$$

## 123. Curvature at the Origin.

When the curve passes through the origin the values of $\frac{dy}{dx}(=p)$ and $\frac{d^2y}{dx^2}(=q)$ at the origin may be deduced without actual differentiation by substituting for $y$ the expression $px+\frac{qx^2}{2!}+\ldots$ (the expansion of $y$ by Maclaurin's Theorem) and equating coefficients of like powers of $x$ in the identity obtained. The radius of curvature at the origin may then be at once deduced from the formula

$$\rho = \pm\frac{(1+p^2)^{\frac{3}{2}}}{q} \qquad \text{[Formula (D)].}$$

**Ex.** Find the curvature of the conic $y-x=x^2+2xy+y^2$ at the origin.

Putting $y=px+q\frac{x^2}{2!}+\ldots$

we have $(p-1)x+\frac{qx^2}{2}+\ldots \equiv x^2+2px^2+p^2x^2+\ldots$ identically;

whence by equating coefficients of like powers of $x$,

$$p=1,\ q=2(p+1)^2=8,$$

and $$\rho=\frac{(1+p^2)^{\frac{3}{2}}}{q}=2^{\frac{-3}{2}}=\cdot 3535\ldots$$

## 124. If we apply the same method to the general curve

$$ax+by+a'x^2+2h'xy+b'y^2+\ldots=0 \qquad \ldots(1),$$

we obtain after substituting $px+\frac{qx^2}{2!}+\ldots$ for $y$, and collecting the powers of $x$, $(a+bp)x+\left(a'+2h'p+b'p^2+\frac{bq}{2}\right)x^2+\ldots\equiv 0.$

Hence $$a+bp=0 \qquad \ldots(2),$$

$$a'+2h'p+b'p^2+\frac{bq}{2}=0 \qquad \ldots(3),$$

etc.,

giving $p=-\frac{a}{b},\ q=-2\frac{a'+2h'p+b'p^3}{b}$, etc.,

whence $$\rho=\pm\frac{(1+p^2)^{\frac{3}{2}}}{q}=\frac{1}{2}\frac{(a^2+b^2)^{\frac{3}{2}}}{a'b^2-2h'ab+b'a^2} \qquad \ldots(4),$$

the value of the radius of curvature of the given curve at the origin.

## 125. Tangents at the origin. Double point.

It will be noted that the equation $p = -\dfrac{a}{b}$

indicating the value of $\dfrac{dy}{dx}$ at the origin proves the equation of the tangent

there to be $\dfrac{Y}{X} = -\dfrac{a}{b}$, or $aX + bY = 0$,

which therefore might be at once *written down* as being the terms of the lowest degree in the equation of the curve (see Art. 87).

When no linear terms occur in the equation of the curve we have $a = 0$ and $b = 0$, and the value of $\dfrac{dy}{dx}$ at the origin takes an undetermined form. We however obtain from equation (3) the quadratic

$$b' p^2 + 2h' p + a' = 0 \qquad \ldots(5),$$

giving two values of $p$ at the origin. It is thus indicated that in this case two branches of the curve pass through the origin in the directions given by equation (5). The tangents to the curve at the origin are therefore

$$a' X^2 + 2h' XY + b' Y^2 = 0,$$

a result which may be written down by inspection from the equation of the curve, by equating to zero the second degree terms; *i.e.* the terms of lowest degree (Art. 87). The origin is now said to be a double point upon the curve.

The curvatures of the two branches at the double point may be obtained by the same method as before (Art. 123) as shown in the following example.

**Ex.** Find the radii of curvature at the origin for the curve

$$y^2 - 3xy + 2x^2 - x^3 + y^4 = 0.$$

Substituting $px + \dfrac{q}{2!}x^2 + \ldots$ for $y$, and collecting the powers of $x$,

we have $(p^2 - 3p + 2)\, x^2 + \left(pq - \dfrac{3}{2}q - 1\right)x^3 + \ldots \equiv 0$,

whence $\quad p^2 - 3p + 2 = 0,$

$$pq - \frac{3}{2}q - 1 = 0,$$

etc.,

whence $\quad p = 1$ or $2$, and $q = -2$ or $2$,

and therefore $\rho = \dfrac{(1+p^2)^{\frac{3}{2}}}{q} = \dfrac{2^{\frac{3}{2}}}{-2} = -\sqrt{2} = -1\cdot 414\ldots,$

or $\qquad = \dfrac{5^{\frac{3}{2}}}{2} = \dfrac{5}{2}\sqrt{5} = 5.590\ldots.$

The difference of sign introduced by the $q$ indicates that the two branches passing through the origin bend in opposite directions.

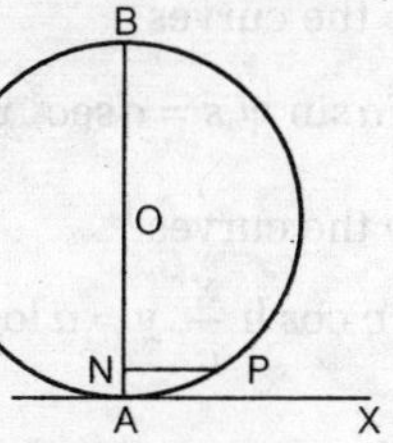


## 126. Newtonian Method.

The Newtonian Method of finding the curvature of the curve at the origin is instructive and interesting. Suppose the axes taken so that the axis of $x$ is a tangent to the curve at the point $A$, and the axis of $y$, viz. $AB$, is therefore the normal. Let $APB$ be the circle of curvature, $P$ the point adjacent to and ultimately co-incident with $A$ in which the curve and the circle intersect; $PN$ a perpendicular upon $AB$. Then

$$PN^2 = AN \cdot NB,$$

or
$$NB = \frac{PN^2}{AN}.$$

Now in the limit

$$NB = AB = \text{twice the radius of curvature.}$$

Hence
$$\rho = Lt\ \frac{1}{2}\frac{PN^2}{AN} = Lt\ \frac{x^2}{2y} \qquad \ldots(E).$$

Similarly, if the axis of $y$ be the tangent at the origin, we have

$$\rho = Lt\ \frac{y^2}{2x}.$$

**Ex.** Find the radius of curvature at the origin for the curve

$$2x^4 + 3y^4 + 4x^2y + xy - y^2 + 2x = 0.$$

In this case the *axis* of $y$ is a tangent at the origin, and therefore we shall endeavour to find $Lt\frac{y^2}{2x}$.

Dividing by $x$,

$$2x^3 + 3y^2 \cdot \frac{y^2}{x} + 4xy + y - \frac{y^2}{x} + 2 = 0.$$

Now, at the origin $Lt\ \frac{y^2}{x} = 2\rho$, $x = 0$, $y = 0$, and the equation becomes

$$-2\rho + 2 = 0,$$

or
$$\rho = 1.$$

## EXAMPLES

**1.** Apply formula (A) to the curves

$$s = a\psi,\ s = a\sin\psi, s = a\sec^3\psi,\ s = a\log\tan\left(\frac{\pi}{4}+\frac{\psi}{2}\right).$$

**2.** Apply formula (D) to the curves

$$y = x^3,\ y = c\cosh\frac{x}{c},\ y = a\log\sec\frac{x}{a}.$$

**3.** Apply formulae (B and C) to the curve for which $\left.\begin{array}{l} x = a\cos\dfrac{s}{a} \\ y = a\sin\dfrac{s}{a}\end{array}\right\}.$

**4.** Prove that in the case of the equiangular spiral whose intrinsic equation is

$$s = a(e^{m\psi}-1),\ \rho = mae^{m\psi}.$$

**5.** For the tractrix $s = c\log\sec\psi$ prove that $\rho = c\tan\psi$.

**6.** Show that in the curve $y = x + 3x^2 - x^3$

the radius of curvature at the origin $= \cdot 4714\ldots$, and that at the point $(1, 3)$ it is infinite.

**7.** Show that in the curve

$$y^2 - 3xy - 4x^2 + x^3 + x^4y + y^5 = 0$$

the radii of curvature at the origin are $\frac{85}{2}\sqrt{17}$ and $5\sqrt{2}$.

**8.** Show that the radii of curvature of the curve

$y^2 = x^2\dfrac{a+x}{a-x}$ for the origin $= \pm a\sqrt{2}$, and for the point $(-a, 0) = \dfrac{a}{4}$.

**9.** Show that the radii of curvature at the origin for the curve $x^3 + y^3 = 3axy$ are each $= \dfrac{3a}{2}$.

**10.** Prove that the chord of curvature parallel to the axis of $y$ for the curve

$y = a\log\sec\dfrac{x}{a}$ is of constant length.

**11.** Prove that for the curve

$$s = m(\sec^3\psi - 1),\ \rho = 3m\tan\psi\sec^3\psi,$$

and hence that $3m\dfrac{dy}{dx}\dfrac{d^2y}{dx^2} = 1$.

Also, that this differential equation is satisfied by the semicubical parabola

$$27my^2 = 8x^3.$$

**12.** Prove that for the curve

$$s = a \log \cot \left( \frac{\pi}{4} - \frac{\psi}{2} \right) + a \frac{\sin \psi}{\cos^2 \psi}, \rho = 2a \sec^3 \psi;$$

and hence that $\frac{d^2y}{dx^2} = \frac{1}{2a}$, and that this differential equation is satisfied by the parabola $x^2 = 4ay$.

**13.** Show that for the curve in which $s = ae^{\frac{x}{e}}$

$$c\rho = s\,(s^2 - c^2)^{\frac{1}{2}}.$$

**14.** Show that the curve for which $s = \sqrt{8ay}$ (the cycloid) has for its intrinsic equation

$$s = 4a \sin \psi.$$

Hence prove $\rho = 4a\sqrt{1 - \frac{y}{2a}}$.

**15.** Prove that the curve for which $y^2 = c^2 + s^2$ (the catenary) has for its intrinsic equation

$$s = c \tan \psi.$$

Hence prove $\rho = \frac{y^2}{c}$ = the part of the normal intercepted between the curve and the $x$-axis.

## 127. Formula for Pedal Equations.

Since a curve and its circle of curvature at any point $P$ intersect in three contiguous and ultimately coincident points they may be regarded as having

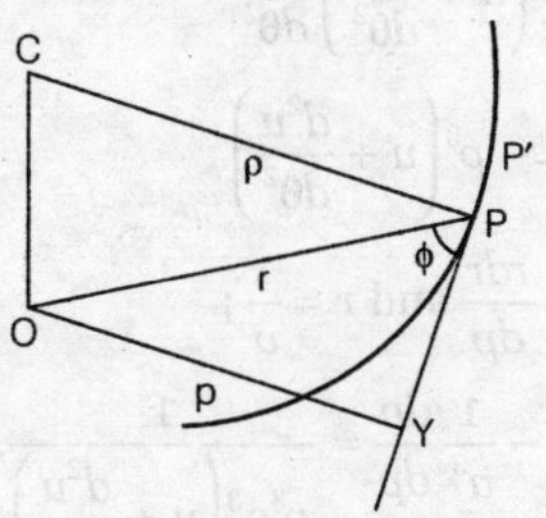


two contiguous tangents common. Therefore the values of $r + \delta r$ and $p + \delta p$ are common in addition to those of $r$ and $p$; *i.e.* the value of $\frac{dr}{dp}$ is common.

Now let $O$ be the pole and $C$ the centre of curvature corresponding to the point $P$ on the curve.

Then $\qquad OC^2 = r^2 + \rho^2 - 2r\rho \cos OPC$

$$= r^2 + \rho^2 - 2r\rho \sin \phi = r^2 + \rho^2 - 2\rho p.$$

Considering this as referring to the circle (for which $OC$ and $\rho$ are constant) we obtain by differentiating

$$0 = 2r\frac{dr}{dp} - 2\rho,$$

and it has been pointed out that the values of $r$ and $\frac{dr}{dp}$ are the same at the point $P$ for the curve and for the circle. Hence for the curve itself we also have

$$\rho = r\frac{dr}{dp} \qquad \text{...(F).}$$

**Ex.** In the equation $p^2 = Ar^2 + B$, which represents any epi- or hypocycloid (p. 89, Ex. 23), we have

$$p = Ar\frac{dr}{dp},$$

and therefore $\rho \propto p$.

The equiangular spiral, in which $p \propto r$, is included as the case in which $B = 0$.

## 128. Polar Curves.

We shall next reduce the formula to a shape suited for application to curves given by their polar equations.

We proved in Art. 95 that

$$\frac{1}{p^2} = u^2 + \left(\frac{du}{d\theta}\right)^2.$$

Hence
$$-\frac{1}{p^3}\frac{dp}{d\theta} = \left(u + \frac{d^2u}{d\theta^2}\right)\frac{dy}{d\theta},$$

or
$$\frac{dp}{du} = -p^3\left(u + \frac{d^2u}{d\theta^2}\right).$$

Now
$$\rho = \frac{rdr}{dp} \text{ and } r = \frac{1}{u};$$

therefore
$$\rho = -\frac{1}{u^3}\frac{du}{dp} = \frac{1}{p^3u^3\left(u + \dfrac{d^2u}{d\theta^2}\right)},$$

or
$$\rho = \frac{\left\{u^2 + \left(\dfrac{du}{d\theta}\right)^2\right\}^{\frac{3}{2}}}{u^3\left(u + \dfrac{d^2u}{d\theta^2}\right)} \qquad \text{...(G).}$$

**129.** This may easily be put in the $r$, $\theta$ form thus:—

Since $$u = \frac{1}{r},$$

we have $$\frac{du}{d\theta} = -\frac{1}{r^2}\frac{dr}{d\theta},$$

and therefore $$\frac{d^2u}{d\theta^2} = \frac{2}{r^3}\left(\frac{dr}{d\theta}\right)^2 - \frac{1}{r^2}\frac{d^2r}{d\theta^2};$$

therefore $$\rho = \frac{\left\{\frac{1}{r^2} + \frac{1}{r^4}\left(\frac{dr}{d\theta}\right)^2\right\}^{\frac{3}{2}}}{\frac{1}{r^3}\left\{\frac{1}{r} + \frac{2}{r^3}\left(\frac{dr}{d\theta}\right)^2 - \frac{1}{r^2}\frac{d^2r}{d\theta^2}\right\}}$$

$$= \frac{\left\{r^2 + \left(\frac{dr}{d\theta}\right)^2\right\}^{\frac{3}{2}}}{r^2 + 2\left(\frac{dr}{d\theta}\right)^2 - r\frac{d^2r}{d\theta^2}} \qquad \text{...(H).}$$

## 130. Tangential Polar Form.

Let the tangent $P_1T$ make an angle $\psi$ with the initial line. Then the perpendicular makes an angle $\alpha = \psi - \frac{\pi}{2}$ with the same line. Let $OY = p$. Let $P_1P_2$ be the normal, and $P_2$ its point of intersection with the normal at the contiguous point $Q$. Let $OY_1$ be the perpendicular from $O$ upon the normal. Call this $p_1$. Let $P_2P_3$ be drawn at right angles to $P_1P_2$, and let the length of $OY_2$, the perpendicular upon it from $O$, be $p_2$.

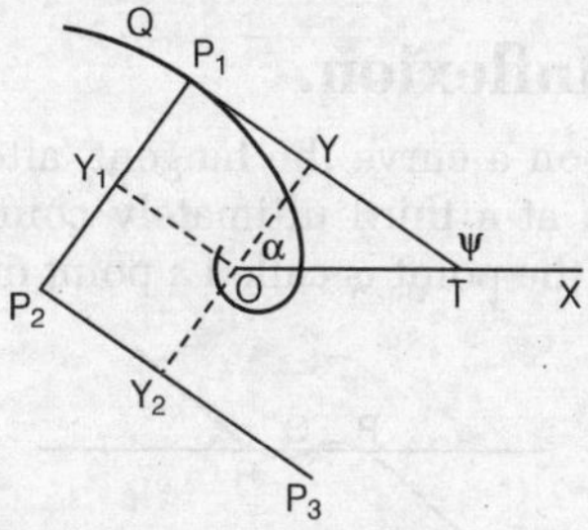


The equation of $P_1T$ is clearly

$$p = x\cos\alpha + y\sin\alpha \qquad \text{...(1).}$$

The contiguous tangent at $Q$ has for its equation

$$p + \delta p = x\cos(\alpha + \delta\alpha) + y\sin(\alpha + \delta\alpha) \qquad \text{...(2).}$$

Hence subtracting and proceeding to the limit it appears that

$$\frac{dp}{d\alpha} = -x\sin\alpha + y\cos\alpha \qquad \ldots(3)$$

is a straight line passing through the point of intersection of (1) and (2); also being perpendicular to (1) it is the equation of the normal $P_1P_2$.

Similarly $$\frac{d^2p}{d\alpha^2} = -x\cos\alpha - y\sin\alpha \qquad \ldots(4)$$

represents a straight line through the point of intersection of two contiguous positions of the line $P_1P_2$ and perpendicular to $P_1P_2$, viz. the line $P_2P_3$, and so on for further differentiations.

From this it is obvious that

$$OY_1 = \frac{dp}{d\alpha} = \frac{dp}{d\psi}, \text{ since } \frac{d\psi}{d\alpha} = 1;$$

$$OY_2 = \frac{d^2p}{d\alpha^2} = \frac{d^2p}{d\psi^2},$$

etc.

Hence $$P_1Y = \frac{dp}{d\psi},$$

and $$\rho = P_1P_2 = OY + OY_2 = p + \frac{d^2p}{d\psi^2} \qquad \ldots(\text{I}).$$

This formula is suitable for the case in which $p$ is given in terms of $\psi$.

**Ex.** It is known that the general $p$, $\psi$ equation of all epi- and hypocycloids can be written in the form

$$p = A\sin B\psi.$$

Hence $\rho = A\sin B\psi - AB^2\sin B\psi$,

and therefore $\rho \propto p$.

## 131. Point of Inflexion.

If at some point upon a curve the tangent, after its cross and recross, crosses the curve again at a third ultimately coincident point, as shewn magnified in the figure, the point is called a point of inflexion. At such a

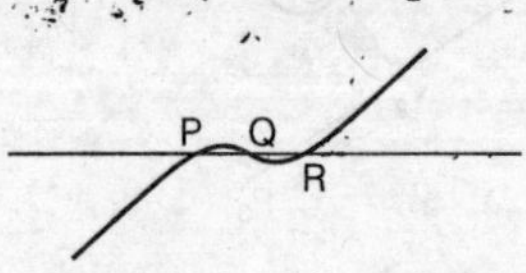


point the two successive chords $PQ$, $QR$ are in line and the angle of contingence vanishes.

At a point of inflexion the circle of curvature passes through three collinear points, and the radius of curvature becomes infinite and changes sign. We may hence deduce various forms of the condition for a point of inflexion; thus if

$$\rho = \infty,$$

we get
$$\frac{d\psi}{ds} = 0 \qquad \text{from (A)},$$

$$\frac{d^2y}{dx^2} = 0 \qquad \text{from (D)},$$

$$u + \frac{d^2u}{d\theta^2} = 0 \qquad \text{from (G)},$$

$$r^2 + 2\left(\frac{dr}{d\theta}\right)^2 - r\frac{d^2r}{d\theta^2} = 0 \qquad \text{from (H)}.$$

## 132. List of Formulae.

The formulae proved above are now collected for convenience.

$$\rho = \frac{ds}{d\psi} \qquad \text{...(A)},$$

$$\frac{1}{\rho} = -\frac{\dfrac{d^2x}{ds^2}}{\dfrac{dy}{ds}} = \frac{\dfrac{d^2y}{ds^2}}{\dfrac{dx}{ds}} \qquad \text{...(B)},$$

$$\frac{1}{\rho^2} = \left(\frac{d^2x}{ds^2}\right)^2 + \left(\frac{d^2y}{ds^2}\right)^2 \qquad \text{...(C)},$$

$$\rho = \frac{(1 + y_1^2)^{\frac{3}{2}}}{y_2} \qquad \text{...(D)},$$

$$\rho = Lt\,\frac{x^2}{2y} \qquad \text{...(E)},$$

$$\rho = r\frac{dr}{dp} \qquad \text{...(F)},$$

$$\rho = \frac{(u^2 + u_1^2)^{\frac{3}{2}}}{u^3(u + u_2)} \qquad \text{...(G)},$$

$$\rho = \frac{(r^2 + r_1^2)^{\frac{3}{2}}}{r^2 + 2r_1^2 - rr_2} \qquad \text{...(H)},$$

$$\rho = p + \frac{d^2p}{d\psi^2} \qquad \text{...(I)}.$$

## EXAMPLES

**1.** Apply formula (F) to the curves $p^2 = ar$, $ap = r^2$, $p = \dfrac{r^{m+1}}{a^m}$.

**2.** Apply formulae (G), (H) to the curves $au = \theta$, $r = a\theta$, $r = a\sin\theta$.

**3.** Apply the polar formula for radius of curvature to show that the radius of the circle $r = a\cos\theta$ is $\dfrac{a}{2}$.

**4.** Show that for the cardioide $r = a(1+\cos\theta)$

$\rho = \dfrac{4a}{3}\cos\dfrac{\theta}{2}$; *i.e.*, $\propto \sqrt{r}$. Also deduce the same result from the pedal equation of the curve, viz., $p\sqrt{2a} = r^{\frac{3}{2}}$.

**5.** Show that at the points in which the Archimedean spiral $r = a\theta$ intersects the reciprocal spiral $r\theta = a$ their curvatures are in the ratio 3 : 1.

**6.** For the equiangular spiral $r = ae^{m\theta}$ prove that the centre of curvature is at the point where the perpendicular to the radius vector through the pole intersects the normal.

**7.** Prove that for the curve

$$r = a\sec 2\theta,\ \rho = -\frac{r^4}{3p^3}.$$

**8.** For any curve prove the formula

$$\rho = \frac{r}{\sin\phi\cdot\left(1+\dfrac{d\phi}{d\theta}\right)} \text{ where } \tan\phi = \frac{rd\theta}{dr}.$$

Deduce the ordinary formula in terms of $r$ and $\theta$.

**9.** Show that the chord of curvature through the pole for the curve $p = f(r)$ is given by chord $= 2p\dfrac{dr}{dp} = 2\dfrac{f(r)}{f'(r)}$.

**10.** Show that the chord of curvature through the pole of the cardioide $r = a(1+\cos\theta)$ is $\dfrac{4}{3}r$.

**11.** Show that the chord of curvature through the pole of the equiangular spiral $r = ae^{m\theta}$ is $2r$.

**12.** Show that the chord of curvature through the pole of the curve $r^m = a^m\cos m\theta$ is $\dfrac{2r}{m+1}$.

Examine the cases when $m = -2, -1, -\frac{1}{2}, \frac{1}{2}, 1, 2$.

**13.** Show that the radius of curvature of the curve $r = a \sin n\theta$ at the origin is $\dfrac{na}{2}$.

**14.** For the curve $r^m = a^m \cos m\theta$, prove that $\rho = \dfrac{a^m}{(m+1)r^{m-1}}$.

Examine the particular cases of a rectangular hyperbola, lemniscate, parabola, cardioide, straight line, circle.

## 133. Centre of Curvature.

The Cartesian co-ordinates of the centre of curvature may be found thus:—

Let $Q$ be the centre of curvature corresponding to the point $P$ of the curve. Let $OX$ be the axis of $x$; $O$ the origin; $x$, $y$ the co-ordinates of $P$; $\bar{x}$, $\bar{y}$ those of $Q$; $\psi$ the angle the tangent makes with the axis of $x$.

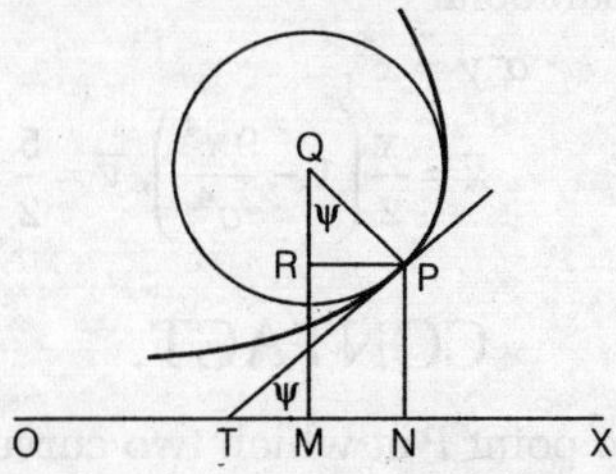


Draw $PN$, $QM$ perpendiculars upon the $x$-axis and $PR$ a perpendicular upon $QM$. Then

$$\bar{x} = OM = ON - RP$$

$\Rightarrow$ $$= ON - QP \sin \psi = x - \rho \sin \psi,$$

and $$\bar{y} = MQ = NP + RQ$$

$$= y + \rho \cos \psi .$$

Now $$\tan \psi = y_1;$$

therefore $$\sin \psi = \frac{y_1}{\sqrt{1 + y_1^2}},$$

and $$\cos \psi = \frac{1}{\sqrt{1 + y_1^2}} .$$

Also $$\rho = \frac{(1 + y_1^2)^{\frac{3}{2}}}{y_2} .$$

Hence $$\left.\begin{aligned} \bar{x} &= x - \frac{y_1(1 + y_1^2)}{y_2} \quad &\ldots(\alpha), \\ \bar{y} &= y + \frac{1 + y_1^2}{y_2} \quad &\ldots(\beta). \end{aligned}\right\}$$

# EXAMPLES

**1.** For the parabola $y = \frac{x^2}{4a}$, prove $\bar{x} = -\frac{x^3}{4a^2}$, $\bar{y} = 2a + \frac{3x^2}{4a}$.

**2.** For the parabola $y^2 = 4ax$, prove $\bar{x} = 2a + 3x$, $\bar{y} = -\frac{2x^{3/2}}{a^{1/2}}$, $\rho = \frac{2SP^{3/2}}{a^{1/2}}$,

*SP* being the focal distance of the point of the parabola whose coordinates are $(x, y)$.

**3.** For the ellipse $\frac{x^2}{a^2} + \frac{y^2}{b^2} = 1$,

prove $\bar{x} = \frac{a^2 - b^2}{a^4} x^3$, $\bar{y} = \frac{b^2 - a^2}{b^4} y^3$, $\rho = \frac{a^2 b^2}{p^3}$,

$p$ being the central perpendicular upon the tangent at $(x, y)$.

**4.** For the cubical parabola

$$a^2 y = x^3,$$

prove
$$\bar{x} = \frac{x}{2}\left(1 - \frac{9x^4}{a^4}\right), \ \bar{y} = \frac{5}{2}\frac{x^3}{a^2} + \frac{a^2}{6x}.$$

# CONTACT.

**134.** Consider the point $P$ at which two curves cut. It is clear that in general each has its own tangent at that point, and that if the curves be of the $m^{th}$ and $n^{th}$ degrees respectively, they will cut in $mn - 1$ other points real or imaginary.

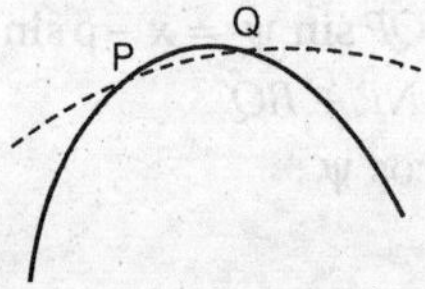


Next, suppose one of these other points (say $Q$) to move along one of the curves up to coincidence with $P$. The curves now cut in two ultimately coincident points at $P$, and therefore have a common tangent. There is then said to be contact *of the first order*. It will be observed that at such a point the curves *do not on the whole cross each other*.

Again, suppose another of the $mn$ points of intersection (viz. $R$) to follow $Q$ along one of the curves to coincidence with $P$.

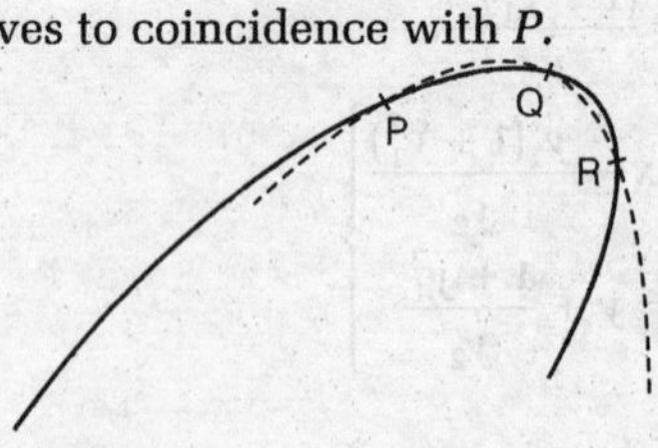

There are now three contiguous points on each curve common, and therefore the curves have two contiguous tangents common, namely, the ultimate position of the chord $PQ$ and the ultimate position of the chord $QR$. Contact of this kind is said to be *of the second order*, and the curves on the whole *cross each other*.

Finally, if other points of intersection follow $Q$ and $R$ up to $P$, so that ultimately $k$ points of intersection coincide at $P$, there will be $k-1$ contiguous common tangents at $P$, and the contact is said to be of the $(k-1)^{\text{th}}$ order. And if $k$ be odd and the contact therefore of an *even order* the curves *will cross*, but if $k$ be even and the contact therefore of *an* odd order they *will not cross*.

## 135. Closest Degree of Contact of the Conic Sections with a Curve.

The simplest curve which can be drawn so as to pass through two given points is a straight line.

| | | | |
|---|---|---|---|
| do. | three | do. | circle. |
| do. | four | do. | parabola. |
| do. | five | do. | conic. |

Hence, if the points be contiguous and ultimately coincident points on a given curve, we can have respectively the

*Straight Line of Closest Contact* (or tangent), having contact of the *first order* and cutting the curve in *two* ultimately coincident points, and therefore *not in general crossing* its curve; the

*Circle of Closest Contact*, having contact of the *second order* and cutting the curve in *three* ultimately coincident points, and therefore in *general crossing* its curve (this is the circle already investigated as the circle of curvature); the

*Parabola of Closest Contact*, having contact of the *third order* and cutting the curve in *four* ultimately coincident points, and therefore in general *not crossing*; and the

*Conic of Closest Contact*, having contact of the *fourth order* and cutting the curve in *five* ultimately coincident points, and therefore in general *crossing*.

It is often necessary to qualify such propositions as these by the words *in general*. Consider for instance the "circle of closest contact" at a given point on a conic section. *A* circle and a conic section intersect in four points, real or imaginary and since three of these are real and coincident, the circle of closest contact cuts the curve again in some one real fourth point.

But *it may happen*, as in the case in which the three ultimately coincident points are at an end of one of the axes of the conic *that the fourth point is coincident with the other three*, in which case the circle of closest contact has a contact of higher order than usual, viz. of the *third* order, cutting the curve in four ultimately coincident points, and therefore on the whole *not crossing* the curve. The student should draw for himself figures of the circle of closest contact at various points of a conic section, remembering that the common chord of the circle and conic and the tangent at the point of contact make equal angles with either axis.

The conic which has the closest possible contact is said to *osculate* its curve at the point of contact, and is called the *osculating conic*. Thus the circle of curvature is called the *osculating circle*, the parabola of closest contact is called the *osculating parabola*, and so on.

## 136. Analytical Conditions for Contact of a given order.

We may treat this subject analytically as follows.

Let
$$\left.\begin{aligned} y &= \phi(x) \\ y &= \psi(x) \end{aligned}\right\}$$
be the equations of two curves which cut at the point $P(x, y)$.

Consider the values of the respective ordinates at the points $P_1$, $P_2$ whose common abscissa is $x + h$.

Let $MN = h$.

Then $NP_1 = \phi(x + h)$,

$NP_2 = \psi(x + h)$,

and
$$P_2P_1 = NP_1 - NP_2 = \phi(x+h) - \psi(x+h)$$
$$= [\phi(x) - \psi(x)] + h\,[\phi'(x) - \psi'(x)] + \frac{h^2}{2!}[\phi''(x) - \psi''(x)] + \ldots$$

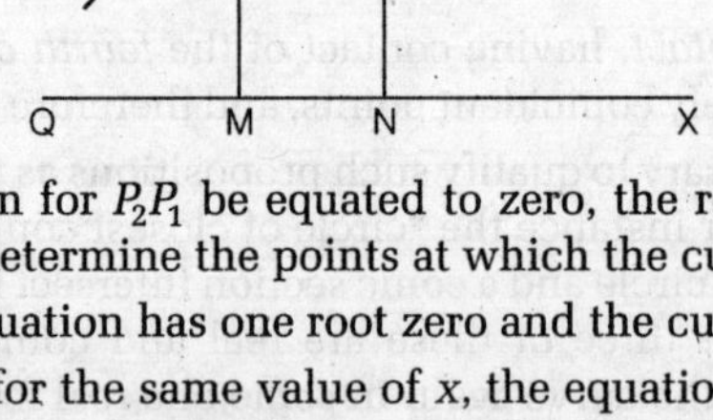


If the expression for $P_2P_1$ be equated to zero, the roots of the resulting equation for $h$ will determine the points at which the curves cut.

If $\phi(x) = \psi(x)$, the equation has one root zero and the curves cut at $P$.

If also $\phi'(x) = \psi'(x)$ for the same value of $x$, the equation has two roots zero and the curves cut in *two* contiguous points at $P$, and therefore have a common tangent. The contact is now of the *first order*.

If also $\phi''(x) = \psi''(x)$ for the same value of $x$, the equation for $h$ has three roots zero and the curves cut in *three* ultimately coincident points at $P$. There are now two contiguous tangents common, and the contact is said to be of the *second order*; and so on.

Similarly for curves given by their polar equations, if $r = f(\theta)$, $r = \phi(\theta)$ be the two equations, there will be $n + 1$ equations to be satisfied for the same value of $\theta$ in order that for that value there may be contact of the $n^{th}$ order, viz.

$$f(\theta) = \phi(\theta),\ f'(\theta) = \phi'(\theta),\ f''(\theta) = \phi''(\theta),\ ....$$
$$f^n(\theta) = \phi^n(\theta).$$

## EXAMPLES

**1.** Shew that the parabola whose axis is parallel to the $y$ axis and which has the closest contact possible with the curve $y = x^4$ at the point (1, 1) is $y = 3 - 8x + 6x^2$.

**2.** Draw carefully the circle of curvature

(1) at an ordinary point on an ellipse,

(2) at the end of the major axis,

(3) at the end of the minor axis,

(4) at an ordinary point on a parabola,

(5) at the vertex of the parabola,

and name the order of contact in each case.

**3.** Shew that the curves $y = x^{n+1}(x - a)(x - b)$, $y = x^{n+1}(x - c)(x - d)$, have contact of the $n^{th}$ order at the origin.

## EXAMPLES

**1.** Find the curvature at the origin in the curves

(*a*) $y = 2x + 3x^2 + 4x^3$, (*b*) $y = 2x + 3x^2 + 4xy$,

(*c*) $(y - x)(y - 2x) = x^3 + y^3$,

(*d*) $(x - y)^2(x - 2y)(x - 3y) = 2a(x^3 - y^3) + 2a^2(x + y)(x - 2y)$.

**2.** In the curve $y = ae^{x/a}$, prove $\rho = a\sec^2\theta\operatorname{cosec}\theta$, where $\theta = \tan^{-1}\dfrac{y}{a}$, and that the curve has no point of inflexion.

**3.** In the limacon $r = a + b\cos\theta$, prove $\rho = \dfrac{(a^2 + 2ab\cos\theta + b^2)^{3/2}}{a^2 + 3ab\cos\theta + 2b^2}$,

and hence shew that if $a$ and $b$ are both positive the limacon can only have points of inflexion when $a$ is intermediate between $b$ and $2b$.

Deduce for a cardioide $(b = a)$, $\rho = \dfrac{4}{3}a\cos\dfrac{\theta}{2}$.

4. Shew that the curve $y = e^{-x^2}$ has points of inflexions where $x = \pm 1\sqrt{2}$.

5. Shew that $y = a \sin \dfrac{x}{a}$ has points of inflexion wherever it cuts the $x$-axis.

6. Shew that the points of inflexion upon $x^2 y = a^2(x - y)$, are given by $x = 0$ and $x = \pm a\sqrt{3}$.

7. Shew that the curve $x(x^2 - ay) = a^3$ has a point of inflexion where it cuts the $x$-axis. Find the equation of the tangent there.

8. Shew that the curve $x^3 + y^3 = a^3$ has inflexions where it cuts the coordinate axes.

9. Shew that the curve $x = \log\left(\dfrac{y}{x}\right)$ has a point of inflexion at $(-2, -2e^{-2})$.

10. Shew that $r\sqrt{\theta} = a$ has a point of inflexion at a distance $a\sqrt{2}$ from the pole.

11. Find the points of inflexion upon $12y = x^4 - 16x^3 + 42x^2 + 12x + 1$.

12. Shew that in a parabola the chord of curvature through the focus and the chord of curvature parallel to the axis are each four times the focal distance of the point of contact.

13. In a parabola the common chord of the curve and its circle of curvature $= 8\sqrt{r(r - a)}$.

14. In the chainette $y = c \cosh \dfrac{x}{c}$ the chord of curvature parallel to the $y$-axis is double of the ordinate, and that parallel to the $x$-axis. $= c \sinh \dfrac{2x}{c}$.

15. If $C_x$ and $C_y$ be the chords of curvature parallel to the axes at any point of the curve $y = ae^{x/a}$,

prove that $\dfrac{1}{C_{x^2}} + \dfrac{1}{C_{y^2}} = \dfrac{1}{2aC_x}$.

16. If $C_r$ and $C_\theta$ be the chords of curvature respectively along and perpendicular to the radius vector, shew that

$$C_r = \frac{2\rho p}{r}, \; C_\theta = \frac{2\rho\sqrt{r^2 - p^2}}{r}.$$

**17.** At the point upon the Archimedean Spiral $r = a\theta$, at which the tangent makes half a right angle with the radius vector,

prove $C_r = C_\theta = \frac{4}{3}a.$

**18.** Shew that for each of the curves $r = a^\theta$, $r\theta = a$, $r \sin n\theta = a$, $r \sinh n\theta = a$, $r \cosh n\theta = a$ (Cotes's Spirals), the curvature $\propto \frac{p^3}{r^4}$.

**19.** Shew that in the curve for which

$y = a\cos^m \psi$,

the radius of curvature is $m$ times the normal.

**20.** Shew that in the curve for which $y = ae^{m\psi}$, the radius of curvature is $m$ times the tangent.

**21.** Shew that in the curve for which $r^2 = a^2 + b^2\psi$, the radius of curvature varies inversely as the perpendicular from the origin upon the normal.

**22.** Shew that in the chainette the radius of curvature varies as the square of its projection upon the $y$-axis.

**23.** In the curve $\theta = \frac{\sqrt{r^2 - a^2}}{a} - \cos^{-1}\frac{a}{r}$, shew that $\rho^2 = 2as$, $s$ being so measured that $\rho$ and $s$ vanish together.

**24.** Prove that in any curve $\frac{d\rho}{ds} = \{3y_1y_2^2 - y_3(1 + y_1^2)\} / y_2^2$, and shew that at every point of a circle $y_3 = \frac{3y_1y_2^2}{(1 + y_1^2)}$.

**25.** For any plane curve prove

(a) $\frac{1}{\rho^3} = \frac{d^2x}{ds^2}\frac{d^3y}{ds^3} - \frac{d^2y}{ds^2}\frac{d^3x}{ds^3}$,

(b) $\frac{1}{\rho^4}\left\{1 + \left(\frac{d\rho}{ds}\right)^2\right\} = \left(\frac{d^3x}{ds^3}\right)^2 + \left(\frac{d^3y}{ds^3}\right)^2$,

(c) $\frac{d^4x}{ds^4}\cdot\frac{dx}{ds} + \frac{d^4y}{ds^4}\frac{dy}{ds} = \frac{3}{\rho^3}\frac{d\rho}{ds}$,

(d) $\frac{d^4x}{ds^4}\frac{d^2y}{ds^2} - \frac{d^4y}{ds^4}\cdot\frac{d^2x}{ds^2} = \frac{3}{\rho^4}\frac{d\rho}{ds}$,

(e) $\rho = \dfrac{\frac{d^4x}{ds^4}\cdot\frac{dx}{ds} + \frac{d^4y}{ds^4}\cdot\frac{dy}{ds}}{\frac{d^4x}{ds^4}\cdot\frac{d^2y}{ds^2} - \frac{d^4y}{ds^4}\cdot\frac{d^2x}{ds^2}}$.

# CHAPTER XI.

# ENVELOPES.

## 137. Families of Curves.

If in the equation $\phi(x, y, c) = 0$ we give any arbitrary numerical values to the constant $c$, we obtain a number of equations representing a certain family of curves; and any member of the family may be specified by the particular value assigned to the constant $c$. The quantity $c$, which is constant for the same curve but different for different curves, is called the *parameter* of the family.

## 138. Envelope. Definition.

Let all the members of the family of curves $\phi(x, y, c) = 0$ be drawn which correspond to a system of infinitesimally close values of the parameter, supposed arranged in order of magnitude. We shall designate as consecutive curves any two curves which correspond to two consecutive values of $c$ from the list. Then the locus of the ultimate points of intersection of consecutive members of this family of curves is called the ENVELOPE of the family.

## 139. The Envelope touches each of the Intersecting Members of the Family.

Let $A, B, C$ represent three consecutive intersecting members of the

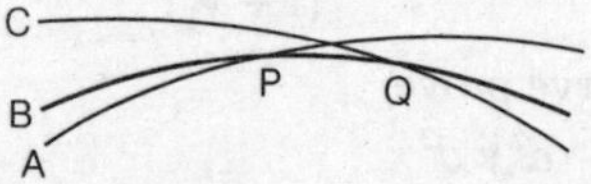


family. Let $P$ be the point of intersection of $A$ and $B$, and $Q$ that of $B$ and $C$.

Now, by definition, $P$ and $Q$ are points on the envelope. Thus the curve $B$ and the envelope have two contiguous points common, and therefore have ultimately a common tangent, and therefore touch each other. Similarly, the envelope may be shown to touch any other curve of the system.

## 140. The Envelope of $A\lambda^2 + 2B\lambda + C = 0$ is $B^2 = AC$.

If $A, B, C$ be any functions of $x, y$ and the equation of any curve be

$$A\lambda^2 + 2B\lambda + C = 0,$$

$\lambda$ being an arbitrary parameter, the envelope of all such curves for different values of $\lambda$ is $B^2 = AC$.

For the equation $A\lambda^2 + 2B\lambda + C = 0$

may be regarded as a quadratic equation to find the values of $\lambda$ for the two particular members of the family which pass through a given point $(x, y)$. Now, if $(x, y)$ be supposed to be a point on the envelope, these members will in the limit be coincident. Hence for such values of $x$, $y$ the quadratic for $\lambda$ must have two equal roots, and the locus of such points is therefore

$$B^2 = AC.$$

**Ex. 1.** Thus the line $y = mx + \dfrac{a}{m}$ may be written in the form

$$m^2x - my + a = 0,$$

whence the equation of the envelope for different values of $m$ is plainly $y^2 = 4ax$.

**Ex. 2.** The line $y = mx + \sqrt{a^2m^2 + b^2}$ may be written in the form

$m^2(x^2 - a^2) - 2mxy + y^2 - b^2 = 0$, and the envelope is

$x^2y^2 = (x^2 - a^2)(y^2 - b^2)$, or $x^2/a^2 + y^2/b^2 = 1$.

## 141. Envelope of $\phi(x, y, c) = 0$.

The envelope of the more general family of curves

$$\phi(x, y, c) = 0$$

may be considered in the same way.

It is proved in Theory of Equations that if $f(c) = 0$ be a rational algebraic equation for $c$ the condition for a pair of equal roots is obtained by eliminating $c$ between $f(c) = 0$ and $f'(c) = 0$.

Hence to find the envelope of $\phi(x, y, c) = 0$ we differentiate with regard to $c$ thus forming $\dfrac{\partial}{\partial c}\phi(x, y, c) = 0$ and then eliminate $c$.

**Ex. 1.** Thus to find the envelope of the line

$$y = cx + \frac{a}{c}$$

for different values of $c$, we have upon differentiating with regard to $c$ $0 = x - \dfrac{a}{c^2}$, whence $cy = a + c^2x = 2a$,

and squaring, $y^2 \cdot \dfrac{a}{x} = 4a^2$, giving $y^2 = 4ax$.

**Ex. 2.** Find the envelope of

$x\cos^3\theta + y\sin^3\theta = a$ for different values of $\theta$.

Differentiating with regard to $\theta$, $-x\cos^2\theta\sin\theta + y\sin^2\theta\cos\theta = 0$,

giving $\dfrac{\cos\theta}{y} = \dfrac{\sin\theta}{x} = \dfrac{\sqrt{\cos^2\theta + \sin^2\theta}}{\sqrt{x^2 + y^2}} = \dfrac{1}{\sqrt{x^2 + y^2}}$.

Hence, the equation of the envelope is

$$x\frac{y^3}{(x^2+y^2)^{3/2}}+y\frac{x^3}{(x^2+y^2)^{3/2}}=a, \text{ or } \frac{xy}{\sqrt{x^2+y^2}}=a,$$

which may be written $\frac{1}{x^2}+\frac{1}{y^2}=\frac{1}{a^2}$.

## EXAMPLES

**1.** Show that the envelope of the line $\frac{x}{a}+\frac{y}{b}=1$,

when $ab=c^2$, a constant, is $4xy=c^2$.

**2.** Find the equation of the curve whose tangent is of the form $y=mx+m^4$, $m$ being independent of $x$ and $y$.

**3.** Find the envelope of the curves $\frac{a^2\cos\theta}{x}-\frac{b^2\sin\theta}{y}=\frac{c^2}{a}$

for different values of $\theta$.

**4.** Find the envelope of the family of trajectories $y=x\tan\theta-\frac{1}{2}g\frac{x^2}{u^2\cos^2\theta}$, $\theta$ being the arbitrary parameter.

**5.** Find the envelopes of straight lines drawn at right angles to tangents to a given parabola and passing through the points in which those tangents cut

(1) the axis of the parabola,

(2) a fixed line parallel to the directrix.

**6.** Find the envelope of straight lines drawn at right angles to normals to a given parabola and passing through the points in which those normals cut the axis of the parabola.

**7.** A series of circles have their centres on a given straight line, and their radii are proportional to the distances of their corresponding centres from a given point in that line. Find the envelope.

**8.** *P* is a point which moves along a given straight line. *PM*, *PN* are perpendiculars on the co-ordinate axes supposed rectangular. Find the envelope of the line *MN*.

**142.** The envelope of $\phi(x,y,c)=0$ ...(1)

may also be obtained as follows:

Let $\phi(x,y,c+\delta c)=0$ ...(2)

be the consecutive member of the family.

This, by Taylor's Theorem, may be expressed in its expanded form as

$$\phi(x,y,c)+\delta c\frac{\partial}{\partial c}\phi(x,y,c)+\ldots=0.$$

Hence in the limit when $\delta c$ is infinitesimally small we obtain

$$\frac{\partial}{\partial c}\phi(x, y, c) = 0$$

as the equation of a curve passing through the ultimate point of intersection of the curves (1) and (2).

If then we eliminate $c$ between and

$$\left.\begin{array}{r}\phi(x, y, c) = 0\\ \frac{\partial}{\partial c}\phi(x, y, c) = 0\end{array}\right\},$$

we obtain the locus of that point of intersection for all values of the parameter $c$. This is the Envelope. Polar curves of the form

$$\phi(r, \theta, c) = 0$$

may be treated in the same manner.

**Ex. 1.** Find the envelope of a circle drawn upon radii vectores of the circle $r = 2a\cos\theta$ as diameters.

Let $d, \alpha$ be the polar co-ordinates of any point on the given circle, then

$$d = 2a\cos\alpha.$$

The equation of a circle on the radius vector $d$ for diameter is

$$r = d\cos(\theta - \alpha) \qquad \ldots(1),$$

or
$$r = 2a\cos\alpha\cos(\theta - \alpha) \qquad \ldots(2).$$

Here, $\alpha$ is the parameter. Differentiating with regard to $\alpha$,

$$-\sin\alpha\cos(\theta - \alpha) + \cos\alpha\sin(\theta - \alpha) = 0,$$

whence $\sin(\theta - 2\alpha) = 0$ or $\alpha = \dfrac{\theta}{2}$ ...(3).

Substituting this value of $\alpha$ in (2),

$$r = 2a\cos^2\frac{\theta}{2} \text{ or } r = a(1 + \cos\theta),$$

the equation of a cardioide.

**Ex. 2.** Find the envelope of a straight line drawn at right angles to radii vectores of the cardioide $r = a(1 + \cos\theta)$ through their extremities.

Here we are to find the envelope of the line

$$x\cos\alpha + y\sin\alpha = d,$$

where $d, \alpha$ are the polar co-ordinates of any point on the cardioide; *i.e.* where $d = \alpha(1 + \cos\alpha)$.

The equation of the line is therefore

$$x\cos\alpha + y\sin\alpha = a(1 + \cos\alpha),$$

or
$$(x - a)\cos\alpha + y\sin\alpha = a,$$

a line which from its form obviously touches the circle

$$(x - a)^2 + y^2 = a^2 \text{ or } r = 2a\cos\theta,$$

which is therefore its envelope.

**Ex. 3.** Find the envelope of

$$\frac{x}{a}+\frac{y}{b}=1 \qquad \text{...(1),}$$

with the condition

$$a^n + b^n = \text{constant} = c^n \text{ say} \qquad \text{...(2).}$$

Here there are *two parameters* with a condition connecting them, so that only one is independent. Imagine $a$ and $b$ to be both functions of some third arbitrary parameter $t$. Differentiating both equations with regard to $t$,

$$\frac{x}{a^2}\frac{da}{dt}+\frac{y}{b^2}\frac{db}{dt}=0,$$

$$a^{n-1}\frac{da}{dt}+b^{n-1}\frac{db}{dt}=0;$$

$$\therefore \qquad \frac{\frac{x}{a^2}}{a^{n-1}}=\frac{\frac{y}{b^2}}{b^{n-1}},$$

$$\text{i.e. } \frac{\frac{x}{a}}{a^n}=\frac{\frac{y}{b}}{b^n}=\frac{\frac{x}{a}+\frac{y}{b}}{a^n+b^n}=\frac{1}{c^n}.$$

Thus $a^{n+1}=c^n x$ and $b^{n+1}=c^n y$.

$\therefore$ substituting in (2),

$$(c^n x)^{\frac{n}{n+1}}+(c^n y)^{\frac{n}{n+1}}=c^n,$$

or

$$x^{\frac{n}{n+1}}+y^{\frac{n}{n+1}}=c^{\frac{n}{n+1}},$$

which is the required envelope.

## EXAMPLES

**1.** Find the envelope of

$y = mx - 2am - am^3$,

*i.e.* of normals of the parabola $y^2 = 4ax$.

**2.** Find the envelope of $\frac{ax}{\cos\theta}-\frac{by}{\sin\theta}=a^2-b^2$,

i.e. of normals of the ellipse $\frac{x^2}{a^2}+\frac{y^2}{b^2}=1$.

**3.** Find the envelopes of

(α) $y = mx + am^2$, (β) $y = mx + am^3$,

(γ) $y = mx + am^p$;

$m$ being the arbitrary parameter.

**4.** Find the envelopes of

(α) $x\cos\theta + y\sin\theta = a$, (β) $x\sqrt{\cos\theta} + y\sqrt{\sin\theta} = a$,

(γ) $\dfrac{x}{\sqrt{\cos\theta}} + \dfrac{y}{\sqrt{\sin\theta}} = a$, (δ) $x\cos^{4/3}\theta + y\sin^{4/3}\theta = a$,

(ε) $x\cos^{\frac{3}{2}}\theta + y\sin^{\frac{3}{2}}\theta = a$, (ζ) $x\cos^4\theta + y\sin^4\theta = a$,

(η) $x\cos^n\theta + y\sin^n\theta = a$;

θ being the arbitrary parameter in each case.

**5.** Find the envelopes of

(α) $x\cos\alpha + y\sin\alpha = a\sqrt{\cos 2\alpha}$, (β) $x\cos 2\alpha + y\sin 2\alpha = a\cos^2\alpha$,

(γ) $x\cos m\alpha + y\sin m\alpha = a(\cos n\alpha)^{\frac{m}{n}}$;

α being the parameter in each case.

**6.** Find the envelopes of circles described on the radii vectores of the following curves as diameters:—

(α) $\dfrac{x^2}{a^2} + \dfrac{y^2}{b^2} = 1$, (β) $y^2 = 4ax$,

(γ) $y^2 = 4a(x + a)$, (δ) $r = a(1 + \cos\theta)$,

(ε) $\dfrac{l}{r} = 1 + e\cos\theta$, (ζ) $r^2\cos 2\theta = a^2$,

(η) $r^2 = a^2\cos 2\theta$, (θ) $r^n = a^n\cos n\theta$.

**7.** Find the envelopes of the circles which pass through the pole and whose centres lie on the several curves of question 6.

**8.** Find the envelopes of straight lines at right angles to the radii vectores of the following curves drawn through their extremities:—

(α) a straight line, (β) a circle through the pole,

(γ) any circle, (δ) a cardioide $r = a(1 + \cos\theta)$,

(ε) a limacon $r = a + b\cos\theta$, (ζ) a lemniscate $r^2 = a^2\cos 2\theta$,

(η) an equiangular spiral $r = ae^{m\theta}$. (θ) $r^n = a^n\cos n\theta$.

**9.** Find the envelopes of the straight line

$\dfrac{x}{a} + \dfrac{y}{b} = 1$ under the several conditions

(α) $a + b = c$, (β) $a^2 + b^2 = c^2$, (γ) $a^m b^n = c^{m+n}$.

**10.** Find the envelopes of the ellipse $\dfrac{x^2}{a^2} + \dfrac{y^2}{b^2} = 1$

under the several conditions

(α) $a^2 + b^2 = c^2$, (β) $a^n + b^n = c^n$, (γ) $a^m b^n = c^{m+n}$.

**11.** Find the envelopes of the parabola

$$\sqrt{\frac{x}{a}}+\sqrt{\frac{y}{b}}=1$$

under the several conditions

(α) $a+b=c,$ (β) $a^n+b^n=c^n,$ (γ) $a^m b^n=c^{m+n}.$

**12.** Find the envelope of

$$\frac{x^m}{a^m}+\frac{y^m}{b^m}=1$$

under the condition $a^p+b^p=c^p$.

**13.** Show that the envelope of the family of curves $A\lambda^3+3B\lambda^2+3C\lambda+D=0,$
where, $\lambda$ is the arbitrary parameter, and $A, B, C, D$ are functions of $x$ and $y$, is $(BC-AD)^2=4(BD-C^2)(AC-B^2)$.

**14.** If $A$, $B$, $C$ be any functions of $x$ and $y$ the envelope of

$A\cos ma+B\sin ma=C(\cos na)^{\frac{m}{n}}$

is $\left(\frac{A^2+B^2}{C^2}\right)^{\frac{n}{m-n}}=\cos^2\frac{n}{m-n}\tan^{-1}\frac{B}{A}.$

**15.** A straight line of given length slides with its extremities on two fixed straight lines at right angles. Find the envelope of a circle drawn on the sliding line as diameter.

**16.** Show that the envelope of straight lines joining the extremities of a pair of conjugate diameters of an ellipse is a similar ellipse.

**17.** The envelope of the polars with respect to the circle $r=2a\cos\theta$ of points which lie upon the circle $r=2b\cos\theta$ is $\{(a-b)x+ab\}^2=b^2\{(x-a)^2+y^2\}$.

**18.** Show that the pedal equation of the envelope of the $x\cos m\theta+y\sin m\theta=a\cos n\theta$ is $m^2r^2=(m^2-n^2)p^2+n^2a^2$.

**19.** Two particles move along parallel lines, the one with uniform velocity and the other with the same initial velocity but with uniform acceleration. Show that the line joining them always touches a fixed hyper-bola.

**20.** Show that the radius of curvature of the envelope of the line $x\cos\alpha+y\sin\alpha=f(a)$ is $f(\alpha)+f''(\alpha)$,
and that the centre of curvature is at the point

$$\left.\begin{aligned}x&=-f'(\alpha)\sin\alpha-f''(\alpha)\cos\alpha\\ y&=f'(\alpha)\cos\alpha-f''(\alpha)\sin\alpha\end{aligned}\right\}.$$

# CHAPTER XII.

# ASSOCIATED LOCI.

**143.** IT is intended in the present chapter to present a brief introduction to a study of several important loci which are intrinsically connected with every curve.

## PEDAL CURVES.

**144.** DEF. If a perpendicular $OY$ be drawn from any fixed point $O$ upon the tangent to any curve the locus of $Y$ is called the "first Positive Pedal" of the original curve with regard to the given point $O$.

Two important cases occur in the Conic Sections :

(1) In a parabola the locus of the foot of the perpendicular from the focus upon a tangent is the tangent at the vertex. This line is therefore the first positive pedal of the parabola with regard to the focus.

(2) In a central conic the locus of the foot of the perpendicular from a focus upon a tangent is the auxiliary circle. This circle is therefore the first positive pedal of the conic with regard to the focus.

### 145. To find the Pedal with regard to the Origin for Cartesian Curves.

When the Cartesian equation of a curve is given, the condition of tangency of

$$X \cos \alpha + Y \sin \alpha = p$$

may be obtained by comparison of this line with the tangent at any point $(x, y)$.

Let this condition when found be $f(p, \alpha) = 0$.

Then since $p, \alpha$ are the polar co-ordinates of the point whose locus is sought we may replace them by the current co-ordinates $r, \theta$, and the equation of the pedal will be

$$f(r, \theta) = 0.$$

**Ex. 1.** The condition that

$x \cos \alpha + y \sin \alpha = p$ touches $x^2 / a^2 + y^2 / b^2 = 1$

is known to be $p^2 = a^2 \cos^2 \alpha + b^2 \sin^2 \alpha$.

Hence the first positive pedal with regard to the origin is

$$r^2 = a^2 \cos^2 \theta + b^2 \sin^2 \theta.$$

**Ex. 2.** Find the first positive pedal of the curve $x^m y^n = a^{m+n}$ with regard to the origin.

The equation of the tangent is plainly

$$X\frac{m}{x} + Y\frac{n}{y} = m + n.$$

Comparing with $X \cos \alpha + Y \sin \alpha = p$,

$$\frac{x \cos \alpha}{m} = \frac{y \sin \alpha}{n} = \frac{p}{m+n},$$

giving $$x = \frac{m}{m+n} \cdot \frac{p}{\cos \alpha},\ y = \frac{n}{m+n} \cdot \frac{p}{\sin \alpha}.$$

Hence the condition of tangency is

$$\left(\frac{m}{m+n} \frac{p}{\cos \alpha}\right)^m \left(\frac{n}{m+n} \frac{p}{\sin \alpha}\right)^n = a^{m+n},$$

and replacing $p$ and $\alpha$ by $r$ and $\theta$, the equation of the pedal becomes

$$r^{m+n} = a^{m+n} \frac{(m+n)^{m+n}}{m^m n^n} \cos^m \theta \sin^n \theta.$$

## 146. To find the Pedal with regard to the Pole of any curve whose Polar Equation is given.

Let $$F(r, \theta) = 0 \qquad ...(1)$$

be the equation of the curve.

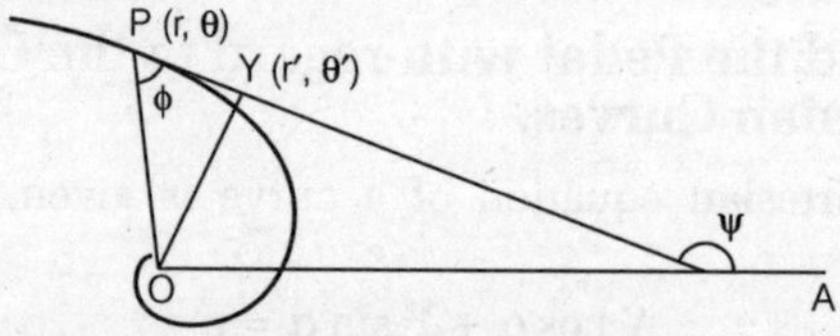


Let $r', \theta'$ be the polar co-ordinates of the point $Y$, which is the foot of the perpendicular $OY$ drawn from the pole on a tangent. Let $OA$ be the initial line.

Then $$\theta = A\hat{O}P = A\hat{O}Y + Y\hat{O}P$$

$$= \theta' + \frac{\pi}{2} - \phi \qquad ... (2),$$

also $$\tan \phi = r\frac{d\theta}{dr} \qquad ... (3).$$

and $$r' = r \sin \phi,$$

or $$\left.\frac{1}{r'^2} = \frac{1}{r^2} + \frac{1}{r^4}\left(\frac{dr}{d\theta}\right)^2\right\} \text{(Art. 95)} \qquad ...(4).$$

If $r, \theta, \phi$ be eliminated from equations 1, 2, 3 and 4, there will remain an equation in $r', \theta'$. The dashes may then be dropped and the required equation will be obtained.

**Ex.** To find the equation of the first positive pedal of the curve

$$r^m = a^m \cos m\theta.$$

Taking the logarithmic differential

$$\frac{m}{r}\frac{dr}{d\theta} = -m \tan m\theta;$$

therefore $\cot\phi = -\tan m\theta;$

therefore $\phi = \dfrac{\pi}{2} + m\theta.$

But $\theta = \theta' + \dfrac{\pi}{2} - \phi,$

therefore $\theta = \theta' - m\theta$, or $\theta = \dfrac{\theta'}{m+1}.$

Again $r' = r\sin\phi = r\cos m\theta = a\cos^{\frac{1}{m}} m\theta \cdot \cos m\theta = a\cos^{\frac{m+1}{m}} \dfrac{m\theta'}{m+1}.$

Hence the equation of the pedal curve is

$$r^{\frac{m}{m+1}} = a^{\frac{m}{m+1}} \cos \frac{m}{m+1}\theta.$$

**147.** DEF. If there be a series of curves which we may designate as

$$A, A_1, A_2, A_3, \ldots A_n, \ldots$$

such that each is the *first positive pedal* curve of the one which immediately precedes it; then $A_2$, $A_3$, etc., are respectively called the *second, third, etc; positive pedals* of $A$. Also, any one of this series of curves may be regarded as the original curve, *e.g.* $A_3$; then $A_2$ is called the *first negative pedal of* $A_3$, $A_1$ the *second negative pedal*, and so on.

**Ex. 1.** Find the $k^{\text{th}}$ positive pedal of

$r^m = a^m \cos m\theta.$

It has been shown that the first positive pedal is

$$r^{m_1} = a^{m_1} \cos m_1\theta,$$

where $m_1 = \dfrac{m}{1+m}.$

Similarly the second positive pedal is

$$r^{m_2} = a^{m_2} \cos m_2\theta,$$

where $m_2 = \dfrac{m_1}{1+m_1} = \dfrac{m}{1+2m};$

and generally the $k^{\text{th}}$ positive pedal is $r^{m_k} = a^{m_k} \cos m_k\theta,$

where $m_k = \dfrac{m}{1+km}.$

# PEDALS.

**Ex. 2.** Find the $k^{th}$ negative pedal of the curve

$$r^m = a^m \cos m\theta.$$

We have shown above that $r^m = a^m \cos m\theta$ is the $k^{th}$ positive pedal of the curve $r^n = a^n \cos n\theta$, provided $m = \dfrac{n}{1+kn}$.

This gives $\quad n = \dfrac{m}{1-km}$.

Hence the $k^{th}$ negative pedal of $r^m = a^m \cos m\theta$ is

$$r^n = a^n \cos n\theta,$$

where $\quad n = \dfrac{m}{1-km}$.

# EXAMPLES

1. Show that the first positive pedal of a circle with regard to any point is a Limacon $(r = a + b\cos\theta)$,which becomes a Cardioide $\{r = a(1+\cos\theta)\}$ when the point is on the circumference.
2. Show that the first positive pedal of a central conic with regard to the centre is of the form $r^2 = A + B\cos 2\theta$, which becomes a Bernoulli's Lemniscate $(r^2 = a^2 \cos 2\theta)$ when the conic is a rectangular hyperbola.
3. Show that the first positive pedal of the parabola $y^2 = 4ax$ with regard to the vertex is the cissoid $x(x^2+y^2) + ay^2 = 0$.
4. Show that

$$r^2 = a^2 \cos 2\theta,\ r^{\frac{2}{3}} = a^{\frac{2}{3}} \cos\frac{2}{3}\theta,\ r^{\frac{2}{5}} = a^{\frac{2}{5}} \cos\frac{2}{5}\theta,\ r^{\frac{2}{7}} = a^{\frac{2}{7}} \cos\frac{2}{7}\theta,$$

$r^{\frac{2}{9}} = a^{\frac{2}{9}} \cos\frac{2}{9}\theta$, are the first, second, third, fourth and fifth pedals of a rectangular hyperbola.

5. Show that the 10th positive and negative pedals of the circle $r = a\cos\theta$ are respectively

$$r = a\cos^{11}\frac{\theta}{11}, \text{ and } r = a\sec^{9}\frac{\theta}{9}.$$

6. Show that the first positive pedal of

$$x^n + y^n = a^n,$$

is $(x^2+y^2)^{\frac{n}{n-1}} = a^{\frac{n}{n-1}}\left(x^{\frac{n}{n-1}} + y^{\frac{n}{n-1}}\right)$.

## 148. Perpendicular on Tangent to Pedal.

Let $PY, QY'$ be tangents at the contiguous points $P, Q$ on the curve, and let $OY, OY'$ be perpendiculars from $O$ upon these tangents. Let $OZ$ be drawn at right angles to $Y'Y$ produced. Let the tangents at $P$ and $Q$ intersect at $T$.

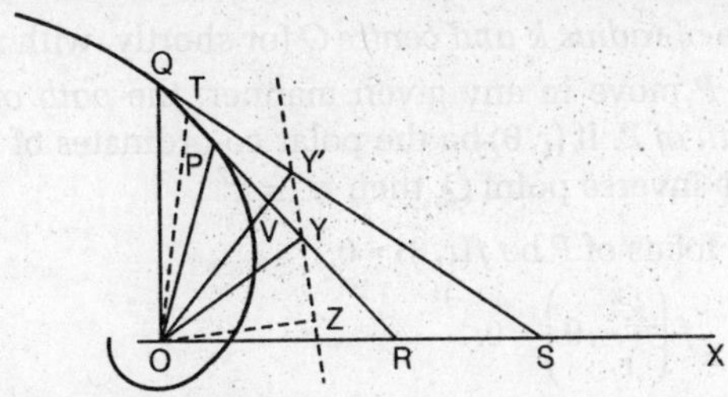


It is clear that since $Y\hat{O}Y' = Y\hat{T}Y'$,

the points $O, Y, Y', T$ are concyclic, and therefore

$$O\hat{Y}Z = \pi - O\hat{Y}Y' = O\hat{T}Y';$$

and the triangles $OYZ$ and $OTY'$ are similar. Therefore

$$\frac{OZ}{OY} = \frac{OY'}{OT};$$

and in the limit when $Q$ comes into coincidence with $P$, $Y'$ comes into coincidence with $Y$, and the limiting position of $YY'$ is the tangent to the pedal curve. Let the perpendicular on the tangent at $Y$ to the pedal curve be called $p_1$, then the above result becomes

$$\frac{p_1}{p} = \frac{p}{r}, \quad \text{or} \quad p_1 r = p^2.$$

## 149. Circle on Radius Vector for diameter touches Pedal.

This fact is clear from the figure of Art. 148, for $OT$ is in the limit a radius vector and the circle on $OT$ for diameter cuts the pedal in the ultimately coincident points $Y$ and $Y'$, and therefore in the limit has the same tangent at $Y$ as the pedal curve.

## 150. Pedals regarded as Envelopes.

It is clear then that the problem of finding the first positive pedal of a given curve is identical with that of finding the envelope of circles described on radii vectores as diameters (see Art. 142).

Again, the first negative pedal is the curve touched by (*i.e.* the envelope of) a straight line drawn through any point of the curve and at right angles to the radius vector to the point.

Thus by Art. 142, Ex. 1, the first positive pedal of $r = 2a\cos\theta$
with regard to the origin is the cardioide $r = a(1 + \cos\theta)$,
and by Ex. 2, the first negative pedal of $r = a(1 + \cos\theta)$
with regard to the origin is the circle $r = 2a\cos\theta$.

# INVERSION.

**151.** DEF. Let $O$ be the pole, and suppose any point $P$ be given; then if a second point $Q$ be taken on $OP$, or $OP$ produced, such that $OP \cdot OQ = \text{constant}, k^2$ say, then $Q$ is said to be the *inverse of the point P with respect to a circle of radius k and centre O* (or shortly, with respect to $O$).

If the point $P$ move in any given manner, the *path of Q is said to be inverse to the path of P*. If $(r, \theta)$ be the polar co-ordinates of the point $P$, and $(r', \theta)$ those of the inverse point $Q$, then $rr' = k^2$.

Hence if the locus of $P$ be $f(r, \theta) = 0$,

that of $Q$ will be $f\left(\dfrac{k^2}{r}, \theta\right) = 0.$

For example the curves $r^m = a^m \cos m\theta$ and $r^m \cos m\theta = a^m$ are inverse to each other with regard to a circle of radius $a$.

## 152. Tangents to Curve and Inverse inclined to Radius Vector at Supplementary Angles.

If $P, P'$ be two contiguous points on a curve, and

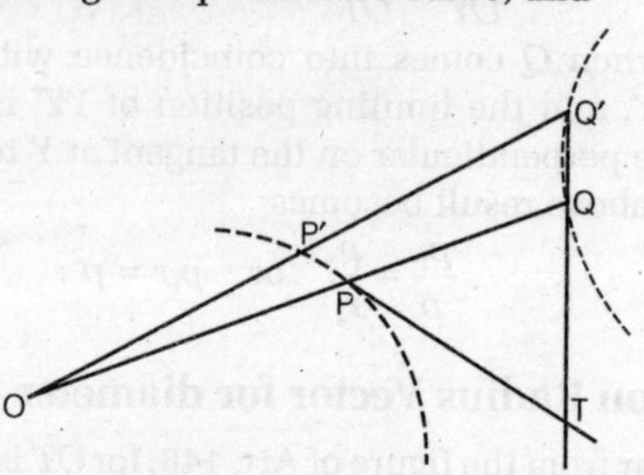


$Q, Q'$ the inverse points, then, since

$$OP \cdot OQ = OP' \cdot OQ',$$

the points $P, P', Q', Q$ are concyclic; and since the angles $OPT$ and $OQ'T$ are therefore supplementary, it follows that in the limit when $P'$ ultimately coincides with $P$ and $Q'$ with $Q$ the tangents at $P$ and $Q$ make supplementary angles with $OPQ$.

# EXAMPLES

1. Show that the inverse of the conic

$$\frac{l}{r} = 1 + e \cos \theta \text{ with regard to the focus is the Limacon}$$

$$\frac{l}{k^2} r = 1 + e \cos \theta$$

which becomes a cardioide

$[r = a(1 + \cos \theta)]$ in the case when the conic is a parabola.

**2.** If the point $x'$, $y'$ be inverse to $(x, y)$, show that

$$x = \frac{k^2x'}{x'^2 + y'^2}, \quad \text{and} \quad y = \frac{k^2y'}{x'^2 + y'^2}.$$

**3.** Show that the inverses of the lines $x = a$, $y = b$ are respectively

$$x^2 + y^2 = \frac{k^2}{a}x, \quad \text{and} \quad x^2 + y^2 = \frac{k^2}{b}y.$$

**4.** Show that the inverse of the conic

$ax^2 + 2bxy + cy^2 = 2y$,

is the cubic $k^2(ax^2 + 2bxy + cy^2) = 2y(x^2 + y^2)$.

**5.** Find the inverses of the straight lines

$3x + 4y = 5$, $4x - 3y = 5$ with regard to the origin, and show that they are circles cutting orthogonally.

# POLAR RECIPROCALS.

## 153. Polar Reciprocal of a Curve with regard to a given Circle.

DEF. If $OY$ be the perpendicular from the pole upon the tangent to a given curve, and if a point $Z$ be taken on $OY$ or $OY$ produced *such that* $OY \cdot OZ$ *is constant* (= $k^2$ say), the locus of $Z$ is called the *polar reciprocal* of the given curve with regard to a circle of radius $k$ and centre at $O$.

From the definition it is obvious that this curve is the *inverse of the first positive pedal* curve, and therefore its equation can at once be found.

**Ex.** *Polar reciprocal of an ellipse with regard to its centre.*

For the ellipse $\dfrac{x^2}{a^2} + \dfrac{y^2}{b^2} = 1$,

the condition that $p = x \cos \alpha + y \sin \alpha$ touches the curve is

$$p^2 = a^2 \cos^2 \alpha + b^2 \sin^2 \alpha.$$

Hence the polar equation of the pedal with regard to the origin is

$$r^2 = a^2 \cos^2 \theta + b^2 \sin^2 \theta.$$

Again, the inverse of this curve is

$$\frac{k^4}{r^2} = a^2 \cos^2 \theta + b^2 \sin^2 \theta,$$

or $\quad a^2x^2 + b^2y^2 = k^4$,

which is therefore the equation of the polar reciprocal of the ellipse with regard to a circle with centre at the origin and radius $k$.

## EXAMPLES

Find the polar reciprocals with regard to a circle of radius $k$ and centre at the origin of the curves.

1. $r = a\cos\theta$.
2. Any circle.
3. $\frac{l}{r} = 1 + e\cos\theta$.
4. $r = a(1+\cos\theta)$.
5. $r^n = a^n \cos n\theta$.
6. $x^m y^n = a^{m+n}$.
7. $x^n + y^n = a^n$.
8. $\left(\frac{x}{a}\right)^m + \left(\frac{y}{b}\right)^m = 1$.

# INVOLUTES AND EVOLUTES.

**154.** DEF. The locus of the centres of curvature of all points on a given curve is called the *evolute*.

If the evolute itself be regarded as the original curve, a curve of which it is the evolute is called an *involute*.

**Ex.** To find the evolute of the parabola

$$y^2 = 4ax.$$

By Ex. 2, 118, the co-ordinates of the centre of curvature are

$$\left.\begin{aligned} \bar{x} &= 2a + 3x \\ \bar{y} &= -2x^{\frac{3}{2}}/a^{\frac{1}{2}} \end{aligned}\right\}$$

The arbitrary abscissa $x$ must be eliminated between these equations. We have

$$(\bar{x} - 2a)^{\frac{3}{2}} = 3^{\frac{3}{2}} x^{\frac{3}{2}} = -3^{\frac{3}{2}} a^{\frac{1}{2}} \bar{y}/2,$$

or squaring and dropping the bar,

$$4(x-2a)^3 = 27ay^2,$$

a semicubical parabola.

## EXAMPLES

1. Show that the locus of the centres of curvature of the ellipse $\frac{x^2}{a^2} + \frac{y^2}{b^2} = 1$,

   is $$(ax)^{\frac{2}{3}} + (by)^{\frac{2}{3}} = (a^2 - b^2)^{\frac{2}{3}}.$$

2. Show that the locus of the centres of curvature of the catenary $y = c\cosh\frac{x}{c}$,

   is $c\log\frac{y + \sqrt{y^2 - 4c^2}}{2c} = x + \frac{y}{4c}\sqrt{y^2 - 4c^2}$.

## 155. Evolute touched by the Normals.

Let $P_1, P_2, P_3$ be contiguous points on a given curve, and let the normals at $P_1, P_2$ and at $P_2, P_3$ intersect at $Q_1, Q_2$ respectively. Then in the limit when $P_2, P_3$ move along the curve to ultimate coincidence with $P_1$ the limiting positions of $Q_1, Q_2$ are the centres of curvature corresponding to the points $P_1, P_2$ of the curve.

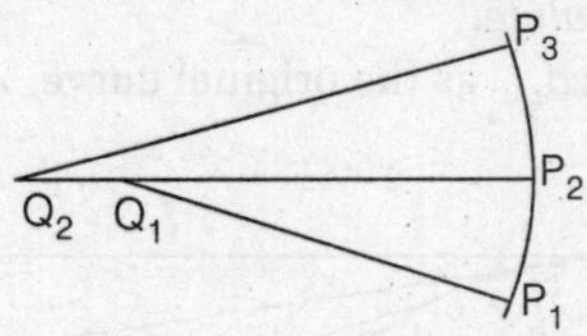


Now $Q_1$ and $Q_2$ both lie on the normal at $P_2$, and therefore it is clear that the normal is a tangent to the locus of such points as $Q_1, Q_2$, *i.e.* each of the normals of the original curve is a *tangent to the evolute*; and in general the best method of investigating the equation of the evolute of any proposed curve is to consider it as the *envelope of the normals* of that curve.

**Ex. 1.** *To find the evolute of the ellipse*

$$\frac{x^2}{a^2}+\frac{y^2}{b^2}=1.$$

The equation of the normal at the point whose eccentric angle is $\phi$ is

$$\frac{ax}{\cos\phi}-\frac{by}{\sin\phi}=a^2-b^2 \quad \text{... (1),}$$

We have to find the envelope of this line for different values of the parameter $\phi$.

Differentiating with regard to $\phi$,

$$ax\frac{\sin\phi}{\cos^2\phi}+by\frac{\cos\phi}{\sin^2\phi}=0 \quad \text{... (2),}$$

or

$$\frac{\sin^3\phi}{by}+\frac{\cos^3\phi}{ax}=0.$$

Hence

$$\frac{\sin\phi}{-\sqrt[3]{by}}=\frac{\cos\phi}{\sqrt[3]{ax}}=\frac{1}{\sqrt{(ax)^{\frac{2}{3}}+(by)^{\frac{2}{3}}}} \quad \text{... (3).}$$

Substituting these values of $\sin\phi$ and $\cos\phi$ in equation (1) we obtain, after reduction

$$(ax)^{\frac{2}{3}}+(by)^{\frac{2}{3}}=(a^2-b^2)^{\frac{2}{3}}.$$

**Ex. 2.** Show that the envelope of $y = mx - 2am - am^3$ (i.e. the normal to $y^2 = 4ax$) is $27ay^2 = 4(x-2a)^3$.

## 156. There is but one Evolute, but an infinite number of Involutes.

Let *ABCD* ... be the original curve on which the successive points $A, B, C, D, \ldots$ are indefinitely close to each other. Let $a, b, c, \ldots$ be the successive points of intersection of normals at $A, B, C, \ldots$ and therefore the centres of curvature of those points. Then looking at *ABC* ... as the original curve, *abcd*... is its *evolute*.

And regarding *abcd*... as the original curve, *ABCD*... is *an involute*.

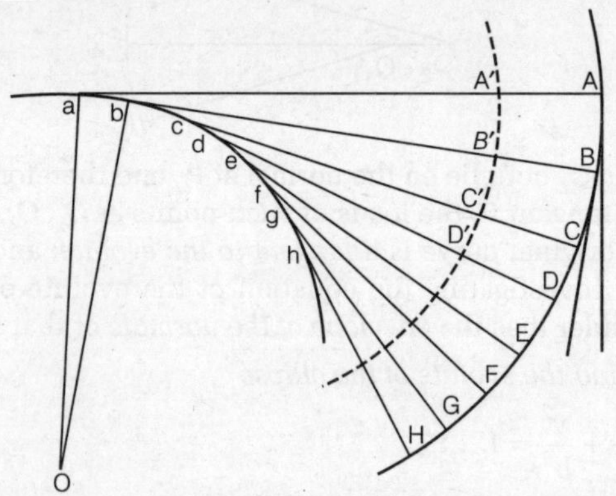


If we suppose any equal lengths $AA'$, $BB'$, $CC'$, ... to be taken along each normal, as shown in the figure, then a new curve is formed, viz. $A'B'C'$..., which may be called a *parallel* to the original curve, having the same normals as the original curve and therefore having the same evolute. It is therefore clear that if any curve be given it can have but *one evolute*, but an infinite number of curves may have the same evolute, and therefore any curve may have an *infinite number of involutes*. The involutes of a given curve thus form a system of *parallel curves*.

## 157. Involutes traced out by the several points of a string unwound from a curve. Length of Arc of Evolute.

Since $a$ is the centre of the circle of curvature for the point $A$ (Fig., Art. 156), $aA = aB = bB +$ elementary arc $ab$ (Art. 81).

Hence $\quad aA - bB = \text{arc } ab$.

Similarly $\quad bB - cC = \text{arc } bc,\ cC - dD = \text{arc } cd$, etc., $fF - gG = \text{arc } fg$.

Hence by addition $aA - gG = \text{arc } ab + \text{arc } bc + \ldots + \text{arc } fg = \text{arc } ag$.

Hence the *difference between the radii of curvature a two points of a curve is equal to the length of the corresponding arc of the evolute*. Also, if the evolute *abc* ... be regarded as a rigid curve and a string be unwound from it, being kept tight, then the *points of the unwinding string describe a system of parallel curves, each of which is an involute of the curve abcd...*, one of them coinciding with the original curve *ABC* ... It is from this property that the names involute and evolute are derived.

## EXAMPLES

1. Show that the whole length of the evolute of the ellipse $\frac{x^2}{a^2}+\frac{y^2}{b^2}=1$, is $4\left(\frac{a^2}{b}-\frac{b^2}{a}\right)$.

2. Show that in the parabola $y^2 = 4ax$ the length of the part of the evolute intercepted within the parabola is $4a\,(3\sqrt{3}-1)$.

## EXAMPLES

1. Show that the fourth negative pedal of the cardioide $r = a\,(1+\cos\theta)$ is a parabola.

2. Show that the fourth and fifth positive pedals of the curve $r = a\left(\sec\frac{2}{9}\theta\right)^{\frac{9}{2}}$ are respectively a rectangular hyperbola and a lemniscate $[r^2 = a^2\cos 2\theta]$.

3. Show that the first positive pedal may be obtained by writing $r$ instead of $p$ and $\frac{r^2}{p}$ instead of $r$ in the pedal equation of the original curve.

4. Show that the first positive pedal of the epicycloid $p^2 = Ar^2 + B$, has for its pedal equation $r^2 = A\frac{r^4}{p^2} + B$.

5. Show that the equation of the $n^{\text{th}}$ pedal of the curve $f(p, r) = 0$, is $f\left(\frac{r^n}{p^{n-1}}, \frac{r^{n+1}}{p^n}\right) = 0$, i.e. it may be obtained from the original equation by writing $\left(\frac{r}{p}\right)^n p$ for $p$, and $\left(\frac{r}{p}\right)^n r$ for $r$.

6. Show that the inverse of the hyperbola $\frac{1}{x}+\frac{1}{y}=\frac{1}{a}$ with regard to the origin is $a\,(x^2+y^2)\,(x+y) = k^2xy$.

7. Show that the inverse of the ellipse $\frac{x^2}{a^2}+\frac{y^2}{b^2}=1$, with regard to the origin is $(x^2+y^2)^2 = k^4\left(\frac{x^2}{a^2}+\frac{y^2}{b^2}\right)$.

**8.** Show that the equation of the inverse of a curve with regard to the pole may be obtained from the pedal equation by writing $\frac{k^2 p}{r^2}$ for $p$ and $\frac{k^2}{r}$ for $r$, i.e. if $f(p, r) = 0$ be the original curve $f\left(\frac{k^2 p}{r^2}, \frac{k^2}{r}\right) = 0$ will be the inverse.

**9.** Show that the inverse of the curve $p^2 = Ar^2 + B$, is $k^4 p^2 = Ak^4 r^2 + Br^4$.

**10.** Show that the pedal equation of the evolute of the curve $p = f(r)$ will be obtained by eliminating $p$ and $r$ between

$$\left.\begin{aligned} p &= f(r), \\ p_1^2 &= r^2 - p^2, \\ r_1^2 &= r^2 + r^2\left(\frac{dr}{dp}\right)^2 - 2pr\,\frac{dr}{dp} \end{aligned}\right\}.$$

**11.** Show that the evolute of the epi- or hypocycloid

$$p^2 = Ar^2 + B \text{ is } p^2 = Ar^2 + \frac{B}{A}(A-1)$$

(i.e. a similar epi- or hypocycloid, see Q. 89).

**12.** Prove the following series of results for the **Equiangular or Logarithmic spiral**

$$r = ae^{\theta \cot \alpha}.$$

(1) $\phi = a$. (Hence the name "Equiangular.")

(2) The pedal equation is $p = r \sin \alpha$.

(3) $\rho = r \operatorname{cosec} \alpha$.

(4) Let $O$ be the pole, $PT$ the tangent at $P$, $OY$ the perpendicular, $OT$ the polar subtangent cutting the normal in $C$. Prove that $C$ is the centre of curvature.

(5) $s = r \sec \alpha$ ($s$ being supposed measured from the pole).

(6) $s = PT$.

(7) Prove geometrically that all the pedals, the inverse, the polar reciprocal, the evolute are *equal* equiangular spirals (i.e. for which $\phi$ is the same).

(8) The equation of the first positive pedal is

$$r = a \sin \alpha\, e^{\left(\frac{\pi}{2} - \alpha\right)\cot \alpha}\, e^{\theta \cot \alpha}.$$

(9) The $n$th pedal is $r = a \sin^n \alpha\, e^{n\left(\frac{\pi}{2} - \alpha\right)\cot \alpha}\, e^{\theta \cot \alpha}$.

(10) The inverse is $r = \frac{k^2}{a} e^{-\theta \cot \alpha}$.

(11) The Polar reciprocal is $r = \frac{k^2}{a \sin \alpha} e^{-\left(\frac{\pi}{2}-\alpha\right)\cot \alpha} e^{-\theta \cot \alpha}$.

(12) The evolute is $r = a \cot \alpha e^{-\frac{\pi}{2}\cot \alpha} e^{\theta \cot \alpha}$.

**13.** Prove the following series of results for **the cardioide**

$$r = a(1 - \cos \theta).$$

(1) The curve may be constructed as the locus of a point on the circumference of a circle of diameter $a$ which rolls without sliding upon the circumference of a circle of equal radius.

(2) Hence prove geometrically $\phi = \frac{\theta}{2}$.

Prove this also from the equation by means of the formula

$$\tan \phi = r \frac{d\theta}{dr}.$$

(3) If $O$ be a fixed point upon a circle of radius $a$ and centre $C$, and $P$ any other point upon the circumference, make the angle $C\hat{P}Q = C\hat{P}O$. Prove that $PQ$ always touches a cardioide formed by the rolling of a circle of radius $\frac{a}{3}$ upon a circle of equal radius (geometrical).

(4) The curve may also be constructed thus:— Take a circle $OQD$ of diameter $a$ and centre $E$. Let a straight rod $PP'$ of length $2a$ move in such a manner that its mid-point $Q$ describes the given circle whilst the rod is constrained to pass through a fixed point $O$ on the circumference. The points $P, P'$ trace out the cardioide. The point $O$ may be called the focus.

(5) Any "focal chord" is of constant length.

(6) The "Instantaneous Centre" for the motion of the rod is at the point $R$ of the circle in (4) diametrically opposite to $Q$.

(7) The lines $RP$, $RP'$ are normals (geometrical).

(8) Normals at the ends of a focal chord intersect at right angles on the circle in (4) (geometrical).

(9) Tangents at the ends of a focal chord intersect at right angles on a concentric circle of three times the radius (geometrical).

(10) If $RP$ cuts the circle in (4) again at $S$ the angle $OSR$ is bisected by $ES$ (geometrical).

(11) Hence show (by 3) that the evolute of the cardioide is a cardioide of one-third the linear dimensions and turned the opposite way (geometrical).

(12) Show (by 11) that the whole length of the arc of the cardioide $r = a(1 - \cos\theta)$ is $8a$.

(13) The cardioide is the first positive pedal of a circle with regard to a point upon the circumference.

(14) The pedal equation is $p = \dfrac{r^{\frac{3}{2}}}{(2a)^{\frac{1}{2}}}$.

(15) The curvature at any point is $3/2\sqrt{2ar}$.

(16) The $n$th pedal of $r = a(1 + \cos\theta)$, is $\dfrac{1}{r^{n+2}} = (2a)^{\frac{1}{n+2}} \cos^{\frac{\theta}{n+2}}$.

(17) The Inverse of the cardioide with regard to the pole is a parabola.

**14.** Show that if $\rho$ be the radius of curvature at any point $p$, $r$ upon the curve $f(p, r) = 0$ and $\rho_1$ that at the corresponding point upon the inverse, then

$$\rho_1 = k^2 \Big/ \left(2p - \frac{r^2}{\rho}\right),$$

where $k^2$ is the constant of inversion.

**15.** With the same notation the radius of curvature at the corresponding point of the polar reciprocal is $\dfrac{k^2 r^3}{p^3 \rho}$, where $k^2$ is the constant of reciprocation.

**16.** With the same notation if $\rho_n$ be the radius of curvature at the corresponding point of the $n$th pedal, prove that

$$\rho_n \frac{r^{n-2}}{p^{n-1}} = \frac{1}{2}\,\frac{1}{-2}\,\frac{1}{-2} \cdots \frac{1}{-2}\,\frac{p\rho}{-r^2}$$

(where there are $n + 1$ quotients)

$$= \frac{nr^2 - (n-1)\,p\rho}{(n+1)\,r^2 - np\rho}.$$

# CHAPTER XIII.

# MAXIMA AND MINIMA. ONE INDEPENDENT VARIABLE.

## 158. Elementary Algebraical and Geometrical methods.

Examples frequently occur in Algebra and Geometry in which it is required to find whether any limitations exist to the admissible values of certain proposed functions for real values of the variable upon which they depend. These investigations can often be conducted in an elementary manner. A few examples follow in illustration.

**Ex. 1.** The function $ax + \frac{b}{x}$ may be written in the form

$\left(\sqrt{ax} - \sqrt{\frac{b}{x}}\right)^2 + 2\sqrt{ab}$, from which it is obvious that the expression can never be less than $2\sqrt{ab}$, the value it attains when $\sqrt{ax} = \sqrt{\frac{b}{x}}$, or $x = \sqrt{\frac{b}{a}}$. For *the square* of a real quantity is essentially positive and therefore any value of $x$ other than $x = \sqrt{\frac{b}{a}}$ will give to the expression a greater value than $2\sqrt{ab}$.

**Ex. 2.** Investigate whether any limitation exists to the real values of the expression $\frac{3x^2 - 4x + 3}{3x^2 + 4x + 3}$ for real values of $x$.

Let $\frac{3x^2 - 4x + 3}{3x^2 + 4x + 3} = y$.

Then $3(1 - y)\,x^2 - 4\,(1 + y)\,x + 3\,(1 - y) = 0$.

If $x$ be real, we must have $4\,(1 + y)^2 - 9(1 - y)^2 > 0$,

*i.e.* $(5y - 1)\,(5 - y)$ must be positive.

Hence $y$ must lie between the values 5 and $\frac{1}{5}$.

Therefore the maximum value of the expression is 5 and the minimum value is $\frac{1}{5}$.

**Ex. 3.** If the sum of two quantities be given, when is their product a maximum?

Let $x + y = a$, a constant,
then $4xy = (x+y)^2 - (x-y)^2 = a^2 - (x-y)^2$.

The right-hand side has its maximum value when $(x-y)^2$ has its minimum, *i.e.* when $x = y$, for being a square it cannot be negative.

Thus the maximum value of $xy$ is $\frac{a^2}{4}$.

This may be shown geometrically as follows:—the problem is to divide a given line $AB$ in such manner that the rectangle of the segments is as great as possible. Let $C$ be the centre and $P$ any other point of the line. Then by Euc. II. 5,
rect. $AP \cdot PB$ + sq. on $CP$ = sq. on $AC$ = rect. $AC \cdot CB$,
*i.e.* the rect. $AP \cdot PB$ is less than the rect. $AC \cdot CB$.

Hence the point of division is the mid-point, or the line must be bisected.

**Ex. 4.** If $x + y + z + w$ be constant, when will $xyzw$ have its maximum value?

So long as any two, say $x$ and $y$, are unequal we can without altering $z$ and $w$ (and thus keeping $x + y$ constant) increase $xy$, and therefore also $xyzw$ by making $x$ and $y$ more nearly equal (by Ex.3).

Hence $xyzw$ does not attain its maximum value until

$$x = y = z = w.$$

The same argument obviously applies to the product of any number of quantities whose sum is constant.

If we are searching for the maximum value of such an expression as $xy^2z^3$, say, with condition $x + y + z = a$, we proceed thus

$$xy^2z^3 = 2^2 3^3 \cdot x \cdot \frac{y}{2} \cdot \frac{y}{2} \cdot \frac{z}{3} \cdot \frac{z}{3} \cdot \frac{z}{3} \text{ and is to be a maximum,}$$

where $x + \frac{y}{2} + \frac{y}{2} + \frac{z}{3} + \frac{z}{3} + \frac{z}{3} = a$;

and by the preceding work we are to make $\frac{x}{1} = \frac{y}{2} = \frac{z}{3} = \frac{a}{6}$,

whence the maximum value is $\frac{2^2 \cdot 3^3 a^6}{6^6} = \frac{a^6}{2^4 \cdot 3^3}$.

**Ex. 5.** In any triangle the maximum value of $\cos A \cos B \cos C$ is $\frac{1}{8}$.

For $2 \cos A \cos B \cos C = \cos A \{\cos(B - C) - \cos A\}$,

and therefore as long as $B$ and $C$ are unequal we may increase the expression by making them more nearly equal and keeping their sum constant. Thus $\cos A \cos B \cos C$ does not attain its maximum value until $A = B = C = \frac{\pi}{3}$, and then its value is $\frac{1}{8}$.

**Ex. 6.** What are the greatest and least values of $a \sin x + b \cos x$?

Let $a = c \cos \alpha$ and $b = c \sin \alpha$,

so that $c^2 = a^2 + b^2$ and $\tan \alpha = \dfrac{b}{a}$.

Thus $a \sin x + b \cos x = c \sin x \cos \alpha + c \cos x \sin \alpha$

$$= \sqrt{a^2 + b^2} \sin (x + \alpha),$$

and as the greatest and least values of a sine are 1 and $-1$, the maximum and minimum values required are $\sqrt{a^2 + b^2}$ and $-\sqrt{a^2 + b^2}$ respectively.

**Ex. 7.** If $A, B, C \ldots$ be a number of points and $P$ any other point, and if $G$ be the centroid of masses $\lambda$ at $A$, $\mu$ at $B$, etc., then it is a known proposition that

$$\lambda PA^2 + \mu PB^2 + \ldots = (\lambda GA^2 + \mu GB^2 + \ldots) + (\lambda + \mu + \ldots)PG^2,$$

or

$$\Sigma\lambda PA^2 = \Sigma\lambda GA^2 + (\Sigma\lambda)PG^2.$$

Hence since $\Sigma\lambda GA^2$ is a fixed quantity for all positions of $P$, $\Sigma\lambda PA^2$ has its minimum value when $P$ is at $G$.

# EXAMPLES

1. Show that the minimum value of $x^2 - 4x + 9$ is 5.
2. Show that the expression $x + \dfrac{1}{x}$ cannot have any value intermediate between 2 and $-2$.
3. Show that $\dfrac{x^2 + x + 1}{x^2 - x + 1}$ has 3 for its maximum value, and $\dfrac{1}{3}$ for its minimum.
4. Show that the value of $\dfrac{x^2 + px + 1}{x^2 - px + 1}$ is intermediate between $\dfrac{2 + p}{2 - p}$ and $\dfrac{2 - p}{2 + p}$.
5. Show that $\dfrac{ax^2 + 2bx + c}{cx^2 + 2bx + a}$ is unlimited in value if $a + c < 2b$.
6. Show that the shortest distance from a given point to a given straight line is the perpendicular distance.
7. Show that the greatest triangle inscribed in a given circle is equilateral.

**8.** Deduce from 7 by projection that a maximum triangle inscribed in an ellipse

(*a*) is such that the tangent at each angular point is parallel to the opposite side,

(*b*) has its centroid at the centre of the ellipse,

(*c*) that its area $= \frac{3\sqrt{3}}{4}ab$, where $a$ and $b$ are the semi-axes.

**9.** Show that the triangle of greatest area with given base and vertical angle is isosceles.

**10.** Show that if $ABC$ be a triangle, and $P$ any point $PA^2 + PB^2 + PC^2$ will be a minimum when $P$ is at the centroid.

**11.** Show that $PA^2 \tan A + PB^2 \tan B + PC^2 \tan C$

has its minimum value when $P$ is at the orthocentre.

**12.** Show that $PA^2 \sin A + PB^2 \sin B + PC^2 \sin C$

has its minimum value when $P$ is at the incentre.

**13.** If $ABCD$ be a quadrilateral, and $P$ any point, $PA^2 + PB^2 + PC^2 + PD^2$

has its minimum value when $P$ is at the intersection of the joins of mid-points of opposite sides.

**14.** Find the maximum rectangle inscribable in a given ellipse, *i.e.* find the maximum value of $xy$, having given $\frac{x^2}{a^2} + \frac{y^2}{b^2} = 1$.

**15.** Find the maximum value of $xyz$, having given $x + y + z = a$.

**16.** Find the maximum value of $xyz$, having given $\frac{x^2}{a^2} + \frac{y^2}{b^2} + \frac{z^2}{c^2} = 1$.

**17.** Find the maximum value of $xy^2$, having given $x + y = a$.

**18.** Find the maximum value of $x^p y^q$, having given $x + y = a$.

**19.** If $\theta + \phi =$ constant, the maximum value of $\sin\theta \sin\phi$ is attained when $\theta = \phi$.

**20.** Find the maximum value of $\sin A \sin B \sin C$ for a triangle.

**21.** Find the maximum and minimum values of $a \sin^2 x + b \cos^2 x$.

**22.** Show that the greatest chord through a point of intersection of two given circles is that which is parallel to the line of centres.

**23.** Find the greatest triangle of given species whose sides pass through three fixed points.

**24.** Find the greatest rectangle whose sides pass through the angular points of a given rectangle.

**25.** Find the two perpendicular focal chords of a given conic whose sum is a maximum.

# THE GENERAL PROBLEM.

**159.** Suppose $x$ to be any independent variable capable of assuming *any real value whatever*, and let $\phi(x)$ be any given function of $x$. Let the curve $y = \phi(x)$ be represented in the adjoining figure, and let $A, B, C, D, \ldots$ be those points on the curve at which the tangent is parallel to one of the co-ordinate axes.

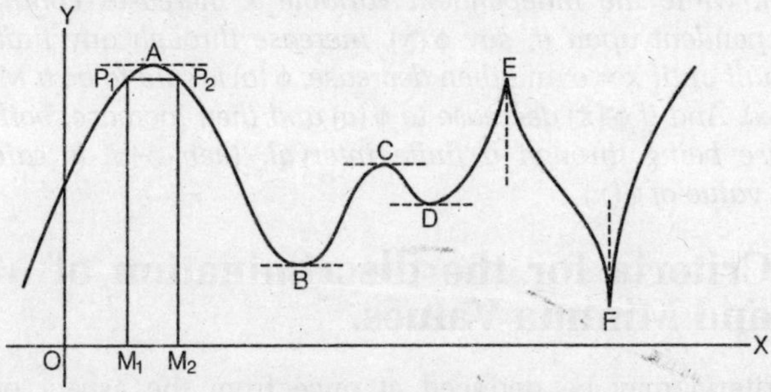


Suppose an ordinate to travel from left to right along the axis of $x$. Then it will be seen that as the ordinate passes such points as $A, C$, or $E$ it *ceases to increase and begins to decrease;* whilst when it passes through $B, D$, or $F$ it *ceases to decrease and begins to increase*. At each of the former sets of points the ordinate is said to have a **maximum** value, whilst at the latter it is said to have a **minimum** value.

## 160. Points of Inflexion.

On inspection of the accompanying figure it will be at once obvious that at such points of inflexion as $G$ or $H$, where the tangent is parallel to one of the co-ordinate axes, there is neither a maximum nor a minimum ordinate.

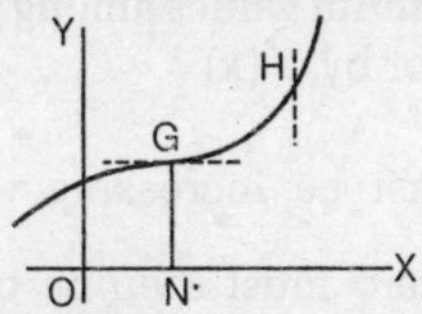


Near $G$, for instance, the ordinate increases up to a certain value $NG$, and then as it passes through $G$ it continues to increase without any prior *sensible* decrease.

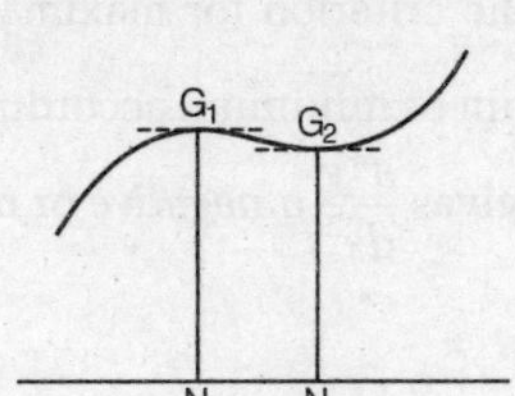

This point may however be considered as a combination of two such points as $A$ and $B$ in the figure of Art. 159, the ordinate increasing up to a certain value $N_1G_1$, then decreasing through an indefinitely small and negligible interval to $N_2G_2$, and then increasing again as shown in the magnified figure, the points $G_1$, $G_2$ being ultimately coincident.

**161.** We are thus led to the following definition:—

DEF. *If, while the independent variable x increases continuously, a function dependent upon it, say* $\phi(x)$, *increase through any finite interval however small until* $x = a$ *and then decrease,* $\phi(a)$ *is said to be a* MAXIMUM *value of* $\phi(x)$. *And if* $\phi(x)$ *decrease to* $\phi(a)$ *and then increase, both decrease and increase being through a finite interval, then* $\phi(a)$ *is said to be a* MINIMUM *value of* $\phi(x)$.

## 162. Criteria for the discrimination of Maxima and Minima Values.

The criteria may be deduced at once from the aspect of $\frac{dy}{dx}$ as a *rate-measurer.* For $\frac{dy}{dx}$ is positive or negative according as $y$ is an increasing or a decreasing function. Now, if $y$ have a *maximum* value it is ceasing to increase and beginning to decrease, and therefore $\frac{dy}{dx}$ must be changing from *positive to negative*; and if $y$ have a *minimum* value it is ceasing to decrease and beginning to increase, and therefore $\frac{dy}{dx}$ must be changing from *negative* to *positive*. Moreover, since a change from positive to negative, or *vice versa*, can only occur by passing through one of the values zero or infinity, we must search for the maximum and minimum values among those corresponding to the values of $x$ given by $\phi'(x) = 0$ or by $\phi'(x) = \infty$.

**163.** Further, since $\frac{dy}{dx}$ must be increasing when it changes from negative to positive, $\frac{d^2y}{dx^2}$ if not zero must then be positive; and similarly, when $\frac{dy}{dx}$ changes from positive to negative $\frac{d^2y}{dx^2}$ must be negative, so we arrive at another form of the criterion for maxima and minima values, viz.

that there will be a maximum or minimum according as the value of $x$ which makes $\frac{dy}{dx}$ zero or infinite, gives $\frac{d^2y}{dx^2}$ *a negative* or *a positive sign.*

## 164. Properties of Maxima and Minima Values. Criteria obtained Geometrically.

The following statements will be obvious from the figures of Arts. 159, 160.

(α) According to the definition given in Art. 161, the term maximum value does not mean the absolutely greatest nor minimum the absolutely least value of the function discussed. Moreover, there may be *several maxima* values *and several minima* values of the same function, some greater and some less than others, as in the case of the ordinates at $A, B, C, \ldots$ (Fig., Art. 159).

(β) Between two equal values of a function at *least one maximum or one minimum must lie*; for whether the function be increasing or decreasing as it passes the value [$M_1P_1$ in Fig., Art. 159] it must, if continuous, respectively decrease or increase again at least once before it attains its original value, and therefore must pass through at least one maximum or minimum value in the interval.

(γ) For a similar reason it is clear that between two maxima at least one minimum must lie; and between two minima at least one maximum must lie. In other words, maxima and minima values must occur **alternately**. Thus we have a maximum at $A$, a minimum at $B$, a maximum at $C$, etc.

(δ) In the immediate neighbourhood of a maximum or minimum ordinate two contiguous ordinates are equal, one on each side of the maximum or minimum ordinate; and these may be considered as ultimately coincident with the maximum or minimum ordinate. Moreover as the ordinate is ceasing to increase and beginning to decrease, or vice versa, its rate of variation is itself in general an infinitesimal. This is expressed by saying that at a maximum or minimum the function discussed has a **stationary** value. This principle is of much use in the geometrical treatment of maxima and minima problems.

(ε) At all points, such as $A, B, C, D, E, \ldots$, at which maxima or minima ordinates occur *the tangent is parallel to one or other of the co-ordinate axes*. At points like $A, B, C, D$ the value of $\frac{dy}{dx}$ vanishes, whilst at the cuspidal points $E, F$, $\frac{dy}{dx}$ becomes infinite.

The positions of maxima and minima ordinates are therefore given by the roots of the equations $\left.\begin{array}{l}\phi'(x)=0\\ \phi'(x)=\infty\end{array}\right\}$.

(ξ) That $\frac{dy}{dx}=0$, or $\frac{dy}{dx}=\infty$, are not in themselves *sufficient* conditions for the existence of a maximum or minimum value is clear from observing the points *G, H* of the figure of Art. 160, at which the tangent is parallel to one of the co-ordinate axes, but at which the

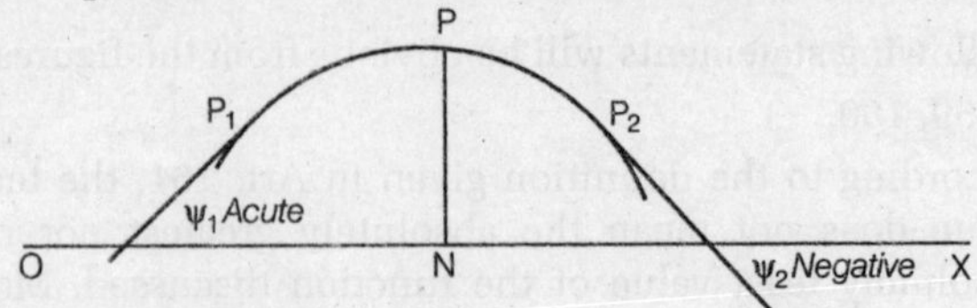


ordinate has not a maximum or minimum value. But in passing a *maximum* value of the ordinate the sign of $\frac{dy}{dx}$, that is the sign of the tangent of the angle which the tangent makes with the *x*-axis, changes from *positive to negative*; while in passing a *minimum* value the change of sign is in the reverse order, namely, from *negative to positive*.

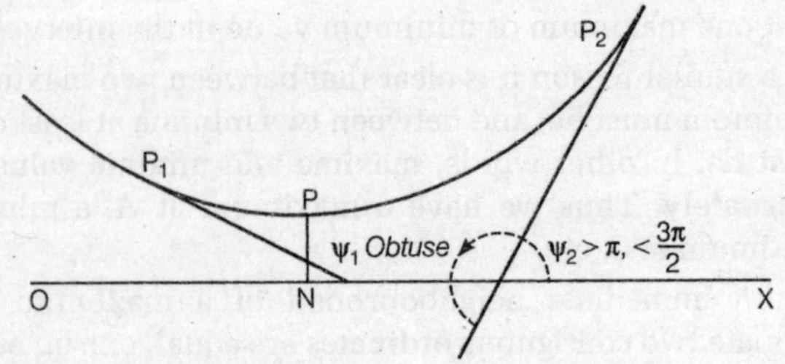


## 165. Working Rule.

We can therefore make the following rule for the **detection and discrimination** of maxima and minima values. First *find* $\frac{dy}{dx}$ and by equating it to zero find for what values of *x* it *vanishes*; also observe if any values of *x* will make it become *infinite*. Then test for each of these values whether the sign of $\frac{dy}{dx}$ *changes from* + *to* − *or from* − *to* + as *x* increases through that value. If the former be the case *y* has a **maximum** value for that value of *x* ; but if the latter, a **minimum**. If no change of sign take place the point is **a point of inflexion** at which the tangent is parallel to one of the co-ordinate axes; *or*, in some cases it may be more convenient to *discriminate* by applying the test of Art. 163. Find the sign of $\frac{d^2y}{dx^2}$ corresponding to the value of *x* under discussion. A *positive* sign indicates a *minimum* value for *y*; a *negative* sign, a *maximum*. When $\frac{d^2y}{dx^2} = 0$ this test fails and there is need of further investigation*.

* See Art. 488 of the author's larger book on the subject.

# EXAMPLES

**1.** Find the maximum and minimum values of $y$ where

$$y = (x - 1)(x - 2)^2.$$

Here

$$\frac{dy}{dx} = (x - 2)^2 + 2(x - 1)(x - 2)$$

$$= (x - 2)(3x - 4).$$

Putting this expression = 0 we obtain for the values of $x$ which give possible maxima or minima values $x = 2$ and $x = \frac{4}{3}$.

To test these: we have

if $x$ be a little less than 2, $\frac{dy}{dx} = (-)(+) =$ negative,

if $x$ be a little greater than 2, $\frac{dy}{dx} = (+)(+) =$ positive.

Hence there is a change of sign, viz., from negative to positive as $x$ passes through the value 2, and therefore $x = 2$ gives $y$ a *minimum* value.

Again, if $x$ be a little less than $\frac{4}{3}$, $\frac{dy}{dx} = (-)(-) =$ positive,

and if $x$ be a little greater than $\frac{4}{3}$, $\frac{dy}{dx} = (-)(+) =$ negative,

showing that there is a change of sign in $\frac{dy}{dx}$, viz. from positive to negative, and therefore $x = \frac{4}{3}$ gives a *maximum* value for $y$. This we might have anticipated from Art. 164, (γ). Otherwise:

$$\frac{dy}{dx} = (x - 2)(3x - 4),$$

so that when $\frac{dy}{dx}$ is put = 0 we obtain $x = 2$ or $\frac{4}{3}$.

And $\frac{d^2y}{dx^2} = 6x - 10$, so that, when $x = 2$, $\frac{d^2y}{dx^2} = 2$, a positive quantity, showing that, when $x = 2$, $y$ assumes a minimum value, whilst, when

$$x = \frac{4}{3}, \frac{d^2y}{dx^2} = -2,$$

which is negative, showing that, for this value of $x$, $y$ assumes a maximum value.

2. If $\dfrac{dy}{dx} = (x-a)^{2n}(x-b)^{2p+1}$, where $n$ and $p$ are positive integers, show that $x = a$ gives neither maximum nor minimum values of $y$, but that $x = b$ gives a minimum.

*It will be clear from this example that neither maxima nor minima values can arise from the vanishing of such factors of* $\dfrac{dy}{dx}$ *as have even indices.*

3. Show that $\dfrac{x^2 - 7x + 6}{x - 10}$ has a maximum value when $x = 4$ and a minimum when $x = 16$.

4. If $\dfrac{dy}{dx} = x(x-1)^2(x-3)^3$,

show that $x = 0$ gives a maximum value to $y$ and $x = 3$ gives a minimum.

5. Find the maxi... m and minimum values of $2x^3 - 15x^2 + 36x + 6$.

6. Show that the expression $(x-2)(x-3)^2$ has a maximum value when $x = \dfrac{7}{3}$, and a minimum value when $x = 3$.

7. Show that the expression $x^3 - 3x^2 + 6x + 3$ has neither a maximum nor a minimum value.

8. Investigate the maximum and minimum values of the expression $3x^5 - 25x^3 + 60x$.

9. For a certain curve $\dfrac{dy}{dx} = (x-1)(x-2)^2(x-3)^3(x-4)^4$; discuss the character of the curve at the points $x = 1$, $x = 2$, $x = 3$, $x = 4$.

10. Find the positions of the maximum and minimum ordinates of the curve for which $\dfrac{dy}{dx} = (x-2)^3(2x-3)^4(3x-4)^5(4x-5)^6$.

11. *To show that a triangle of maximum area inscribed in any oval curve is such that the tangent at each angular point is parallel to the opposite side.*

If $PQR$ be a maximum triangle inscribed in the oval, its vertex $P$ lies between the vertices $L$, $M$ of two equal triangles $LQR$, $MQR$

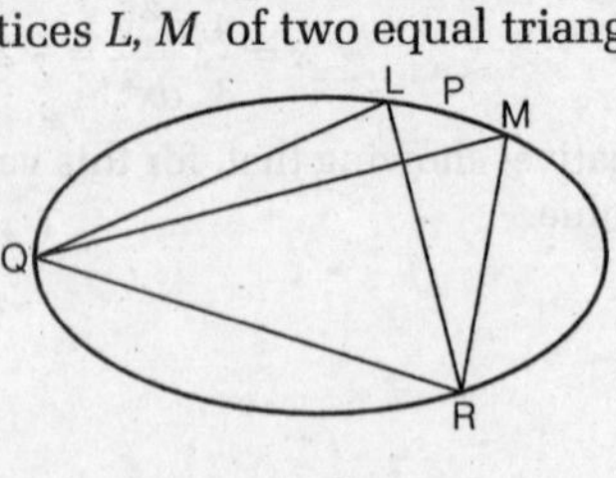

inscribed in the oval. Now, the chord $LM$ is parallel to $QR$ and the tangent at $P$ is the limiting position of the chord $LM$, which proves the proposition.

It follows that, if the oval be an ellipse, the medians of the triangle are diameters of the curve, and therefore the centre of gravity of the triangle is at the centre of the ellipse.

**12.** *Show that the sides of a triangle of minimum area circumscribing any oval curve are bisected at the points of contact; and*

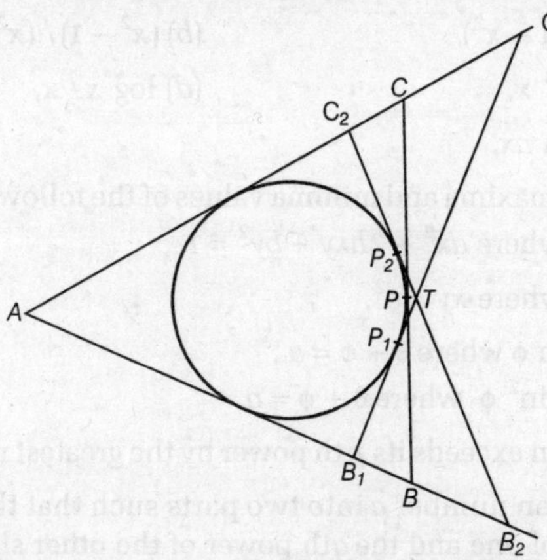


*hence that, if the oval be an ellipse, the centre of gravity of such a triangle coincides with the centre of the ellipse.*

Let $ABC$ be a triangle of minimum area circumscribing the oval. Suppose $P$ the point of contact of $BC$. Let $AB_1C_1$, $AB_2C_2$ be two equal circumscribing triangles such that $B_1C_1$, $B_2C_2$ touch the oval at $P_1$, $P_2$ on opposite sides of $P$ and intersect in $T$. Then

$$\text{triangle } TB_1B_2 = \text{triangle } TC_1C_2$$

or $$\frac{1}{2} TB_1 \cdot TB_2 \sin B_1TB_2 = \frac{1}{2} TC_1 \cdot TC_2 \sin C_1TC_2 .$$

If we bring $P_1$ and $P_2$ nearer and nearer to $P$ so as to entrap the minimum triangle, the above equation ultimately becomes $TB^2 = TC^2$; and $T$ being ultimately the point of contact $P$, the side $BC$ is bisected at its point of contact. The remainder of the question follows as in Ex. 11.

## EXAMPLES

**1.** Find the position of the maximum and minimum ordinates of the curves

(*a*) $y = (x-1)(x-2)(x-3)$, (*b*) $4y = x^4 - 8x^3 + 22x^2 - 24x$,

(*c*) $a^2y = (x-a)^2(x-b)$, (*d*) $a^3y^2 = (x-a)^4(x-b)$.

**2.** Find the maxima and minima radii vectores of the curves

(a) $r = a \sin \theta + b \cos \theta$, (b) $r = a \sin^2 \theta + b \cos^2 \theta$,

(c) $(x^2 + y^2)^2 = ax^2 + 2hxy + by^2$, (d) $\dfrac{c^4}{r^2} = \dfrac{a^2}{\sin^2 \theta} + \dfrac{b^2}{\cos^2 \theta}$,

(e) $\dfrac{a^2}{x^2} + \dfrac{b^2}{y^2} = 1$, (f) $r = a \sin^3 \theta \cos^4 \theta$.

**3.** Discuss the maxima and minima values of the following expressions:

(a) $x(1 - x)(1 - x^2)$, (b) $(x^2 - 1)/(x^2 + 3)^3$,

(c) $\sin x \cos^3 x$, (d) $\log x / x$,

(e) $\sin^n x \sin nx$.

**4.** Discuss the maxima and minima values of the following expressions:

(a) $x^2 + y^2$ where $ax^2 + 2hxy + by^2 = 1$,

(b) $ax + by$ where $xy = c^2$,

(c) $\sin \theta + \sin \phi$ where $\theta + \phi = a$,

(d) $\sin^2 \theta + \sin^2 \phi$ where $\theta + \phi = a$.

**5.** What fraction exceeds its $p$th power by the greatest number possible?

**6.** Divide a given number $a$ into two parts such that the product of the $p$th power of one and the $q$th power of the other shall be as great as possible.

**7.** Given the length of an arc of a circle, find the radius when the corresponding segment has a maximum or minimum area.

**8.** In a submarine telegraph cable the speed of signalling varies as $x^2 \log \dfrac{1}{x}$ where $x$ is the ratio of the radius of the core to that of the covering. Show that the greatest speed is attained when this ratio is $1 : \sqrt{e}$.

**9.** An open tank is to be constructed with a square base and vertical sides so as to contain a given quantity of water. Show that the expense of lining it with lead will be least, if the depth is made half of the width.

**10.** From a fixed point $A$ on the circumference of a circle of radius $c$ the perpendicular $AY$ is let fall on the tangent at $P$; prove that the maximum area of the $\Delta\, APY$ is $\dfrac{3}{8} c^2 \sqrt{3}$.

**11.** The sum of the perimeters of a circle and a square is $l$. Show that when the sum of the areas is least the side of the square is double the radius of the circle.

**12.** The sum of the surfaces of a sphere and a cube is given. Show that when the sum of the volumes is least, the diameter of the sphere is equal to the edge of the cube.

**13.** Show that the cone of greatest volume which can be inscribed in a given sphere is such that three times its altitude is twice the diameter of the sphere. Show also that this is the cone of greatest convex surface inscribable in the sphere.

**14.** Find the cylinder of greatest volume which can be inscribed in a given cone.

**15.** Show that the right circular cylinder of given surface and maximum volume is such that its height is equal to the diameter of its base.

**16.** Show that the semivertical angle of the right cone of given surface and maximum volume is $\sin^{-1}\frac{1}{3}$.

**17.** Show that a triangle of maximum perimeter inscribed in any oval curve is such that the tangent at any angular point makes equal angles with the sides which meet at that point. Show also that if the oval be an ellipse, the sides of the triangle will touch a confocal.

**18.** If a triangle of minimum perimeter circumscribe an oval show that the points of contact of the sides are also the points where they are touched by the e-circles of the triangle.

**19.** Show that the chord of a given curve which passes through a given point and cuts off a maximum or minimum area is bisected at the point.

**20.** Find the area of the greatest triangle which can be inscribed in a given parabolic segment having for its base the bounding chord of the segment.

**21.** In any oval curve the maximum or minimum chord which is normal at one end is either a radius of curvature at that end or normal at both ends.

**22.** Show that if a triangle of minimum area be circumscribed about an ellipse the normals at the points of contact meet in a point, and find the equation of its locus.

**23.** Find the co-ordinates of the limiting position, when $a' = a, b' = b$ of the intersection of the straight lines

$$\frac{x}{a} + \frac{y}{b} = 1, \ \frac{x}{a'} + \frac{y}{b'} = 1,$$

where $$a^n + b^n = a'^n + b'^n = 2c^n.$$

Find the co-ordinates of the point on the locus of the limiting position of the intersection, which is at a maximum distance from the origin, and prove that the maximum distance is $\frac{c}{\sqrt{2}}$. [I.C.S., 1892.]

# CHAPTER XIV.

# UNDETERMINED FORMS.

**166.** ELEMENTARY methods of procedure have been explained in the first chapter.

We propose now to show how the processes of the Differential Calculus may be employed in the determination of the true values of functions assuming singular forms, and shall discuss each singularity in order (see Art. 16).

## 167. I. Form $\dfrac{0}{0}$.

Consider a curve passing through the origin and defined by the equations $\left.\begin{array}{l} x = \psi(t), \\ y = \phi(t). \end{array}\right\}$

Let $x$, $y$ be the co-ordinates of a point $P$ on the curve very near the origin,

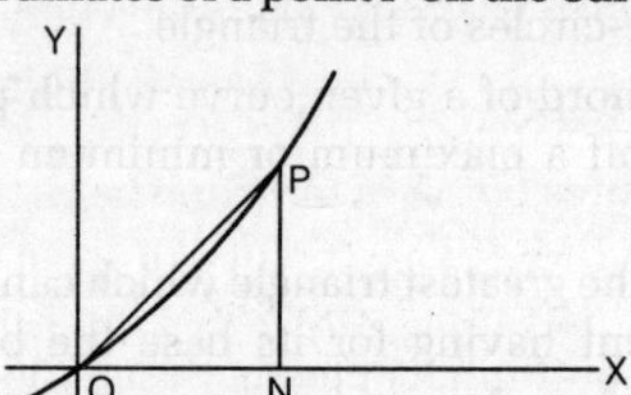


and suppose $a$ to be the value of $t$ corresponding to the origin, so that

$$\phi(a) = 0 \text{ and } \psi(a) = 0.$$

Then ultimately we have

$$Lt\,\frac{y}{x} = Lt\,\tan PON = Lt_{x=0}\,\frac{dy}{dx} = Lt_{t=a}\,\frac{\phi'(t)}{\psi'(t)}.$$

Hence $$Lt_{t=a}\,\frac{\phi(t)}{\psi(t)} = Lt_{t=a}\,\frac{\phi'(t)}{\psi'(t)};$$

and if $\dfrac{\phi'(t)}{\psi'(t)}$ be not of the form $\dfrac{0}{0}$ when $t$ takes its assigned value $a$, we therefore obtain $Lt_{t=a}\,\dfrac{\phi(t)}{\psi(t)} = \dfrac{\phi'(a)}{\psi'(a)}$. But, It $\dfrac{\phi'(t)}{\psi'(t)}$ be also of undetermined form, we may repeat the process; thus

$$Lt_{t=a}\,\frac{\phi'(t)}{\psi'(t)} = Lt_{t=a}\,\frac{\phi''(t)}{\psi''(t)} = \text{etc.},$$

proceeding in this manner until we arrive at a fraction such that when the value $a$ is substituted for $t$ its numerator and denominator *do not both vanish*, and thus obtaining an intelligible result—zero, finite, or infinite.

**Ex. 1.** $Lt_{\theta=0} \dfrac{1-\cos\theta}{\theta^2}$.

Here $\phi(\theta) = 1 - \cos\theta$ and $\psi(\theta) = \theta^2$, which both vanish when $\theta$ vanishes.

$$\phi'(\theta) = \sin\theta \text{ and } \psi'(\theta) = 2\theta,$$

which again both vanish when $\theta$ vanishes.

$$\phi''(\theta) = \cos\theta \text{ and } \psi''(\theta) = 2,$$

whence $\phi''(0) = 1$ and $\psi''(0) = 2$.

Therefore $$Lt_{\theta=0} \frac{1-\cos\theta}{\theta^2} = \frac{1}{2}.$$

**Ex. 2.** $Lt_{\theta=0} \dfrac{e^\theta + e^{-\theta} + 2\cos\theta - 4}{\theta^4} \left[\text{form } \dfrac{0}{0}\right]$

$$= Lt_{\theta=0} \frac{e^\theta - e^{-\theta} - 2\sin\theta}{4\theta^3} \left[\text{form } \frac{0}{0}\right]$$

$$= Lt_{\theta=0} \frac{e^\theta + e^{-\theta} - 2\cos\theta}{12\theta^2} \left[\text{form } \frac{0}{0}\right]$$

$$= Lt_{\theta=0} \frac{e^\theta - e^{-\theta} + 2\sin\theta}{24\theta} \left[\text{form } \frac{0}{0}\right]$$

$$= Lt_{\theta=0} \frac{e^\theta + e^{-\theta} + 2\cos\theta}{24} = \frac{4}{24} = \frac{1}{6}.$$

## EXAMPLES

*Find by the above method the following limits:*

1. $Lt_{x=0} \dfrac{a^x - 1}{b^x - 1}$.

2. $Lt_{x=0} \dfrac{\sin ax}{\sin bx}$.

3. $Lt_{x=0} \dfrac{xe^x - \log(1+x)}{x^2}$.

4. $Lt_{x=0} \dfrac{x\cos x - \log(1+x)}{x^2}$.

5. $Lt_{x=0} \dfrac{\cosh x - \cos x}{x \sin x}$.

6. $Lt_{x=0} \dfrac{x - \sin x \cos x}{x^3}$.

7. $Lt_{x=0} \dfrac{x^5 - 2x^3 - 4x^2 + 9x - 4}{x^4 - 2x^3 + 2x - 1}$.

8. $Lt_{x=0} \dfrac{e^x \sin x - x - x^2}{x^3}$.

9. $Lt_{x=0} \dfrac{3\tan x - 3x - x^3}{x^5}$.

10. $Lt_{x=\frac{\pi}{4}} \dfrac{\sin\left(x + \frac{\pi}{4}\right) - 1}{\log \sin 2x}$.

## 168. II. Form $0 \times \infty$.

Let $\phi(a) = 0$ and $\psi(a) = \infty$, so that $\phi(x)\,\psi(x)$ takes the form $0 \times \infty$ when $x$ approaches and ultimately coincides with the value $a$.

Then $$Lt_{x=a}\, \phi(x)\,\psi(x) = Lt_{x=a} \frac{\phi(x)}{\dfrac{1}{\psi(x)}},$$

and since $$\frac{1}{\psi(a)} = \frac{1}{\infty} = 0,$$

the limit may be supposed to take the form $\frac{0}{0}$ and may be treated like Form I.

**Ex. 1.** $Lt_{\theta=0}\, \theta \cot\theta = Lt_{\theta=0} \dfrac{\theta}{\tan\theta} = Lt_{\theta=0} \dfrac{1}{\sec^2\theta} = 1.$

**Ex. 2.** $Lt_{x=0}\, x \sin\dfrac{a}{x} = Lt_{\theta=\infty} \dfrac{\sin\dfrac{a}{x}}{\dfrac{1}{x}} = Lt_{\frac{a}{x}=0}\, a \dfrac{\sin\dfrac{a}{x}}{\dfrac{a}{x}} = a.$

## 169. III. Form $\frac{\infty}{\infty}$.

Let $\phi(a) = \infty$, $\psi(a) = \infty$, so that $\dfrac{\phi(x)}{\psi(x)}$ takes the form $\frac{\infty}{\infty}$ when $x$ approaches indefinitely near the value $a$.

The artifice adopted in this case is to write

$$\frac{\phi(x)}{\psi(x)} = \frac{\dfrac{1}{\psi(x)}}{\dfrac{1}{\phi(x)}}$$

Then since $\dfrac{1}{\psi(a)} = \dfrac{1}{\infty} = 0$,

and $\dfrac{1}{\phi(a)} = \dfrac{1}{\infty} = 0$, we may consider this as taking the form $\frac{0}{0}$,

and therefore we may apply the rule of Art. 167

$$Lt_{x=a} \frac{\phi(x)}{\psi(x)} = Lt_{x=a} \frac{\dfrac{1}{\psi(x)}}{\dfrac{1}{\phi(x)}} = Lt_{x=a} \frac{\dfrac{\psi'(x)}{[\psi(x)]^2}}{\dfrac{\phi'(x)}{[\phi(x)]^2}}$$

$$= Lt_{x=a} \left[\frac{\phi(x)}{\psi(x)}\right]^2 \frac{\psi'(x)}{\phi'(x)}.$$

Therefore $$Lt_{x=a}\frac{\phi(x)}{\psi(x)}=\left[Lt_{x=a}\frac{\phi(x)}{\psi(x)}\right]^2 Lt_{x=a}\frac{\psi'(x)}{\phi'(x)}.$$

Hence, *unless* $Lt_{x=a}\dfrac{\phi(x)}{\psi(x)}$ *be zero or infinite*, we have

$$1=\left\{Lt_{x=a}\frac{\phi(x)}{\psi(x)}\right\}\left\{Lt_{x=a}\frac{\psi'(x)}{\phi'(x)}\right\},$$

or $$Lt_{x=a}\frac{\phi(x)}{\psi(x)}=Lt_{x=a}\frac{\phi'(x)}{\psi'(x)}.$$

**170.** If, however, $Lt_{x=a}\dfrac{\phi(x)}{\psi(x)}$ be zero, then

$$Lt_{x=a}\frac{\phi(x)+\psi(x)}{\psi(x)}=1,$$

and therefore, by the former case (the limit being neither zero nor infinite),

$$=Lt_{x=a}\frac{\phi'(x)+\psi'(x)}{\psi'(x)}.$$

Hence, subtracting unity from each side, $Lt_{x=a}\dfrac{\phi(x)}{\psi(x)}=Lt_{x=a}\dfrac{\phi'(x)}{\psi'(x)}$.

Finally, in the case in which $Lt_{x=a}\dfrac{\phi(x)}{\psi(x)}=\infty$, then $Lt_{x=a}\dfrac{\psi(x)}{\phi(x)}=0$,

and therefore by the last case $=Lt_{x=a}\dfrac{\psi'(x)}{\phi'(x)}$;

therefore $$Lt_{x=a}\frac{\phi(x)}{\psi(x)}=Lt_{x=a}\frac{\phi'(x)}{\psi'(x)}.$$

This result is therefore proved true in all cases.

**171.** *If any function become infinite for any finite value of the independent variable, then all its differential coefficients will also become infinite for the same value.* An algebraical function only becomes infinite by the vanishing of some factor in the denominator.

Now, the process of differentiating never removes such a factor, but raises it to a higher power in the denominator.

Hence all differential coefficients of the given function will contain that vanishing factor in the denominator, and will therefore become infinite when such a value is given to the independent variable as will make that factor vanish.

It is obvious too that the circular functions which admit of infinite values, viz., $\tan x, \cot x, \sec x, \operatorname{cosec} x$, are really fractional forms and become infinite by the vanishing of a sine or cosine *in the denominator*, and therefore these follow the same rule as the above.

The rule is also true for the logarithmic function $\log(x-a)$ when $x = a$, or for the exponential function $b^{\frac{1}{x-a}}$ when $x = a$, $b$ being supposed greater than unity.

**172.** From the above remarks it will appear that if $\phi(a)$ and $\psi(a)$ become infinite so also *in general* will $\phi'(a)$ and $\psi'(a)$. Hence at first sight it would appear that the formula $Lt_{x=0} = \dfrac{\phi'(x)}{\psi'(x)}$ is no better than the original form $Lt_{x=a} \dfrac{\phi(x)}{\psi(x)}$. But it *generally* happens that the limit of the expression $\dfrac{\phi'(x)}{\psi'(x)}$, when $x = a$, can be more easily evaluated.

**Ex. 1.** *Find* $Lt_{\theta=\frac{\pi}{2}} \dfrac{\log\left(\theta - \frac{\pi}{2}\right)}{\tan\theta}$ *which is of the form* $\dfrac{\infty}{\infty}$.

Following the rule of differentiating numerator for new numerator, and denominator for new denominator, we may write the above limit

$$= Lt_{\theta=\frac{\pi}{2}} \frac{\frac{1}{\theta - \frac{\pi}{2}}}{\sec^2\theta},$$

which is still of the form $\dfrac{\infty}{\infty}$. But it can be written

$$= Lt_{\theta=\frac{\pi}{2}} \frac{\cos^2\theta}{\theta - \frac{\pi}{2}} \quad \left(\text{which is of the form } \frac{0}{0}\right)$$

$$= Lt_{\theta=\frac{\pi}{2}} \frac{-2\cos\theta\sin\theta}{1} = 0.$$

**Ex. 2.** *Evaluate* $Lt_{x=\infty} \dfrac{x^n}{e^x}$, *which is of the form* $\dfrac{\infty}{\infty}$.

$$Lt_{x=\infty} \frac{x^n}{e^x} = Lt_{x=\infty} \frac{nx^{n-1}}{e^x} = \dots$$

$$= Lt_{x=\infty} \frac{n!}{e^x} = \frac{n!}{\infty} = 0.$$

It is obvious that the same result is true when $n$ is fractional.

**Ex. 3.** *Evaluate* $Lt_{x=0} \underset{x=0}{Lt}\ x^m (\log x)^n$, *m and n being positive.*

This is of the form $0 \times \infty$, but may be written

$$Lt_{x=0} \left\{ \frac{\log x}{x^{-\frac{m}{n}}} \right\}^n \qquad \left[\text{Form} \frac{\infty}{\infty}\right]$$

and by putting $x^{\frac{m}{n}} = e^{-y}$ this expression is reduced to

$$Lt_{x=\infty} \left\{ \frac{-\frac{n}{m} y}{e^y} \right\}^n = 0 \text{ as in Ex. 2 .}$$

## 173. Form $\infty - \infty$.

Next, suppose $\phi(a) = \infty$ and $\psi(a) = \infty$, so that $\phi(x) - \psi(x)$ takes the form $\infty - \infty$, when $x$ approaches and ultimately coincides with the value $a$.

Let $\quad u = \phi(x) - \psi(x) = \psi(x) \left\{ \frac{\phi(x)}{\psi(x)} - 1 \right\}.$

From this method of writing the expression it is obvious that unless $Lt_{x=a} \frac{\phi(x)}{\psi(x)} = 1$ the limit of $u$ becomes

$\psi(a) \times$ (a quantity which does not vanish); and therefore the limit sought is $\infty$.

But if $Lt_{x=a} \frac{\phi(x)}{\psi(x)} = 1$, the problem is reduced to the evaluation of an expression which takes the form $\infty \times 0$, a form which has already been already discussed (II.).

**Ex.** $Lt_{x=0} \left( \frac{1}{x} - \cot x \right) = Lt_{x=0} \frac{1}{x} (1 - x \cot x)$

$$= Lt_{x=0} \frac{\sin x - x\cos x}{x\sin x} \qquad \left(\text{which is of the form } \frac{0}{0}\right)$$

$$= Lt_{x=0} \frac{x \sin x}{\sin x + x\cos x} \quad \text{(which is of the same form still)}$$

$$= Lt_{x=0} \frac{\sin x + x\cos x}{2\cos x - x\sin x} = 0.$$

## EXAMPLES

1. Find $Lt_{x=\infty}\ 2^x \sin \dfrac{a}{2^x}$.

2. Find $Lt_{x=1} \sec \dfrac{\pi}{2x} . \log x$.

3. Find $Lt_{x=0} \operatorname{cosec}^n x - \dfrac{1}{x^n}$ for the values $n = 1, 2, 3$.

4. Find $Lt_{x=0} \log_{\tan x} \tan 2x$.

5. Find $Lt_{x=1} \left\{\dfrac{\pi \cot \pi x}{x} + \dfrac{(3x^2-1)}{x^2 - x^4}\right\}$.

## 174. V. Forms $0^0$, $\infty^0$, $1^\infty$.

Let $y = u^v$, $u$ and $v$ being functions of $x$; then

$$\log_e y = v \log_e u.$$

Now $\log_e 1 = 0$, $\log_e \infty = \infty$, $\log_e 0 = -\infty$; and therefore when the expression $u^v$ takes one of the forms $0^\circ$, $\infty^\circ$, $1^\infty$, $\log y$ takes the undetermined form $0 \times \infty$. The rule is therefore to *take the logarithm and proceed as in Art.* 168.

**Ex. 1.** Find $Lt_{x=0}\ x^x$, *which takes the undetermined form* $0^\circ$.

$$Lt_{x=0} \log_e x^x = Lt_{x=0} \frac{\log_e x}{\frac{1}{x}} = Lt_{x=0} \frac{\frac{1}{x}}{-\frac{1}{x^2}} = Lt_{x=0} (-x) = 0,$$

Hence $\qquad Lt_{x=0}\ x^x = e^0 = 1$.

**Ex. 2.** *Find* $Lt_{x=\frac{\pi}{2}} (\sin x)^{\tan x}$.

*This takes the form* $1^\infty$.

$$Lt_{x=\frac{\pi}{2}} (\sin x)^{\tan x} = Lt_{x=\frac{\pi}{2}} e^{\tan x \log \sin x},$$

and $$Lt_{x=\frac{\pi}{2}} \tan x \log \sin x = Lt_{x=\frac{\pi}{2}} \frac{\log \sin x}{\cot x} = Lt_{x=\frac{\pi}{2}} \frac{\cot x}{-\operatorname{cosec}^2 x}$$

$$= Lt_{x=\frac{\pi}{2}} (-\sin x \cos x) = 0,$$

whence required limit $= e^0 = 1$.

A slightly different arrangement of the work is exemplified here.

**175.** The following example is worthy of notice, viz.

$$Lt_{x=a}\{1+\phi(x)\}^{\psi(x)},$$

given that $\phi(a)=0$, $\psi(a)=\infty$,

$$Lt_{x=a}\phi(x)\,\psi(x)=m.$$

We can write the above in the form

$$Lt_{x=a}\left[\{1+\phi(x)\}^{\frac{1}{\phi(x)}}\right]^{\phi(x).\,\psi(x)},$$

which is clearly $e^m$ by Art. 14, Chap I.

It will be observed that many examples take this form, such, for example, as

$$Lt_{x=0}\left(\frac{\tan x}{x}\right)^{\frac{1}{x^2}}$$

on p. 7, and Exs. 21 to 26 on p. 10.

## 176. $\dfrac{dy}{dx}$ or doubtful value at a Multiple Point.

The value of $\frac{dy}{dx}$ takes the undetermined form $\frac{0}{0}$ at a multiple point.

The rule of Art. 167 may be applied to find the true limiting values of $\frac{dy}{dx}$ for such cases, but it is generally better to proceed otherwise.

If the multiple point be at the origin, the equations of the tangents at that point can be at once written down by inspection and the required values of $\frac{dy}{dx}$ thus found.

If the multiple point be not at the origin, the equation of the curve should be transformed to parallel axes through the multiple point and the problem is then solved as before.

**Ex.** *Consider the value of $\frac{dy}{dx}$ at the origin for the curve*

$$x^4+ax^2y+bxy^2+y^4=0.$$

The tangents at the origin are obviously

$$x=0,\ y=0,\ ax+by=0,$$

making with the axis of $x$ angles whose tangents are respectively

$$\infty,\ 0,\ -\frac{a}{b},$$

which are therefore the required values of $\frac{dy}{dx}$.

# EXAMPLES

*Investigate the following limiting forms:—*

**1.** $Lt_{x=0} \dfrac{\log(1-x^2)}{\log \cos x}$.

**2.** $Lt_{x=1} \dfrac{2x^3-3x^2+1}{3x^5-5x^3+2}$.

**3.** $Lt_{x=\frac{\pi}{4}} \dfrac{1-\tan x}{1-\sqrt{2}\sin x}$.

**4.** $Lt_{x=1} \dfrac{1+\cos \pi x}{\tan^2 \pi x}$.

**5.** $Lt_{x=a} \log\left(2-\dfrac{x}{a}\right)\cot(x-a)$.

**6.** $Lt_{x=0} \dfrac{\log_{\sin x} \cos x}{\log_{\sin \frac{x}{2}} \cos \dfrac{x}{2}}$.

**7.** $Lt_{\theta=0} \dfrac{\cot\theta \tan^{-1}(m\tan\theta) - m\cos^2\dfrac{\theta}{2}}{\sin^2\dfrac{\theta}{2}}$.

**8.** $Lt_{x=0} (\cos x)^{\cot^2 x}$.

**9.** $Lt_{x=1} (1-x^2)^{\frac{1}{\log(1-x)}}$.

**10.** $Lt_{x=0} (\log x)^{\log(1-x)}$.

**11.** $Lt_{x=\infty} \dfrac{Ax^n+Bx^{n-1}+Cx^{n-2}+\ldots}{ax^m+bx^{m-1}+cx^{m-2}+\ldots}$ according as $n$ is >, =, or < $m$.

**12.** Find $Lt_{x=0} \dfrac{\sin h^2 x}{x^2 \cos x}$.

**13.** Find $Lt_{x=0} \dfrac{\text{vers}^{-1} x}{\sqrt{2x-x^2}}$.

**14.** Find $Lt_{x=0} \dfrac{\sqrt{a^2+ax+x^2}-\sqrt{a^2-ax+x^2}}{\sqrt{a+x}-\sqrt{a-x}}$.

**15.** Find $Lt_{x=0} \dfrac{x-1}{2x^2}+\dfrac{e^{-x}}{2x\sinh x}$.

**16.** If $Lt_{x=0} \dfrac{\sin 2x + a\sin x}{x^3}$ be finite, find the value of $a$ and the limit.

**17.** If $Lt_{x=0} \dfrac{\sinh 3x + a_1 \sinh 2x + a_2 \sinh x}{x^5}$ have a finite limit, find it and determine the necessary values of $a_1$ and $a_2$.

**18.** If $Lt_{x=0} \dfrac{\cos 4x + a_1 \cos 2x + a_2}{x^4}$ have a finite limit, find it and determine the necessary values of $a_1$ and $a_2$.

**19.** If $Lt_{x=0} \dfrac{\sin x + a_1 e^x + a_2 e^{-x} + a_3 \log \overline{1+x}}{x^3}$ have a finite limit, find it and determine the values of $a_1, a_2, a_3$.

**20.** Show that $Lt_{x=0} \dfrac{(1+x)^{\frac{1}{x}} - e + \dfrac{ex}{2}}{x^2} = \dfrac{11e}{24}$.

**21.** Find $Lt_{x=0} \dfrac{d^2y}{dx^2}$,

where $y = \theta / \sin\theta$

and $\theta = \text{vers}^{-1} x$.

**22.** Find $Lt_{x=0} \left(\dfrac{\sinh x}{x}\right)^{\frac{1}{x^2}}$.

**23.** Find $Lt_{x=0} \left(6 \dfrac{\sinh x - x}{x^3}\right)^{\frac{1}{x^2}}$.

**24.** Find (*a*) $Lt_{x=0} (\cosh x)^{\frac{1}{x^2}}$,

(*b*) $Lt_{x=0} \left\{2 \dfrac{\cosh x - 1}{x^2}\right\}^{\frac{1}{x^2}}$,

(*c*) $Lt_{x=0} \left\{\dfrac{24\cosh x - 24 - 12x^2}{x^4}\right\}^{\frac{1}{x^2}}$.

# CHAPTER XV.

# LIMITATIONS OF TAYLOR'S THEOREM.

## CONTINUITY.

**177.** SUPPOSE that portion of the curve $y = \phi\, x$ which lies between two given ordinates $AL$ $(x = a)$ and $BM$ $(x = b)$

to be drawn. Then if we find that as $x$ increases through some value, as $ON$, the ordinate $\phi x$ *suddenly changes* from $NP$ to $NQ$ (say) without going through the intermediate values, the function is said to be discontinuous for the value $x = ON$ of the independent variable.

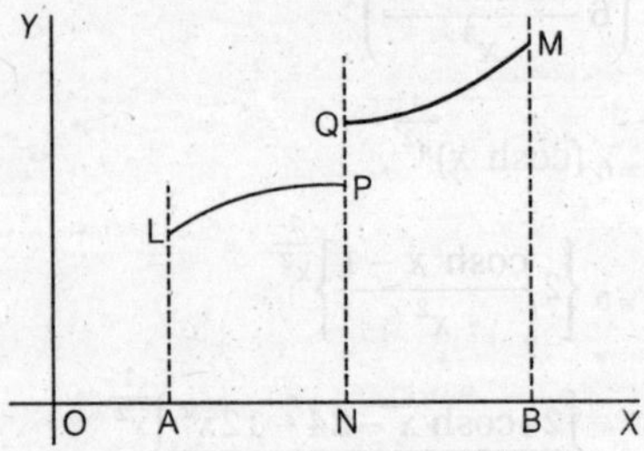


Thus for a function $\phi x$ to be continuous between two values $a$ and $b$ of the independent variable, it is necessary that its Cartesian graph $y = \phi x$ shall be able to be described by the motion of a particle travelling *along it* from the point $(a, \phi a)$ to the point $(b, \phi b)$ without moving off the curve.

**178.** In the same way, if at a point $P$ on a curve, if the tangent suddenly changes its inclination to the axis of $x$ without going through the intermediate positions there, as shown in the accompanying figure, there is said to be a discontinuity in the value of $\phi' x$.

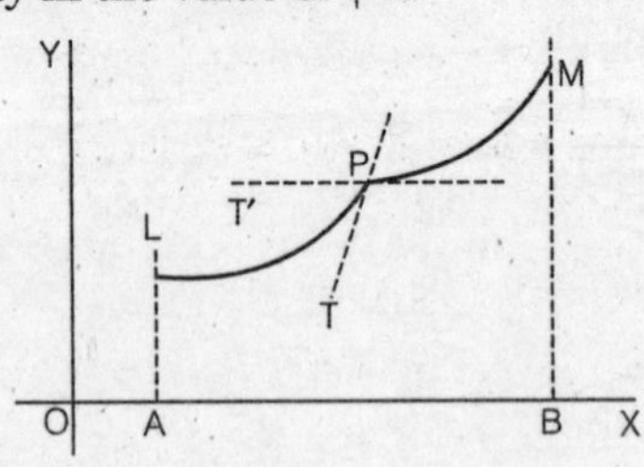

**179.** If the curve $y = \phi x$ cut the $x$-axis at two points $A(x = a, y = 0)$ and $B(x = b, y = 0)$, it is obvious that provided that the curve $y = \phi x$ and the inclination of its tangent be finite and continuous between $A$ and $B$, the tangent to the curve must be parallel to the $x$-axis at some intermediate point $P$ between $A$ and $B$.

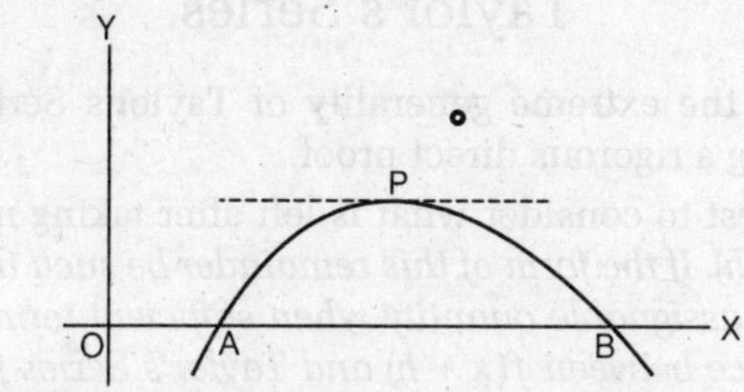


It is also evident from a figure that the tangent may be parallel to the $x$-axis at more than one intermediate point.

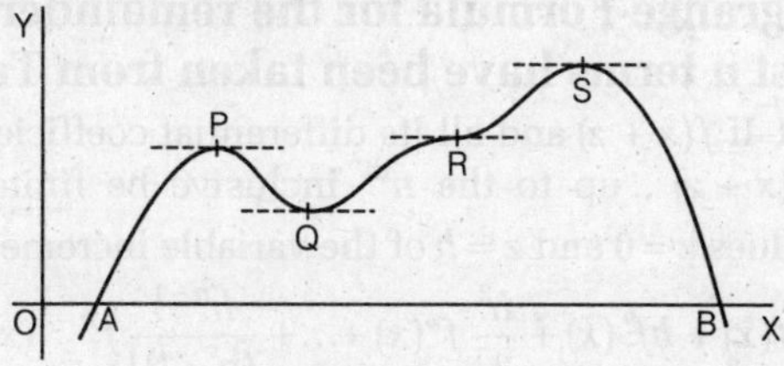


**180.** We thus arrive at the following important result :

*If any function of x, say $\phi x$, vanish when $x = a$ and also when $x = b$, and is finite and continuous, as also its first differential coefficient $\phi' x$ between those values, then $\phi' x$ must vanish for at least one intermediate value.*

## EXAMPLES

1. Show that $e^{\frac{-1}{x}}$ takes the form 0 or $\infty$ according as $x$ is very small and positive, or very small and negative. Give a graphical illustration by tracing the curve $y + 1 = e^{\frac{-1}{x}}$.
2. Show that if a rational integral function of $x$ vanish for $n$ values between given limits, its first and second differential coefficients will vanish for at least $(n - 1)$ and $(n - 2)$ values of $x$ respectively between the same limits. Illustrate these results geometrically.
3. Prove that no more than one root of an equation $f(x) = 0$ can lie between any adjacent two of the roots of the equation

$$f'(x) = 0.$$

4. Establish the result of Art. 179 from the aspect of a differential coefficient as a measurer of the rate of increase.
5. Show that no algebraic curve ever stops abruptly at a point.

## Taylor's Series.

**181.** From the extreme generality of Taylor's Series there is much difficulty in giving a rigorous direct proof.

It is found best to consider what is left after taking $n$ terms of Taylor's series from $f(x+h)$. *If the form of this remainder be such that it can be made smaller than any assignable quantity when sufficient terms of the series are taken the difference between $f(x+h)$ and Taylor's Series for $f(x+h)$ will be indefinitely small, and under these circumstances we shall be able to assert the truth of the Theorem.*

### 182. Lagrange-Formula for the remainder after the first n terms have been taken from Taylor's Series.

THEOREM–If $f(x+z)$ and all its differential coefficients, viz. $f'(x+z)$, $f''(x+z)$, ....$f^n(x+z)$, up to the $n^{\text{th}}$ inclusive be finite and continuous between the values $z=0$ and $z=h$ of the variable increment $z$ then will

$$f(x+h)=f(x)+hf'(x)+\frac{h^2}{2!}f''(x)+\ldots+\frac{h^{n-1}}{(n-1)!}f^{n-1}(x)+\frac{h^n}{n!}f^n(x+\theta h)$$

where $\theta$ is some positive proper fraction.

Let
$$f(x+h)=f(x)+hf'(x)+\frac{h^2}{2!}f''(x)+\ldots+\frac{h^{n-1}}{(n-1)!}f^{n-1}(x)+\frac{h^n}{n!}R \qquad \ldots(1),$$

$R$ being some function of $x$ and $h$, whose form remains to be discovered. Consider the function

$$f(x+z)-f(x)-zf'(x)-\frac{z^2}{2!}f''(x)-\ldots-\frac{z^{n-1}}{(n-1)!}f^{n-1}(x)-\frac{z^n}{n!}R\equiv\phi(z),\text{ say;}$$

then differentiating $n$ times with regard to $z$ (keeping $x$ constant),

$$f'(x+z)\quad -f'(x)-zf''(x)-\ldots-\frac{z^{n-2}}{(n-2)!}f^{n-1}(x)-\frac{z^{n-1}}{(n-1)!}R\equiv\phi'(z),$$

$$f''(x+z)\quad -f''(x)-\ldots-\frac{z^{n-3}}{(n-3)!}f^{n-1}(x)-\frac{z^{n-2}}{(n-2)!}R\equiv\phi''(z),$$

etc., etc., etc.,

$$f^{n-1}(x+z)\quad -f^{n-1}(x)-\quad zR\equiv\phi^{n-1}(z),$$

$$f^n(x+z)\quad -\quad R\equiv\phi^n(z).$$

All the functions $\phi(z), \phi'(z)\ldots, \phi^n(z)$ are finite and continuous between the values 0 and $h$ of the variable z, and evidently $\phi(0), \phi'(0), \phi''(0)\ldots, \phi^{n-1}(0)$ are all zero. Also from equation (1) $\phi(h) = 0$. Therefore by Art. 180,

$\phi'(z) = 0$ for some value $(h_1)$ of $z$ between 0 and $h$,

$\therefore$ $\phi''(z) = 0$ for some value $(h_2)$ of $z$ between 0 and $h_1$,

$\therefore$ $\phi'''(z) = 0$ for some value $(h_3)$ of $z$ between 0 and $h_2$,

and so on; and finally

$\phi^n(z) = 0$ for some value $(h_n)$ of $z$ between 0 and $h_{n-1}$.

Thus $$f^n(x + h_n) - R = 0 .$$

Now since $h_n < h_{n-1} < h_{n-2} \ldots < h_2 < h_1 < h,$

we may put $h_n = \theta h$ where $\theta$ is some positive proper fraction.

Thus $$R = f^n(x + \theta h) .$$

Hence substituting in equation (1)

$$f(x + h) = f(x) + hf'(x) + \frac{h^2}{2!} f''(x) + \ldots + \frac{h^{n-1}}{(n-1)!} f^{n-1}(x) + \frac{h^n}{n!} f^n(x + \theta h) \quad \ldots(2).$$

This method of establishing the result is a modification of one due to Mr Homersham Cox *(Camb. and Dublin Math. Journal).*

**183.** If then the form of the function $f(x)$ be such that by making $n$ sufficiently great the expression

$$\frac{h^n}{n!} f^n(x + \theta h)$$

can be made less than any assignable quantity however small, we can make the true series for $f(x + h)$ *differ by as little as we please from Taylor's form* $f(x) + hf'(x) + \frac{h^2}{2!} f''(x) + \ldots$ to $\infty$.

The above form of the remainder is due to Lagrange, and the investigation is spoken of as *Lagrange's Theorem on the Limits of Taylor's Theorem.*

**184.** The corresponding Lagrange-formula for the remainder after $n$ terms of Maclaurin's Series is obtained by writing 0 for $x$ and $x$ for $h$ and becomes $\frac{x^n}{n!} f^n(\theta x)$,

thus giving

$$f(x) = f(0) + xf'(0) + \frac{x^2}{2!} f''(0) + \ldots + \frac{x^{n-1}}{(n-1)!} f^{n-1}(0) + \frac{x^n}{n!} f^n(\theta x) .$$

**185.** The student should notice the special cases of equation (2), Art. 182, when $n = 1, 2, 3$, etc., viz.

$$f(x+h) = f(x) + hf'(x+\theta_1 h),$$

$$f(x+h) = f(x) + hf'(x) + \frac{h^2}{2!} f''(x+\theta_2 h),$$

etc.;

all that is known with respect to the $\theta$ in each case being that it is a *positive proper fraction.*

## 186. Geometrical Illustration.

It is easy to give a geometrical illustration of the equation

$$f(x+h) = f(x) + hf'(x+\theta h).$$

For let $x$, $f(x)$, be the co-ordinates of a point $P$ on the curve $y = f(x)$, and let $x + h$, $f(x+h)$ be the co-ordinates of another point $Q$, also on the curve. And suppose the curve and the inclination of the tangent to the curve to the axis of $x$ to be continuous and finite between $P$ and $Q$; draw $PM$, $QN$ perpendicular to $OX$ and $PL$ perpendicular to $QN$, then

$$\frac{f(x+h) - f(x)}{h} = \frac{NQ - MP}{MN} = \frac{LQ}{PL} = \tan LPQ.$$

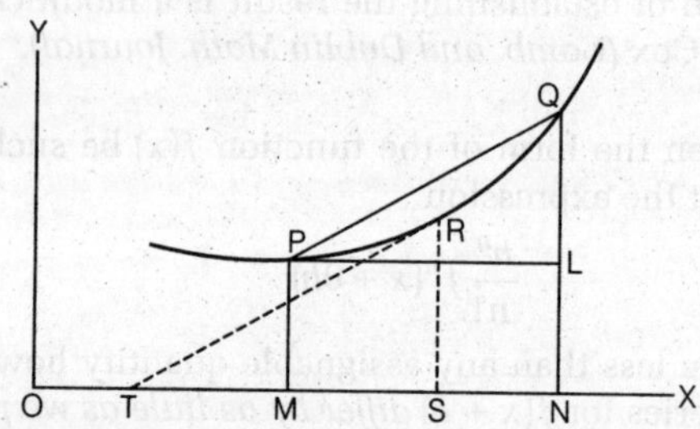


Also, $x + \theta h$ is the abscissa of some point $R$ on the curve between $P$ and $Q$, and $f'(x+\theta h)$ is the tangent of the angle which the tangent line to the curve at $R$ makes with the axis of $x$.

$$\frac{f(x+h) - f(x)}{h} = f'(x+\theta h)$$

Hence the assertion that is equivalent to the obvious geometrical fact that *there must be a point R somewhere between P and Q at which the tangent to the curve is parallel to the chord PQ.*

## 187. Failure of Taylor's Theorem.

The cases in which Taylor's Theorem is said to fail are those in which it happens

(1) That $f(x)$, or one of its differential coefficients, *becomes infinite* between the values of the variable considered;

(2) Or that $f(x)$, or one of its differential coefficients, becomes *discontinuous* between the same values;

(3) Or that the remainder $\frac{h^n}{n!} f^n(x + \theta h)$, *cannot be made to vanish in the limit* when $n$ is taken sufficiently large, so that the series does not approach a finite limit.

**Ex.** If $f(x) = \sqrt{x}$, $f(x+h) = \sqrt{x+h}$, $f'(x) = \frac{1}{2\sqrt{x}}$, etc.

Hence Taylor's Theorem gives

$$f(x+h) = \sqrt{x+h} = \sqrt{x} + \frac{1}{2\sqrt{x}} h + \ldots$$

If, however, we put $x = 0$, $\frac{1}{2\sqrt{x}}$ becomes infinite, while $\sqrt{x+h}$ becomes $\sqrt{h}$.

Thus, as we might expect, we fail at the second term to expand $\sqrt{h}$ in a series of integral powers of $h$.

**188.** In Art. 70 the proof of Taylor's Theorem is not general, the assumption being made that a convergent expansion in ascending positive integral powers of $x$ is possible. The above article shews when this assumption is legitimate.

For any continuous function $f(x)$ in which the $(p+1)^{\text{th}}$ differential coefficient is the first to become infinite or discontinuous between the values $x$ and $x + h$ of the variable, the theorem

$$f(x+h) = f(x) + hf'(x) + \ldots + \frac{h^p}{p!} f^p(x + \theta h),$$

which involves no differential coefficients of higher order than the $p^{\text{th}}$, is rigorously true, although Taylor's Theorem,

$$f(x+h) = f(x) + hf'(x) + \ldots + \frac{h^p}{p!} f^p(x) + \frac{h^{p+1}}{(p+1)!} f^{p+1}(x) + \ldots$$

fails to furnish us with an intelligible result.

**189.** The remarks made with respect to the failure of Taylor's Theorem obviously also apply to the particular form of it, Maclaurin's Theorem, so that Maclaurin's Theorem is said to fail when any of the expressions $f(0)$, $f'(0)$, $f''(0)$, ... become *infinite*, or if there be a *discontinuity* in the function or any of its differential coefficients as $x$ passes through the value zero and increases to the value $x$, or if the remainder $\frac{x^n}{n!} f^n(\theta x)$ *does not become infinitely small* when $n$ becomes infinitely large, for in this case the series is divergent and does not tend to any finite limit.

# EXAMPLES

**1.** Prove that

$$a^x = 1 + x\log_e a + \frac{x^2}{2!}(\log_e a)^2 + \ldots$$

$$+ \frac{x^{n-1}}{(n-1)!}(\log_e a)^{n-1} + \frac{x^n}{n!}a^{\theta x}(\log_e a)^n.$$

[Here $f(x) = a^x$, $f^n(x) = a^x(\log_e a)^n$, $f^n(0) = (\log_e a)^n$,

and $$\frac{x^n}{n!}f^n(\theta x) = \frac{x^n}{n!}a^{\theta x}(\log_e a)^n.$$

Hence the result follows by Art. 184.

The student should notice that

$$\frac{x^n a^{\theta x}(\log_e a)^n}{n!}$$

can be made *smaller than any assignable quantity* by sufficiently increasing $n$. Hence the remainder after $n$ terms of Maclaurin's expansion have been taken ultimately vanishes when $n$ is taken very large. Therefore Maclaurin's Theorem is applicable and gives

$$a^x = 1 + x\log_e a + \frac{x^2}{2!}(\log_e a)^2 + \ldots + \text{to } \infty.]$$

**2.** Shew that

$$\sin ax = ax - \frac{a^3x^3}{3!} + \frac{a^5x^5}{5!} - \ldots + \frac{a^nx^n}{n!}\sin\frac{n\pi}{2} + \ldots,$$

and that the remainder after $r$ terms may be expressed as

$$\frac{a^rx^r}{r!}\sin\left(a\theta x + \frac{r\pi}{2}\right).$$

**3.** Shew that the remainder after $r$ terms of $e^{ax}\cos bx$ have been taken is

$$\frac{(a^2+b^2)^{r/2}}{r!}x^r e^{a\theta x}\cos\left(b\theta x + r\tan^{-1}\frac{b}{a}\right).$$

**4.** Shew for what values of $x$ and at what differential coefficient Taylor's Theorem will fail if

$$f(x) = \frac{(x-a)^{10}(x-b)^{13/2}(x-c)^{23/3}}{(x-d)^5}.$$

**5.** How does Maclaurin's Theorem fail to expand

$\log x$, $\tan^{-1}\sqrt{x}$, or $e^{-1/x}$

in ascending positive integral powers of $x$? Is $e^{-1/x}$ continuous as $x$ passes through zero?

## MISCELLANEOUS EXAMPLES

**1.** A circle is drawn with its centre on a given parabola and touching its axis, shew that if the point of contact recede with a constant velocity from the vertex, the rate of increase of the area of the circle is also constant.

**2.** If $V$ be the volume of a sphere of radius $r$ and $S$ its surface, shew that $\dfrac{dV}{dr} = S$, and interpret this equation geometrically.

**3.** If $V$ be the volume of a cube whose edge is $x$, and $S$ its surface, interpret geometrically the equations

$$\frac{dV}{dx} = 3x^2; \; \frac{dS}{dx} = 12x.$$

**4.** If $V$ be the volume of a rectangular parallelepiped of edges $x$, $y$, $z$ interpret the equations $\dfrac{\partial V}{\partial x} = yz, \dfrac{\partial V}{\partial y} = zx, \dfrac{\partial V}{\partial z} = xy.$

**5.** Evaluate the limits:

(1) $Lt_{x=\infty}\left(x \tan \dfrac{1}{x}\right)^{x^2}$.  (2) $Lt_{x=\infty} 2^x \tan \dfrac{a}{2^x}$.

(3) $Lt_{x=\infty} \dfrac{d}{dx}\left(\dfrac{ax^2 + bx + c}{ex + f}\right)$.

**6.** Prove that $Lt_{x=\frac{1}{2}} \dfrac{\cos^2 \pi x}{e^{2x} - 2ex} = \dfrac{\pi^2}{2e}$.

**7.** Evaluate $Lt_{x=0} \dfrac{\tan(a + x) - \tan(a - x)}{\tan^{-1}(a + x) - \tan^{-1}(a - x)}$.

**8.** Prove that $Lt_{x=0}\left(\dfrac{1}{2x^2} - \dfrac{1}{2x \tan x}\right) = \dfrac{1}{6}$.

**9.** Find the limiting values of the following functions

(i) $\dfrac{a \sin \theta - \sin a\theta}{\theta(\cos \theta - \cos a\theta)}$ when $\theta = 0$.  (ii) $\dfrac{x \sin x - \frac{\pi}{2}}{\cos x}$ when $x = \dfrac{\pi}{2}$.

(iii) $(\sin x)^{\tan x}$ when $x = 0$.

(iv) $\dfrac{\sqrt{x} - \sqrt{a} + \sqrt{x - a}}{\sqrt{x^2 - a^2}}$ when $x = a$.

**10.** Find the intercept made by the curve $y = x \cot \dfrac{\pi x}{2a}$ (The Quadratrix) upon the $y$-axis.

**11.** If $u = x\sqrt{x^2 + a^2} + a^2 \log(x + \sqrt{x^2 + a^2})$,

shew that $\dfrac{du}{dx} = 2\sqrt{x^2 + a^2}$.

**12.** If $x + \sqrt{a^2 - y^2} = a \log \dfrac{a + \sqrt{a^2 - y^2}}{y}$,

shew that $\dfrac{dy}{dx} = -\dfrac{y}{\sqrt{a^2 - y^2}}$.

**13.** Find $\dfrac{d}{dx}\begin{vmatrix} 1, & 1, & 1, & 1 \\ 1, & x, & 1, & 1 \\ 1, & 1, & x, & 1 \\ 1, & 1, & 1, & x \end{vmatrix}$

**14.** If $y = \begin{vmatrix} x, & a, & b, & c \\ -a, & x, & -c, & b \\ -b, & c, & x, & -a \\ -c, & -b, & a, & x \end{vmatrix}$,

shew that $\dfrac{d^2 y}{dx^2} - 12x^2 = 4(a^2 + b^2 + c^2)$.

**15.** If $\sqrt{1 - x^2} + \sqrt{1 - y^2} = a(x - y)$, prove that $\dfrac{dy}{dx} = \dfrac{\sqrt{1 - y^2}}{\sqrt{1 - x^2}}$.

**16.** If $y = \dfrac{1}{4\sqrt{2}} \log \dfrac{1 + x\sqrt{2} + x^2}{1 - x\sqrt{2} + x^2} + \dfrac{1}{2\sqrt{2}} \tan^{-1} \dfrac{x\sqrt{2}}{1 - x^2}$,

prove that $\dfrac{dy}{dx} = \dfrac{1}{1 + x^4}$.

Hence expand $y$ in powers of $x$.

**17.** If $y = 1 + \dfrac{a_1}{x - a_1} + \dfrac{a_2 x}{(x - a_1)(x - a_2)} + \dfrac{a_3 x^2}{(x - a_1)(x - a_2)(x - a_3)} + \dots$

to $n + 1$ terms,

shew that $\dfrac{dy}{dx} = \dfrac{y}{x}\left\{\dfrac{a_1}{a_1 - x} + \dfrac{a_2}{a_2 - x} + \dots + \dfrac{a_n}{a_n - x}\right\}$.

**18.** Differentiate $\dfrac{(x - 1)^4}{(x + 2)^3}$ twice with respect to $x$, and find the value of the result when $x = 0$.

**19.** If $u_n = \cos h^n x$ and $v_n = \sin h^n x$, prove that

$\dfrac{d^2 u_n}{dx^2} = n^2 u_n - n(n - 1) u_{n-2}$, and $\dfrac{d^2 v_n}{dx^2} = n^2 v_n + n(n - 1) v_{n-2}$.

**20.** If $x = \cos \log y$, shew that $(1 - x^2) y_2 - x y_1 = y$.

**21.** If $y = \dfrac{(ax^2 + bx + c)}{(1 - x)}$, shew that $(1 - x) y_3 = 3 y_2$.

**22.** Prove that $\dfrac{d^n}{dx^n}(e^{ax}\cdot u)=e^{ax}\left(\dfrac{d}{dx}+a\right)^n u$.

**23.** Find $\dfrac{d^n y}{dx^n}$ where $y=\dfrac{1}{x^2+6x+8}$.

**24.** Shew that $\dfrac{d^n}{dx^n}\dfrac{px^2+qx+r}{(x-a)(x-b)(x-c)}$

$$=(-1)^n n!\,\Sigma\,\frac{pa^2+qa+r}{(a-b)(a-c)}\frac{1}{(x-a)^{n+1}}.$$

**25.** If $y=x^m\sin x$, find $\dfrac{d^n y}{dx^n}$.

**26.** Shew that $\left(\dfrac{d}{dx}\right)^n\dfrac{(1+x)^n}{(1-2x)^3}$

$$=\frac{3^n}{2}\frac{(n+2)!}{(1-2x)^{n+3}}-n\cdot 3^{n-1}\frac{(n+1)!}{(1-2x)^{n+2}}+\frac{n(n-1)3^{n-2}}{2}\frac{n!}{(1-2x)^{n+1}}.$$

**27.** Shew that $\dfrac{d^m}{dx^m}x^{-1}(x+1)^{-1}(x+2)^{-1}\ldots(x+n)^{-1}$

$$=(-1)^m\frac{m!}{n!}\left\{\frac{{}^nC_0}{x^{m+1}}-\frac{{}^nC_1}{(x+1)^{m+1}}+\frac{{}^nC_2}{(x+2)^{m+1}}-\ldots+(-1)^n\frac{{}^nC_n}{(x+n)^{m+1}}\right\}.$$

**28.** If $\phi(x)=(1-x)^{-1}(1-cx)^{-1}\,(1-c^2x)^{-1}\ldots$ to $\infty$, where $c$ is less than unity, shew that

$$\phi^n(0)=\frac{n!}{(1-c)(1-c^2)\ldots(1-c^n)}.$$

**29.** Prove that if $ac>b^2$, $\dfrac{d^n}{dx^n}\dfrac{b+cx}{a+2bx+cx^2}$

$$=(-1)^n n!\left(\frac{c}{a+2bx+cx^2}\right)^{\frac{n+1}{2}}\cos\left\{(n+1)\tan^{-1}\frac{\sqrt{ac-b^2}}{b+cx}\right\}.$$

**30.** If $y=\dfrac{e^x+e^{-x}}{x^2}$ then $x^2\dfrac{d^2y}{dx^2}+4x\dfrac{dy}{dx}+2y=x^2y$, and if $n$ be any *even* integer, $x^2\dfrac{d^ny}{dx^n}+2nx\dfrac{d^{n-1}y}{dx^{n-1}}+n(n-1)\dfrac{d^{n-2}y}{dx^{n-2}}=x^2y$.

**31.** If $y=(x^2-1)^n$, prove

(*a*) $(x^2-1)y_1=2nxy$,

(*b*) $(x^2-1)y_{n+2}+2xy_{n+1}-n(n+1)y_n=0$.

Hence if $P_n=A\dfrac{d^n}{dx^n}(x^2-1)^n$, shew that

$$\frac{d}{dx}\left\{(1-x^2)\frac{dP_n}{dx}\right\}+n(n+1)P_n=0.$$

**32.** Prove that $e^{a+bx+cx^2+dx^3+\ldots}$

$$=e^a\left\{1+bx+\frac{b^2+2c}{2!}x^2+\frac{b^3+6bc+6d}{3!}x^3+\ldots\right\}.$$

**33.** If $u=f(x)$, shew that

$$f\left(\frac{x}{2}\right)=u-\frac{x}{2}\frac{du}{dx}+\frac{1}{2!}\left(\frac{x}{2}\right)^2\frac{d^2u}{dx^2}-\frac{1}{3!}\left(\frac{x}{2}\right)^3\frac{d^3u}{dx^3}+\ldots$$

**34.** If $e^x\sin x=\Sigma a_nx^n$, shew that

$$a_n-\frac{a_{n-1}}{1!}+\frac{a_{n-2}}{2!}-\frac{a_{n-3}}{3!}+\ldots=\frac{\sin\dfrac{n\pi}{2}}{n!}.$$ [I. C. S.]

**35.** If $e^x=\log(a_0+a_1x+a_2x^2+\ldots+a_nx^n+\ldots)$, prove that

$$(n+1)a_{n+1}=a_n+\frac{a_{n-1}}{1!}+\frac{a_{n-2}}{2!}+\frac{a_{n-3}}{3!}+\ldots+\frac{a_0}{n!}.$$

**36.** If $A_0$, $A_1$, etc. be the successive coefficients in the expansion of $y=e^{\cos mx+\sin mx}$, prove

$$A_{n+1}=\frac{m}{n+1}\left\{A_n+\sum_1^n\frac{m^r}{r!}A_{n-r}\left(\cos\frac{r\pi}{2}-\sin\frac{r\pi}{2}\right)\right\}.$$ [I. C. S.]

**37.** Given that

$$\sin\log(1+x)=\frac{A_1}{1!}x+\frac{A_2}{2!}x^2+\frac{A_3}{3!}x^3+\ldots$$

$$\cos\log(1+x)=1+\frac{B_1}{1!}x+\frac{B_2}{2!}x^2+\frac{B_3}{3!}x^3+\ldots$$

calculate the first eight coefficients of each expansion. [M. TRIPOS.]

**38.** From the expansion of $\sin^{-1}\dfrac{x}{\sqrt{1-x^2}}$, deduce

$$\tan^{-1}x=\frac{x}{1+x^2}\left\{1+\frac{2}{3}\frac{x^2}{1+x^2}+\frac{2\cdot4}{3\cdot5}\left(\frac{x^2}{1+x^2}\right)^2+\ldots\right\}.$$

Also establish the series

(a) $$\frac{\pi}{2}=1+\frac{1}{3}+\frac{1\cdot2}{3\cdot5}+\frac{1\cdot2\cdot3}{3\cdot5\cdot7}+\ldots$$

(b) $$\frac{2\pi}{3\sqrt3}=1+\frac{1}{3}\left(\frac{1}{2}\right)+\frac{1\cdot2}{3\cdot5}\left(\frac{1}{2}\right)^2+\frac{1\cdot2\cdot3}{3\cdot5\cdot7}\left(\frac{1}{2}\right)^3+\ldots$$

**39.** Establish the expansions

(a) $$\frac{\pi^2}{8}=1+\frac{1}{2}\cdot\frac{1}{3}+\frac{1}{3}\cdot\frac{1\cdot2}{3\cdot5}+\frac{1}{4}\frac{1\cdot2\cdot3}{3\cdot5\cdot7}+\ldots\ldots$$

(b) $$\frac{\pi^2}{9}=1+\frac{1}{2}\frac{1}{3}\left(\frac{1}{2}\right)+\frac{1}{3}\frac{1\cdot2}{3\cdot5}\left(\frac{1}{2}\right)^2+\frac{1}{4}\frac{1\cdot2\cdot3}{3\cdot5\cdot7}\left(\frac{1}{2}\right)^3+\ldots\ldots$$

**40.** Prove that $\dfrac{4\pi}{3\sqrt{3}} = 1 + \dfrac{3}{6} + \dfrac{3\cdot 6}{6\cdot 10} + \dfrac{3\cdot 6\cdot 9}{6\cdot 10\cdot 14} + \ldots\ldots$

**41.** Show that if $f(x+h)$ be expanded by Taylor's Theorem and then $h$ be put equal to $-x$, the sum of the first $n+1$ terms may be expressed as

$$(-1)^n \frac{x^{n+1}}{n!} \frac{d^n}{dx^n}\left[\frac{f(x)}{x}\right].$$

**42.** In the curve $\dfrac{x^3}{a} + \dfrac{y^3}{b} = xy$, find the points at which the tangent is parallel to one of the co-ordinate axes.

**43.** Find at what angle the circle $x^2 + y^2 = a(x - y)$ cuts the co-ordinate axes.

**44.** In the curve $y = \log \coth \dfrac{x}{2}$ shew that $\dfrac{ds}{dx} = \coth x$.

**45.** In any curve prove that

(a) $p = \dfrac{r^2 d\theta}{ds}$. (b) $\sqrt{r^2 - p^2} = \dfrac{rdr}{ds}$.

**46.** Find the sine of the angle of intersection of the rectangular hyperbola $x^2 - y^2 = a^2$ and the circle $x^2 + y^2 = 4a^2$.

**47.** Shew that the points of inflexion on the cubic $y = \dfrac{a^2 x}{a^2 + x^2}$ are given by $x = 0$ and $x = \pm a\sqrt{3}$.

Shew that these three points of inflexion lie on the straight line $x = 4y$.

**48.** If a line be drawn through any point of a given curve at right angles to the radius vector (and therefore touching the first negative pedal), then the portion of it intercepted between the two curves is equal to the polar subnormal of the point on the original curve through which it is drawn.

What is the geometrical meaning of $\dfrac{dr}{d\theta}$?

**49.** In any curve the radius of curvature of the evolute at a point corresponding to the point $p$, $r$ on the original curve is

$$\sqrt{r^2 - p^2}\, \frac{d}{dp}\left(r \frac{dr}{dp}\right).$$

**50.** If $\rho$ and $\rho'$ be the radii of curvature at corresponding points of a curve and its evolute, and $p, q, r$ are the first, second and third differential coefficients of $y$ with respect to $x$, prove that

$$\frac{\rho'}{\rho} = \frac{\{3pq^2 - r(1 + p^2)\}}{q^2}.$$

**51.** If $\rho$, $\rho'$ be the radii of curvature at the extremities of two conjugate diameters of an ellipse, then $(\rho^{2/3} + \rho'^{2/3})(ab)^{2/3} = a^2 + b^2$.

**52.** The projections on the $x$-axis of the radii of curvature at corresponding points of $y = \log \sec x$ and its evolute are equal.

**53.** In the curve for which

$$y^{2m}\left(\frac{dy}{dx}\right)^2 = a^{2m} - y^{2m},$$

prove that the normal is $m$ times the radius of curvature.

**54.** Shew that there is an infinite series of parallel asymptotes to the curve $(r-b)\theta = a \operatorname{cosec} \theta$, whose distances from the pole are in Harmonical Progression. Find also the circular asymptote.

**55.** Shew that the asymptotes of the curve

$$4(x^4 + y^4) - 17x^2y^2 - 4x(4y^2 - x^2) + 2(x^2 - 2) = 0$$

cut the curve in eight points lying upon an ellipse whose eccentricity $= \dfrac{\sqrt{3}}{2}$.

**56.** In the curve

$$r \cos \frac{\sqrt{a^2 - b^2}}{a}\theta = \sqrt{a^2 - b^2}, \text{ shew that } p = \frac{ar}{\sqrt{b^2 + r^2}}.$$

**57.** Find the asymptotes of the curves

(1) $x^4 - y^4 = a^2xy$.

(2) $(x^2 - 2ax)(x^2 + y^2) = b^2x^2$.

**58.** Find the asymptotes of the curve

$(x-y)^2(x-2y)(x-3y) - 2a(x^3 - y^3) - 2a^2(x+y)(x-2y) = 0$.

**59.** Determine from the equation $(x-a)^3 + 7(y-b)^3 = (x+y-a-b)^3$, the values of $\dfrac{dy}{dx}$ when $x = a, y = b$.

**60.** Find that point on the curve $\left(\dfrac{y}{b}\right)^n = \dfrac{x}{a}$

where the angle which the tangent makes with a radius vector from the origin has a maximum or minimum value.

**61.** Find the area and position of the maximum triangle having a given angle which can be inscribed in a given circle and prove that the area cannot have a minimum value.

**62.** If four straight rods be freely hinged at their extremities, the greatest quadrilateral they can form is inscribable in a circle.

**63.** Find the triangle of minimum area which can be described about a given ellipse, having a side parallel to the major axis of the ellipse. Also shew that the triangle formed by joining the points of contact is an inscribed triangle of maximum area.

**64.** A tree in the form of a frustum of a cone is $n$ feet long and the greater and less diameters are $a$ and $b$ feet respectively, shew that the greatest beam of square section that can be cut out of it is $\dfrac{na}{3(a-b)}$ feet long.

**65.** Find the maximum radius vector of the spiral $r\cos h\,\theta = a$.

**66.** Investigate the maximum value of $\cos mx \cdot \cos^m x$.

**67.** Investigate the maxima and minima of

$$\cos x + \cos 2x + \cos 3x.$$

**68.** Find the maximum and minimum values of $e^x \cos x$ and trace the curve $y = e^x \cos x$.

**69.** The corner of a leaf is turned down, so as just to reach the other edge of the page; find when the length of the crease is a minimum; also when the part turned down is a minimum.

**70.** If the angle $C$ of a triangle $ABC$ be acute and constant, prove that $\sin^2 A + \sin^2 B$ is a maximum and $\cos^2 A + \cos^2 B$ a minimum, when $A = B$.

**71.** Shew that the shortest normal chord of the parabola $y^2 = 4ax$ is $6a\sqrt{3}$ and its inclination to the axis is $\tan^{-1}\sqrt{2}$.

**72.** Find the maximum value of

$$(x-a)^2(x-b), \begin{cases} (1) \text{ when } a > b, \\ (2) \text{ when } a < b. \end{cases}$$

What happens if $a = b$? Illustrate your answers by diagrams of the curve

$y = (x-a)^2(x-b)$

in the three different cases. [I. C. S.]

**73.** Prove that the pedal equation of the envelope of the line $x\cos 2\theta + y\sin 2\theta = 2a\cos\theta$ is $p^2 = \frac{4}{3}(r^2 - a^2)$.

**74.** A square slides with two of its adjacent sides passing through two fixed points. Shew that its remaining sides touch a pair of fixed circles, one diagonal passes through a fixed point, and that the envelope of the other is a circle.

**75.** The tangent at any point $P$ of a parabola meets the tangent at the vertex in $Q$, and the normal at $P$ meets the axis in $R$; find the envelope of $QR$.

**76.** Ellipses of given eccentricity $e$, have for their major axes parallel chords of a circle of radius $c$. Shew that their envelope is an ellipse whose eccentricity is $\sqrt{\dfrac{1-e^2}{2-e^2}}$.

**77.** Shew that the expansion of $\frac{x}{2}\frac{e^x+1}{e^x-1}$ is

$$1 + B_1\frac{x^2}{2!} - B_3\frac{x^4}{4!} + B_5\frac{x^6}{6!} - B_7\frac{x^8}{8!} + \ldots\ldots$$

where $B_1 = \frac{1}{6}, B_3 = \frac{1}{30}, B_5 = \frac{1}{42}, B_7 = \frac{1}{30}$, etc.

[These numbers are called Bernoulli's numbers.]

**78.** Shew that if, $\tan x = S_1\frac{x}{1!} + S_3\frac{x^3}{3!} + S_5\frac{x^5}{5!} + \ldots\ldots$

then $S_{2n-1} = B_{2n-1}\frac{2^{2n}(2^{2n}-1)}{2n}$.

**79.** Shew that $\sec x = 1 + S_2\frac{x^2}{2!} + S_4\frac{x^4}{4!} + S_6\frac{x^6}{6!} + \ldots\ldots$

where $S_2 = 1, S_4 = 5, S_6 = 61$, etc.

[These numbers are called Euler's numbers.]

**80.** If $\sec x + \tan x = 1 + S_1\frac{x}{1!} + S_2\frac{x^2}{2!} + S_3\frac{x^3}{3!} + \ldots\ldots$

prove

(a) $S_{p+1} = S_p + \frac{p(p-1)}{1\cdot 2}S_{p-2}S_2 + \frac{p(p-1)(p-2)(p-3)}{1\cdot 2\cdot 3\cdot 4}S_{p-4}S_4 + \ldots\ldots$

(which when $p$ is even expresses any Bernoulli's number in terms of lower order Euler's numbers).

(b) $S_p - \frac{p(p-1)}{1\cdot 2}S_{p-2} + \frac{p(p-1)(p-2)(p-3)}{1\cdot 2\cdot 3\cdot 4}S_{p-4} - \ldots$

$$+ \cos\frac{p\pi}{2} = \sin\frac{p\pi}{2}.$$

(c) $S_1 = 1, S_2 = 1, S_3 = 2, S_4 = 5, S_5 = 16, S_6 = 61, S_7 = 272,$
$S_8 = 1385, S_9 = 7936$, etc.

(d) $S_p = \frac{2^{p+2}p!}{\pi^{p+1}}\left\{\left(\frac{1}{1}\right)^{p+1} + \left(-\frac{1}{3}\right)^{p+1} + \left(\frac{1}{5}\right)^{p+1} + \left(-\frac{1}{7}\right)^{p+1} + \left(\frac{1}{9}\right)^{p+1} + \ldots\right\}.$

(e) Deduce the several results

$$1 - \frac{1}{3} + \frac{1}{5} - \frac{1}{7} + \ldots\ldots = \frac{\pi}{4};\quad 1 + \frac{1}{3^2} + \frac{1}{5^2} + \frac{1}{7^2} + \ldots\ldots = \frac{\pi^2}{8};$$

$$1 - \frac{1}{3^3} + \frac{1}{5^3} - \frac{1}{7^3} + \ldots\ldots = \frac{\pi^3}{32};\quad 1 + \frac{1}{3^4} + \frac{1}{5^4} + \frac{1}{7^4} + \ldots\ldots = \frac{\pi^4}{96};$$

$$1 - \frac{1}{3^5} + \frac{1}{5^5} - \frac{1}{7^5} + \ldots\ldots = \frac{5\pi^5}{1536};$$

etc.

# ANSWERS TO THE EXAMPLES.

## CHAPTER I.

### PAGE 4.

1. (a) $\infty$, (b) $\frac{1}{a}$, (c) $\infty$. 2. (i) $\frac{b}{a}$, (ii) $\frac{a}{b}$.

3. $3a^2, 4a^3, 5a^3/2$. 4. $\frac{b}{d}, \frac{a}{c}$. 5. $-1$.

7. $-\infty, 0, 0, -1, -\infty, \infty, 0, \infty$. 8. $\frac{3}{2}, \frac{1}{2}$.

### PAGE 9, 10.

1. $\log_b a$. 2. $\frac{3}{5}$. 3. $\frac{m}{n}$. 4. $\frac{1}{n}$. 5. 4.

6. 4. 7. 2. 8. 1. 9. $\frac{1}{2}$. 10. $\frac{3}{2}$.

11. $\frac{2}{3}$. 12. $\frac{1}{6}$. 13. 1. 14. 1. 15. $\frac{1}{15}$.

16. $-\frac{11}{6}$. 17. $\frac{13}{60}$. 18. $-\frac{2}{3}$. 19. $\frac{1}{2}$. 20. 1.

21. $\infty$. 22. 1. 23. $e^{-\frac{1}{6}}$. 24. 0. 25. $e^{-1}$.

26. $e^{\frac{1}{2}}$.

## CHAPTER II.

### PAGE 13.

1. $Y - y = 3x^2 (X - x)$. 2. $Y - y = 4x^3 (X - x)$.

3. $2\sqrt{x} (Y - y) = X - x$. 4. $Y - y = (2x + 3x^2)(X - x)$.

5. $Y - y = \cos x (X - x)$. 6. $Y - y = e^x (X - x)$.

7. $x(Y - y) = X - x$. 8. $Y - y = \sec^2 x (X - x)$.

9. $Xx + Yy = c^2$. 10. $Xx/a^2 + Yy/b^2 = 1$.

### PAGE 14.

1. 2. 2. 1. 3. 3. 4. $6x$.

5. $-\frac{1}{x^2}$. 6. $-\frac{1}{x^2}$. 7. $-\frac{2}{x^3}$. 8. $\frac{a}{2\sqrt{x}}$.

9. $\frac{x}{\sqrt{x^2 + a^2}}$. 10. $\frac{e^{\sqrt{x}}}{2\sqrt{x}}$. 11. $e^{\sin x} \cos x$. 12. $\tan x$.

**13.** $\sin x + x\cos x$. **14.** $\dfrac{(x\cos x - \sin x)}{x^2}$.

**15.** $x^x(\log x + 1)$.

## CHAPTER III.

### PAGE 21.

**1.** $x^2(3\sin x + x\cos x)$; $(3+x)\,x^2e^x$; $x^2(3\log_e x + 1)$;

$x^2(3\tan x + x\sec^2 x)$; $x^2(3\log_e \sin x + x\cot x)$.

**2.** $x^3(4 - x\cot x)\operatorname{cosec} x$; $(x\cos x - 4\sin x)/x^5$;

$(\cos x - \sin x)/e^x$; $e^x(\sin x - \cos x)\operatorname{cosec}^2 x$.

**3.** $\sec^2 x\log_e \sin x + 1$; $e^x\left(\log_e x + \dfrac{1}{x}\right)$; $\sin x(2 + \tan^2 x)$.

**4.** $x^2e^x \sin x(3 + x + x\cot x)$; $\tan x\log_e x + x\sec^2 x\log_e x + \tan x$.

**5.** $x^2e^{-x}\{(3-x)\sin x + x\cos x\}$; $x^2e^{-x}\operatorname{cosec} x\{3 - x - x\cot x\}$;

$-(3 + x + x\cot x)/x^4e^x\sin x$.

**6.** $(\sin x + 2x\cos x)/\sqrt{x}$; $3(2x\sec^2 x - \tan x)/2x^{\frac{3}{2}}$; $2e^x(2x-1)/x^{\frac{3}{2}}$.

**7.** $e^x(2x^{\frac{7}{2}} + 6x^{\frac{5}{2}} + 2x + 1)/2x^{\frac{1}{2}}$; $e^x\log_e x(x^4 + 5x^3 + 3x^2) + e^x(x^3 + x^2)$.

### PAGE 23.

**1.** $3e^{3x}$; $-e^{-x}$; $3\sin^2 x\cos x$; $\dfrac{\cos x}{2\sqrt{\sin x}}$; $\dfrac{1}{2x\sqrt{\log_e x}}$; $\dfrac{\sec^2 x}{2\sqrt{\tan x}}$; $\dfrac{\cos\sqrt{x}}{2\sqrt{x}}$.

**2.** $e^{\sin x}\cos x$; $e^{\tan x}\sec^2 x$; $3x^2e^{x^3}$; $e^{\sqrt{x}}/2\sqrt{x}$; 1.

**3.** $\cot x$; $2\operatorname{cosec} 2x$; $\dfrac{1}{2x}$; $\dfrac{3}{x}$.

**4.** $\dfrac{\cos(\log x)}{x}$; $\dfrac{\sec^2(\log_e x)}{x}$; $\dfrac{\cos(\log_e x)}{2x\sqrt{\sin(\log_e x)}}$; $\dfrac{\cos\sqrt{x}}{4\sqrt{x}\sqrt{\sin\sqrt{x}}}$; $\dfrac{\cot\sqrt{x}}{2\sqrt{x}}$.

**5.** $\dfrac{\sqrt{e^x}}{4}\cot\sqrt{e^x}$; $\sec^2 \log_e \sin e^{\sqrt{x}}\cdot\cot e^{\sqrt{x}}\cdot e^{\sqrt{x}}\cdot\dfrac{1}{2\sqrt{x}}$.

## CHAPTER IV.

### PAGE 25.

**1.** 1; $10x^9$; $-x^{-2}$; $-10x^{-11}$; $\dfrac{3}{2}x^{\frac{1}{2}}$; $\dfrac{1}{2x^{\frac{1}{2}}}$; $\dfrac{1}{3x^{\frac{2}{3}}}$; $-\dfrac{5}{6}x^{-\frac{11}{6}}$; $-\dfrac{5}{4}x^{-\frac{9}{4}}$.

**2.** $n(x+a)^{n-1}$; $nx^{n-1}$; $\dfrac{1}{2x^{\frac{1}{2}}}$; $-\dfrac{1}{(x+a)^2}$; $-\dfrac{1}{2}\dfrac{1}{(x+a)^{\frac{3}{2}}}$.

**3.** $na(ax+b)^{n-1}$; $nax^{n-1}$; $na^n x^{n-1}$; $na(x+b)^{n-1}$; $a^n$.

**4.** $1+x+\frac{x^2}{2!}+\frac{x^3}{3!}+\frac{x^4}{4!}+\ldots$ .

**5.** $-(15a+11b\sqrt[3]{x})/12c\sqrt[4]{x^9}$; $\sqrt{a}/\sqrt{x}\,(\sqrt{a}-\sqrt{x})^2$;

$2\sqrt[3]{a}/3\sqrt[3]{x^2}\,(\sqrt[3]{a}-\sqrt[3]{x})^2$; $a/(a-x)^{\frac{3}{2}}(a+x)^{\frac{1}{2}}$; $2a/3(a-x)^{\frac{4}{3}}(a+x)^{\frac{2}{3}}$.

**6.** $\frac{(a-c)\{bx^2+2(a+c)x+b\}}{(cx^2+bx+a)^2}$;

$(x+a)^{p-1}(x+b)^{q-1}\{(p+q)x+pb+qa\}$;

$\frac{(x+a)^{p-1}}{(x+b)^{q+1}}\{(p-q)x+pb-qa\}$.

## PAGE 26.

**1.** $2e^{2x}$; $-e^{-x}$; $ne^{nx}$; $\sin h\ x$; $\cos h\ x$; $3e^{3x}$.

**2.** $\frac{1}{2x}$; $\frac{1}{x+a}$; $\frac{a}{ax+b}$; $\frac{2ax+b}{ax^2+bx+c}$; $\frac{2}{1-x^2}$; $\frac{4x}{1-x^4}$; $-\frac{(\log_x a)^2}{x\log_e a}$.

**3.** $e^x\phi'(e^x)$; $\frac{1}{x}\phi'(\log x)$; $\frac{1}{2}\frac{\phi'(x)}{\sqrt{\phi(x)}}$; $n[\phi(a+x)]^{n-1}\phi'(a+x)$;

$n(a+x)^{n-1}\phi'[(a+x)^n]$.

**4.** $e^x\left[\log(x+a)+\frac{1}{x+a}\right]$; $x^{n-1}e^x(x+n)$; $(1+\log a)a^x\cdot e^x$; $2^x\log_e 2$; $1°$.

**5.** $\frac{1+e^x}{x+e^x}$; $e^x+\frac{1}{x}$; $\frac{e^x}{x(\log x)^2}(x\log x-1)$.

**6.** $e^{x\log x}\cdot\log ex$; $\frac{x+1}{x}$; $\log ex$.

## PAGE 27.

**1.** $2\cos 2x$; $n\cos nx$; $n\sin^{n-1}x\cos x$; $n\cos x^n\cdot x^{n-1}$; $\frac{\cos\sqrt{x}}{2\sqrt{x}}$.

**2.** $\frac{\cos\sqrt{x}}{4\sqrt{x}\sqrt{\sin\sqrt{x}}}$; $\cot x$; $\frac{1}{2\sqrt{x}}\cot\sqrt{x}$; $\cos xe^{\sin x}$; $\frac{\cos xe^{\sqrt{\sin x}}}{2\sqrt{\sin x}}$.

**3.** $\sin^{m-1}x\cos^{n-1}x\,(m\cos^2 x-n\sin^2 x)$; $\frac{\sin^{m-1}x}{\cos^{n+1}x}(m\cos^2 x+n\sin^2 x)$;

$n^3x^{n-1}\sin^{n-1}(nx^n)\cos(nx^n)$; $e^{ax}(a\sin bx+b\cos bx)$.

**4.** $\frac{1}{2}(\cos 2x+2\cos 4x-3\cos 6x)$ ; $\sin x(\sin 3x+3\sin x)/\sin^2 3x$ .

**5.** $-\frac{1}{2}(\sin 2x+2\sin 4x+3\sin 6x)$ ;

$$-\cos^p ax\cdot\cos^q bx\cdot\cos^r cx\ (ap\tan ax+bq\tan bx+cr\tan cx).$$

## PAGE 30.

**1.** $2x\sec x^2\cdot\tan x^2;\frac{2}{x\sqrt{x^4-1}};2x\sec^2 x^2;\frac{2x}{1+x^4};2x\sin x^2;\frac{2}{\sqrt{2-x^2}}$ .

**2.** $\frac{1}{2\cos h\, x}$; $e^x\sec^2 e^x;2\operatorname{cosec} 2x;\frac{1}{(1+x^2)\tan^{-1}x};-2\operatorname{cosec} 2x$ .

**3.** $\frac{1}{\sqrt{2ax-x^2}};\frac{1}{\sqrt{a(2-a)+2x(1-a)-x^2}};\frac{a}{a^2+x^2};\frac{2}{1+x^2}$.

**4.** $-\cos\frac{x}{2}\sqrt{\text{covers } x};pq\ x^{q-1}\tan^{p-1}x^q\cdot\sec^2 x^q$;

$$pq\,x^{p-1}(\tan^{-1}x^p)^{q-1}/(1+x^{2p});\ \log\tan^{-1}x+\frac{x}{(1+x^2)\tan^{-1}x}.$$

**5.** $\sec^2 x\cdot\sin^{-1}x+\frac{\tan x}{\sqrt{1-x^2}};\frac{1}{\sin x\sqrt{\sin^2 x-\cos^2 x}}$;

$$\frac{\sin x}{1+\cos^2 x};e^x\left(\sin^{-1}x+\frac{1}{\sqrt{1-x^2}}\right).$$

## PAGE 32.

**1.** $x^{\sin x}\left(\frac{\sin x}{x}+\cos x\cdot\log x\right)$;

$$(\sin^{-1}x)^x\left(\log\sin^{-1}x+\frac{x}{\sin^{-1}x\cdot\sqrt{1-x^2}}\right);x^{x^2+1}\log ex^2;2x^{2x}\log ex.$$

**2.** $(\sin x)^{\cos x}\left(\frac{\cos^2 x}{\sin x}-\sin x\log\sin x\right)$

$$+(\cos x)^{\sin x}\left(\cos x\log\cos x-\frac{\sin^2 x}{\cos x}\right)$$

$$(\tan x)^x(\log\tan x+2x\operatorname{cosec} 2x)+x^{\tan x}\left(\sec^2 x\log x+\frac{1}{x}\tan x\right).$$

**3.** $\tan x\cdot\log x\cdot e^x\cdot x^x\cdot\sqrt{x}\left(2\operatorname{cosec} 2x+\frac{1}{x\log x}+2+\log x+\frac{1}{2x}\right)$.

## PAGE 33.

**1.** $\frac{3}{1+x^2}$. **2.** $-\frac{1}{1+x^2}$. **3.** $\frac{1}{2}\frac{1}{1+x^2}$. **4.** $\frac{1}{\sqrt{1-x^2}}$.

**5.** 1. **6.** $\frac{2}{\sqrt{1-x^2}}$. **7.** $\frac{x}{\sqrt{1+x^2}}$. **8.** $-\frac{2}{1+x^2}$.

**9.** $\frac{3}{\sqrt{1-x^2}}$. **10.** $\frac{x^2-2x^{\frac{3}{2}}-2x^{\frac{1}{2}}+1}{2x^{\frac{1}{2}}(1+x)(1+x^2)}$. **11.** $\frac{2}{\sqrt{1-x^2}}$.

**12.** $\frac{x^2-1}{x^2-4}$.

## PAGE 36.

**1.** $-\frac{x^2}{y^2}$. **2.** $-\frac{x^{n-1}}{y^{n-1}}$. **3.** $\frac{y}{x(y-1)}$. **4.** $-\frac{y}{x}\frac{2x^2-1}{2y^2-1}$.

**5.** $-y^2\log\frac{e}{x}/x^2\log\frac{e}{y}$. **6.** $-\frac{yx^{y-1}+y^x\log y}{xy^{x-1}+x^y\log x}$.

## PAGE 37- 40.

**1.** $\frac{x^2+2x-2}{(x+1)^2}$. **2.** $\frac{1}{n}(a+x)^{\frac{1-n}{n}}$.

**3.** $\frac{2x}{n}(a^2+x^2)^{\frac{1-n}{n}}$. **4.** $-\frac{1}{(1-x)^{\frac{1}{2}}(1+x)^{\frac{3}{2}}}$.

**5.** $-\frac{3x+x^3}{(1+x^2)^{\frac{3}{2}}}$. **6.** $\frac{x^4-2a^2x^2+4a^4}{(x^2-a^2)^{\frac{3}{2}}(x^2-4a^2)^{\frac{1}{2}}}$.

**7.** $-\frac{2+2x-x^2}{2(1-x)^{\frac{1}{2}}(1+x+x^2)^{\frac{3}{2}}}$. **8.** $\frac{2(1-x^2)}{1+x^2+x^4}$.

**9.** $\frac{1}{x\{1+(\log x)^2\}}$. **10.** $\frac{\pi}{180}\cos x^\circ$.

**11.** $\cos e^x\cdot e^x\cdot\log x+\frac{\sin e^x}{x}$. **12.** $\frac{\log\sqrt{\cot x}}{\cos h\, x}-\frac{2\tan^{-1}e^x}{\sin 2x}$.

**13.** $\frac{\sin h\, x}{\cos h\, x}$, *i.e.* $\tan h\, x$. **14.** $-\frac{2\operatorname{cosec} 2x}{\sqrt{2\log\cot x-(\log\cot x)^2}}$.

**15.** $\dfrac{\cos x}{1+\sin^2 x}$. **16.** $-\dfrac{1}{1+x^2}$. **17.** $-\dfrac{1}{x\sqrt{x^2-1}}$.

**18.** $\dfrac{(\sin^{-1} x)^{m-1}(\cos^{-1} x)^{n-1}}{\sqrt{1-x^2}}(m\cos^{-1} x - n\sin^{-1} x)$.

**19.** $\cos(e^x \log x)\, e^x \log(xe^{\frac{1}{x}})\sqrt{1-(\log x)^2} - \sin(e^x \log x)\dfrac{\log x^{\frac{1}{x}}}{\sqrt{1-(\log x)}}$.

**20.** $\left(\dfrac{x}{n}\right)^{nx}\left\{n\left(\log\dfrac{ex}{n}\right)^2+\dfrac{1}{x}\right\}$.

**21.** $\dfrac{ab}{a^2+x^2\left(\tan^{-1}\dfrac{x}{a}\right)^2}\left\{\tan^{-1}\dfrac{x}{a}+\dfrac{ax}{a^2+x^2}\right\}$.

**22.** $\dfrac{\cos^{-1} x - x\sqrt{1-x^2}}{(1-x^2)^{\frac{3}{2}}}$. **23.** $\dfrac{a\sin(a\,\text{cosec}^{-1} x)}{x\sqrt{x^2-1}}$.

**24.** $-\dfrac{\sqrt{b^2-a^2}}{b+a\cos x}$. **25.** $2e^{\tan^{-1} x}\left\{\dfrac{\log\sec x^3}{1+x^2}+3x^2\tan x^3\right\}$.

**26.** $e^{ax}\left\{a\cos(b\tan^{-1} x)-\dfrac{b}{1+x^2}\sin(b\tan^{-1} x)\right\}$.

**27.** $\dfrac{xa^{cx}(2+cx\log_e a)}{1+x^4a^{2cx}}$. **28.** $\dfrac{x\log_a e\sin(\log_a\sqrt{a^2+x^2})}{(a^2+x^2)\cos^2(\log_a\sqrt{a^2+x^2})}$.

**29.** $\dfrac{2}{1-x^4}$. **30.** $\dfrac{1}{x\log x}$.

**31.** $\dfrac{1}{x\log x\log^2 x\log^3 x\ldots\log^{n-1} x}$.

**32.** $\dfrac{1}{a+b\cos x}$. **33.** $\dfrac{1}{\sqrt{1-x^2}}-\dfrac{1}{2\sqrt{x-x^2}}$.

**34.** $10^x\cdot 10^{10x}(\log_e 10)^2$. **35.** $e^x\cdot e^{e^x}$.

**36.** $e^{x^x}\cdot x^x\cdot\log(ex)$. **37.** $x^{e^x}\cdot e^x\log(xe^{\frac{1}{x}})$.

**38.** $x^{x^x}\cdot x^x\cdot\left\{(\log x)^2+\log x+\dfrac{1}{x}\right\}$.

**39.** $x^x\log(ex) - x^{\frac{1}{x}-2}\log\dfrac{x}{e}$.

**40.** $-(\cot x)^{\cot x}\,\text{cosec}^2 x\log(e\cot x)$
$+(\cos h\,x)^{\cos h\,x}\sin h\,x\log(e\cos h\,x)$.

41. $\dfrac{x^{\frac{1}{2}}}{1+x^{\frac{3}{2}}}\dfrac{a^{cx}\,x^{\sin x}}{1+a^{2cx}\,x^{2\sin x}}\log\left(a^c x^{\cos x}\,e^{\frac{\sin x}{x}}\right)$

$+\tan^{-1}(a^{cx}x^{\sin x})-\dfrac{1-2x^{\frac{3}{2}}}{2x^{\frac{1}{2}}(1+x^{\frac{3}{2}})^2}.$

42. $\dfrac{1}{\sqrt{1-e^{2\tan^{-1}x}}}\dfrac{e^{\tan^{-1}x}}{1+x^2}.$

43. $\dfrac{\left(\sin\dfrac{m}{x}+\cos\dfrac{m}{x}\right)\left(1-\sin\dfrac{m}{x}+\cos\dfrac{m}{x}\right)\dfrac{m}{x^2}}{2\sqrt{\left(1+\cos\dfrac{m}{x}\right)\left(1-\sin\dfrac{m}{x}\right)}}.$

44. $\dfrac{\sqrt{1-x^2-2\sqrt{x}}}{4\sqrt{x}\,\sqrt{1-x^2}\,\sqrt{\sqrt{x}+\cos^{-1}x}\,(1+\sqrt{x}+\cos^{-1}x)}.$

45. $y\left[2xe^{x^2}\cos e^{x^2}\log\dfrac{1+\sqrt{x}}{1+2\sqrt{x}}-\dfrac{\sin e^{x^2}}{2\sqrt{x}\,(1+\sqrt{x})(1+2\sqrt{x})}\right].$

46. $-y\cot x\,(1+2\operatorname{cosec}^2 x\log\cos x).$

47. $-y\left\{\dfrac{\log\cot^{-1}x}{x^2}+\dfrac{1}{x(1+x^2)\cot^{-1}x}\right\}.$

48. $\left(1+\dfrac{1}{x}\right)^x\left\{\log\dfrac{x+1}{x}-\dfrac{1}{x+1}\right\}+x^{\frac{1}{x}-1}\{x+1-\log x\}.$

49. $\dfrac{b}{a}\dfrac{x^2+y^2-ay}{(x^2+y^2)\sec^2\dfrac{y}{b}-bx}.$

50. $\cos x\cdot\cos 2x\cdot\cos^2 y\cdot e^{\cos^2 x}.$

51. $-\dfrac{ax+hy}{hx+by}.$

52. $\dfrac{n}{2x}\left(\dfrac{a}{a+bx^n}\right)^{\frac{1}{2}}.$

53. $\dfrac{y\tan x+\log\sin y}{\log\cos x-x\cot y}.$

54. $x(3+2\tan\log x+\tan^2\log x).$

55. $\dfrac{y}{x}\dfrac{x-y}{x+y}.$

56. $\dfrac{y^2}{x-xy\log x}.$

57. $\dfrac{y\log y}{x\log x}\dfrac{1+x\log x\log y}{1-x\log y}.$

58. $\dfrac{y\{(a+bx)y-bx^2\}}{x(y-x)(a+bx)}.$

59. $-\dfrac{ax+hy+g}{hx+by+f}.$

**60.** $\frac{y}{x}$. **61.** $\frac{6x^2(1+y^2)\tan x^3 e^{\tan^{-1} y}}{1+y^2-\log\sec^2 x^3 e^{\tan^{-1} y}}$. **63.** $\frac{\log_{10} e}{2x^2}$.

**64.** $-(1+a^2\cos^2 bx)(x^2+ax+a^2)^{n-1}$

$[n(2x+a)\log\cot\frac{x}{2}-\text{cosec}\, x\,(x^2+ax-a^2)]/\,ab\sin bx$.

**65.** $x^{\sin^{-1}x}\left(\log x+\frac{\sqrt{1-x^2}}{x}\sin^{-1}x\right)$. **66.** $\frac{1}{2}$.

**67.** $\frac{1}{x^4}\frac{\sqrt{1+x^2}+\sqrt{1-x^2}}{\sqrt{1+x^2}-\sqrt{1-x^2}}$. **68.** $\frac{2}{x}$. **69.** $-\frac{1}{2}$. **70.** 1.

**71.** $2\frac{n(1+x^2)\tan^{-1}x\log\tan^{-1}x+x}{(1+x^2)\tan^{-1}x(\sqrt{x}\cos\sqrt{x}-3\sin\sqrt{x})}x^{\frac{2n+3}{2}}$.

**80.** $\frac{e^{-xz}}{4z^3+x^2}\left[\frac{8z^4+5x^5}{2xz\sqrt{x^2z-1}}-(5z^4+4x^5)\sec^{-1}x\sqrt{z}\right]$.

**85.** $\frac{1}{\log x}-\frac{2}{x^2-1}$. [Deduce from first result of 83 by putting $x$ for $x$, then using exponential values and writing $z^{\frac{1}{2}}$ for $e^x$, or otherwise.]

**86.** (b) Prove $H_n=\frac{x^{n+2}(y-z)+y^{n+2}(z-x)+z^{n+2}(x-y)}{x^2(y-z)+y^2(z-x)+z^2(x-y)}$, and then differentiate.

## CHAPTER V.

### PAGE 43, 44.

**1.** $\frac{(-1)^n a^n n!}{(ax+b)^{n+1}}$. **2.** $\frac{n!}{(a-x)^{n+1}}$. **3.** $\frac{b^n\cdot n!}{(a-bx)^{n+1}}$.

**4.** $\frac{(-1)^{n-1}ab^{n-1}n!}{(a+bx)^{n+1}}$. **5.** $\frac{(-1)^n(bc-ad)c^{n-1}n!}{(cx+d)^{n+1}}$. **6.** $\frac{(-1)^n a^2 n!}{(x-a)^{n+1}}$ $(n>1)$.

**7.** $\frac{(-1)^n(n+3)!}{3!(x+a)^{n+4}}$. **8.** $(-1)^{n-1}\frac{1\cdot3\cdot5\ldots(2n-3)}{2^n}\frac{1}{(x+a)^{\frac{2n-1}{2}}}$.

**9.** $\frac{3\cdot8\cdot13\cdot18\ldots(5n-2)}{5^n}\cdot\frac{(-1)^n}{(x+a)^{\frac{5n+3}{5}}}$.

**10.** $(-1)^{n-1}\frac{pa^n(n-1)!}{(ax+b)^n}$.

**11.** $\frac{1}{2}\left\{\cos\left(x+\frac{n\pi}{2}\right)-3^n\cos\left(3x+\frac{n\pi}{2}\right)\right\}.$

**12.** $\frac{e^x}{2}\left\{2^{\frac{n}{2}}\cos\left(x+\frac{n\pi}{4}\right)-10^{\frac{n}{2}}\cos(3x+n\tan^{-1}3)\right\}.$

**13.** $\frac{e^x}{2}\{1-5^{\frac{n}{2}}\cos(2x+n\tan^{-1}2)\}.$

**14.** $\frac{e^{ax}}{2}\left\{a^n+(a^2+4b^2)^{\frac{n}{2}}\cos\left(2bx+n\tan^{-1}\frac{2b}{a}\right)\right\}.$

**15.** $\frac{1}{4}\left\{2^n\sin\left(2x+\frac{n\pi}{2}\right)+4^n\sin\left(4x+\frac{n\pi}{2}\right)-6^n\sin\left(6x+\frac{n\pi}{2}\right)\right\}.$

**16.** $$\frac{e^{3x}}{16}\left\{2\cdot(10)^{\frac{n}{2}}\cos\left(x+n\tan^{-1}\frac{1}{3}\right)\right.$$
$$\left.-(18)^{\frac{n}{2}}\cos\left(3x+\frac{n\pi}{4}\right)-(34)^{\frac{n}{2}}\cos\left(5x+n\tan^{-1}\frac{5}{3}\right)\right\}.$$

**17.** $\left\{2^{n-1}\sin\left(2x+\frac{n\pi}{2}\right)-4^{n-1}\sin\left(4x+\frac{n\pi}{2}\right)\right\}.$

**18.** $\frac{e^x}{4}\left\{2\cdot5^{\frac{n}{2}}\sin(2x+n\tan^{-1}2)-(17)^{\frac{n}{2}}\sin(4x+n\tan^{-1}4)\right\}.$

## PAGE 46.

**1.** $(-1)^n2^{n-1}n!\left\{\frac{1}{(2x-1)^{n+1}}-\frac{1}{(2x+1)^{n+1}}\right\}.$

**2.** $(-1)^n\cdot2^n n!\sin(n+1)\theta\sin^{n+1}\theta$, where $\tan\theta=\frac{1}{2x}$.

**3.** $\frac{(-1)^{n-1}(n-1)!}{2}\left\{\frac{1}{(x+a)^n}-\frac{1}{(x-a)^n}\right\}.$

**4.** $\frac{(-1)^n n!}{4a^3}\left[\frac{1}{(x-a)^{n+1}}-\frac{1}{(x+a)^{n+1}}-\frac{2}{a^{n+1}}\sin(n+1)\theta\sin^{n+1}\theta\right],$

where $x=a\cot\theta$.

**5.** $$\frac{(-1)^n n!}{a^2-b^2}\left[\frac{1}{2a}\left\{\frac{1}{(x-a)^{n+1}}-\frac{1}{(x+a)^{n+1}}\right\}\right.$$
$$\left.-\frac{1}{2b}\left\{\frac{1}{(x-b)^{n+1}}-\frac{1}{(x+b)^{n+1}}\right\}\right].$$

**6.** $\frac{(-1)^n n!}{a^2-b^2}\left[\frac{\sin(n+1)\phi\sin^{n+1}\phi}{b^{n+2}}-\frac{\sin(n+1)\theta\sin^{n+1}\theta}{a^{n+2}}\right],$

where $x=a\cot\theta=b\cot\phi$.

**7.** $2(-1)^{n-1}(n-1)!\sin n\theta \sin^n \theta$, where $x = \cot \theta$.

**8.** $\dfrac{(-1)^n \cdot 2^{n+2} n!}{3^{\frac{n+2}{2}}} \sin(n+1)\theta \sin^{n+1}\theta$, where $x = \dfrac{\cos\left(\theta + \dfrac{\pi}{6}\right)}{\sin\theta}$.

**9.** $\dfrac{(-1)^n 2^{n+1} n!}{3^{\frac{n+2}{2}}} \{\sin(n+1)\theta \sin^{n+1}\theta - \sin(n+1)\phi \sin^{n+1}\phi\}$,

where $x = \dfrac{\cos\left[\theta - \dfrac{\pi}{6}\right]}{\sin\theta} = \dfrac{\cos\left(\phi + \dfrac{\pi}{6}\right)}{\sin\phi}$.

**10.** $(-1)^n n!\left\{\sin(n+1)\theta \sin^{n+1}\theta - \sec^{n+2}\dfrac{\pi}{6} \sin(n+1)\phi \sin^{n+1}\phi\right\}$,

where $x = \cot\theta = \dfrac{\cos\left(\phi + \dfrac{\pi}{6}\right)}{\sin\phi}$.

## PAGE 48.

**1.** $e^x (x+n)$. **2.** $a^{n-2}e^{ax}\{a^2x^2 + 2nax + n(n-1)\}$.

**3.** $\dfrac{2(-1)^{n-1}(n-3)!}{x^{n-2}}$.

**4.** $x^2 \sin\left(x + \dfrac{n\pi}{2}\right) + 2nx \sin\left(x + \dfrac{\overline{n-1}\,\pi}{2}\right) + n(n-1)\sin\left(x + \dfrac{\overline{n-2}\,\pi}{2}\right)$.

**5.** $e^{ax}(P\sin bx + Q\cos bx)$, where $P + iQ = (a+ib)^n$.

**6.** $\dfrac{n!}{(x+1)^{n+1}}$.

**7.** $(-1)^{n-1}(n-2)!\sin^{n-1}\theta\cos\theta\cos n\theta\ \{n\tan\theta - \tan n\theta\}$,
where $x = \cot\theta$.

**8.** $(-1)^{n-1}(n-3)!\sin^{n-2}\theta\ \{(n-1)(n-2)\sin n\theta\cos^2\theta$
$-2n(n-2)\sin(n-1)\theta\cos\theta + n(n-1)\sin(n-2)\theta\}$, where $x = \cot\theta$.

## PAGE 51-53.

**1.** $y_4 = (16x^4 - 12)\sin x^2 - 48x^2\cos x^2$. **2.** $y_4 = x\sin x - 4\cos x$.

**3.** $y_6 = -8e^x\cos x$.

**4.** $y_n = a^{n-3}e^{ax}\{a^3x^3, + 3na^2x^2 + 3n(n-1)ax + n(n-1)(n-2)\}$.

**10.** $y_n = \dfrac{(-1)^n n!}{c-d}\left\{\dfrac{(c-a)(c-b)}{(x-c)^{n+1}} - \dfrac{(d-a)(d-b)}{(x-d)^{n+1}}\right\}$.

**11.** $y_n = (-1)^{n-1} n! \left\{ \frac{(n+2)(n+1)}{2(x-1)^{n+3}} + \frac{(n+1)}{(x-1)^{n+2}} + \frac{1}{(x-1)^{n+1}} - \frac{1}{(x-2)^{n+1}} \right\}.$

**12.** $y_3 = n(n-1)(n-2)\, x^{n-3} \left\{ \log x + \frac{1}{n} + \frac{1}{n-1} + \frac{1}{n-2} \right\}.$

$y_n = n! \left\{ \log x + \frac{1}{1} + \frac{1}{2} + \frac{1}{3} + \ldots + \frac{1}{n} \right\}.\; y_{n+1} = \frac{n!}{x}.$

**14.** $y_n = \frac{(-1)^n\, n!}{3^{\frac{n+3}{2}}} \sin^{n+1}\theta \left\{ \operatorname{cosec}^{n+1}\left(\theta + \frac{\pi}{6}\right) + 2^{n+2} \sin\left(\overline{n+1}\,\theta - \frac{\pi}{6}\right) \right\},$

where $x + 1 = \sqrt{3} \sin\left(\theta + \frac{\pi}{6}\right) / \sin\theta$.

**15.** $y_n = \frac{1}{2}(-1)^n\, n! \sin^{n+1}\theta \,\{\sin(n+1)\theta - \cos(n+1)\theta$

$+ (\sin\theta + \cos\theta)^{-n-1}\}$, where $\theta = \cot^{-1} x$.

**16.** $y_n = \frac{(-1)^n n!}{4} \left\{ \frac{(n+1)(n+2)}{(x-1)^{n+3}} + \frac{3(n+1)}{(x-1)^{n+2}} \right.$

$\left. + \frac{1}{2}\frac{1}{(x-1)^{n+1}} - \frac{1}{2}\frac{1}{(x+1)^{n+1}} \right\}.$

## CHAPTER VI.

### PAGE 56.

**8.** $x^3 + x^4 + \frac{x^5}{2} \ldots$ .

**9.** (*a*) $\tan^{-1} \frac{p - qx}{q + px} = \tan^{-1} \frac{p}{q} - \tan^{-1} x =$ etc.

(*b*) $\tan^{-1} \frac{3x - x^3}{1 - 3x^2} = 3 \tan^{-1} x =$ etc.

(*c*) $\sin^{-1} \frac{2x}{1 + x^2} = 2 \tan^{-1} x =$ etc.

(*d*) $\cos^{-1} \frac{x - x^{-1}}{x + x^{-1}} = 2 \cot^{-1} x = \pi - 2 \tan^{-1} x =$ etc.

## CHAPTER VII.

### PAGE 71.

**8.** ·0027 of an inch.

# CHAPTER VIII.

## PAGE 76.

### *Tangents.*

**1.** (1) $Xx + Yy = c^2$. (2) $Yy = 2a(X + x)$.

(3) $\frac{X}{x} + \frac{Y}{y} = 2$. (4) $Y - y = \sinh\frac{x}{c}(X - x)$.

(5) $X(2xy + y^2) + Y(x^2 + 2xy) = 3a^3$.

(6) $Y - y = \cot x(X - x)$.

(7) $X(x^2 - ay) + Y(y^2 - ax) = axy$.

(8) $X\{2x(x^2 + y^2) - a^2x\} + Y\{2y(x^2 + y^2) + a^2y\} = a^2(x^2 - y^2)$.

### *Normals.*

(1) $\frac{X}{x} = \frac{Y}{y}$. (2) $\frac{X - x}{2a} + \frac{Y - y}{y} = 0$, etc.

**2.** Tangents are $Y = \pm\frac{3\sqrt{3}}{8}X - \frac{a}{8}$.
Normals are $Y = \mp\frac{8\sqrt{3}}{9}X + \frac{41}{36}a$.

**4.** ($\alpha$) Parallel at points of intersection with $ax + hy = 0$.
Perpendicular at points of intersection with $hx + by = 0$.

($\beta$) Parallel at $\left(-\frac{a}{\sqrt[3]{2}}, \frac{3a\sqrt[3]{2}}{2}\right)$.
Perpendicular where $x = 0$.

($\gamma$) Parallel at $\left(\frac{4a}{3}, \frac{2\sqrt[3]{4}}{3}a\right)$.
Perpendicular at $(0, 0)$, $(2a, 0)$.

**5.** ($\alpha$) Tangent, $\frac{x}{a}\cos\theta + \frac{y}{b}\sin\theta = 1$.
Normal, $ax\sec\theta - by\operatorname{cosec}\theta = a^2 - b^2$.

($\beta$) Tangent, $x\sin\frac{\theta}{2} - y\cos\frac{\theta}{2} = a\theta\sin\frac{\theta}{2}$.
Normal, $x\cos\frac{\theta}{2} + y\sin\frac{\theta}{2} = a\theta\cos\frac{\theta}{2} + 2a\sin\frac{\theta}{2}$.

($\gamma$) Tangent, $x\sin\frac{A + B}{2B}\theta - y\cos\frac{A + B}{2B}\theta = (A + B)\sin\frac{A - B}{2B}\theta$.
Normal, $x\cos\frac{A + B}{2B}\theta + y\sin\frac{A + B}{2B}\theta = (A - B)\cos\frac{A - B}{2B}\theta$.

**6.** For an ellipse, $r^2 = a^2\cos^2\theta + b^2\sin^2\theta$.

For a rectangular hyperbola, $r^2 = a^2\cos 2\theta$.

**7.** $\frac{1}{a} - \frac{1}{b} = \frac{1}{a'} - \frac{1}{b'}$, i.e. they must be confocal.

**9.** The axes are tangents at the origin. Also at the point $(2^{\frac{1}{3}}a, 2^{\frac{2}{3}}a)$ the tangents to the parabolas make angles $\tan^{-1}2^{\frac{4}{3}}$, $\tan^{-1}2^{-\frac{2}{3}}$ respectively with the tangent to the Folium.

## PAGE 77.

**2.** ($\alpha$) $ax = \pm by$, ($\beta$) $x = 0$ and $y = 0$, ($\gamma$) $ax = \pm y\sqrt{b^2 - a^2}$.

## PAGE 81.

**1.** $c^4 / \sqrt{x^6 + y^6}$. **8.** area $= \frac{1}{2}\sqrt[3]{a^4xy}$. **9.** $n = -2; n = 1$.

## PAGE 88, 89.

**1.** At $x = 2 \pm \frac{1}{\sqrt{3}}$. **6.** Where $x = \pm \frac{a}{\sqrt{2}}$.

**12.** If normal $= y^3 / b^2$, subtangent $= b^2y / \sqrt{y^4 - b^4}$,

subnormal $= y\sqrt{y^4 - b^4} / b^2$.

**19.** $\frac{\pi}{2}$. **20.** $\frac{\pi}{4}$.

# CHAPTER IX.

## PAGE 91.

**1.** $y = x; y = 2x; y = 3x$. **2.** $y = x; y = \pm (2x - 1)$.

**3.** $y + x = 0; y + 1 = \pm x\sqrt{3}$.

**4.** $y = x; y + x + 1 = 0; y + 2x + 2 = 0; y + 3x + 3 = 0$.

**5.** $2x + 3y + 1 = 0; 3x + 4y + 1 = 0; 4x + 5y + 1 = 0$.

## PAGE 92.

**1.** $y + x = 0; y - x = 0; y - x = 1$.

**2.** $y + x = 0; y - x = 0; y - x = 1; y - x = 2$. **3.** $y \pm x = \pm 1$.

## PAGE 97.

**1.** $x + y = \frac{2a}{3}$. **2.** $x + y = 0$. **3.** $x + y = 0$. **4.** $y = 0$.

**5.** $x = 0$. **6.** $x = 2a$. **7.** $x + y + a = 0$.

**8.** $x = 0; y = 0; x + y = 0$. **9.** $y = 0$. **10.** $x = \pm a$.

**11.** $x = a; y = a; x = y$. **12.** $x = \pm a$. **13.** $x = 0$.

**14.** $x = a$. **15.** $x = \pm 1; y = x$. **16.** $x = 0; y = \pm\left(x + \frac{m}{2}\right)$.

**17.** $x + 2y = 0; x + y = 1; x - y = -1.$ **18.** $x = 0; x - y = 0; x - y + 1 = 0.$

**19.** $y = 0; x = y; x = y \pm 1.$ **20.** ; $x + 2y = \pm 2.$

**21.** $x + y = \pm 2\sqrt{2}; x + 2y + 2 = 0.$ **22.** $y = 3x - 2a; x + 3y = \pm a.$

## PAGE 98.

**1.** $x^3 - 6x^2y + 11xy^2 - 6y^3 = x.$ **3.** $\dfrac{x^2}{a^2} + \dfrac{y^2}{b^2} = 1.$

## PAGE 100.

**1.** $\theta = 0.$ **2.** $r \sin \theta = a.$

**3.** $nr \sin \left(\theta - \dfrac{k\pi}{n}\right) = a \sec k\pi$, where $k$ is any integer.

**4.** $r \sin \theta = a.$ **5.** $r \cos \theta = 2a.$ **6.** $\theta = \dfrac{\pi}{2}, r \sin \theta = \dfrac{a}{2}.$

**7.** $r \sin \left(\theta - \dfrac{k\pi}{n}\right) = \dfrac{b}{n}$, where $k$ is any integer.

**8.** $n\theta = k\pi$, where $k$ is any integer.

## PAGE 101, 102.

**1.** $x = y.$ **2.** $x - y = \dfrac{a}{5}.$ **3.** $x - y = \dfrac{a}{5}.$ **4.** $x = \pm 1, y = x.$

**5.** $x = a.$ **6.** $x = 1, x = 2, y = 0.$

**7.** $x = 2, y = 1, y = x + 1.$ **8.** $y = 0, y = 2x.$

**9.** $x \pm y = \pm \sqrt{a^2 - b^2} / 2.$ **10.** $x = \pm a.$

**11.** $y - x + a = 0, y + x - a = 0.$ **12.** $x = y + 2.$

**13.** $x = \pm 2, y - x = 0.$ **14.** $x \pm 2y = \pm \sqrt{\dfrac{5}{8}}.$

**15.** $x = 0, y - x\sqrt{a} = \dfrac{b}{2\sqrt{a}}, y + x\sqrt{a} = -\dfrac{b}{2\sqrt{a}}.$

**16.** $3x + 4y = 0, y - 2x = 0, y - 2x + 3 = 0.$

**17.** $3x + 4y = 0, y - 2x + 1 = 0, y - 2x + 2 = 0.$

**18.** $y = \pm x, y - 2x + 1 = 0, y - 2x + 2 = 0.$

**19.** $r \sin \left\{(2k + 1)\dfrac{\pi}{2a} - \theta\right\} = \dfrac{b}{a} \operatorname{cosec} (2k + 1)\dfrac{\pi}{2}$, where $k$ is any integer.

**20.** $r \sin \theta = 2a, r = a.$ **21.** $r \sin (1 \pm \theta) + \dfrac{a}{2} = 0, r = a.$

**22.** $r \cos \theta = a.$ **23.** $\dfrac{a}{2r} = \pm \cos \theta - \sin \theta.$

# CHAPTER X.

## PAGE 110.

**1.** $\rho = a; \rho = a\cos\psi; \rho = 3a\sec^4\psi\sin\psi; \rho = a\sec\psi.$

**2.** $\rho = (1+9x^4)^{\frac{3}{2}}/6x; \rho = y^2/c; \rho = a\sec\frac{x}{a}.$ **3.** $\rho = a.$

## PAGE 116.

**1.** $\rho = 2r^{\frac{3}{2}}/a^{\frac{1}{2}}; \rho = a/2; \rho = a^m/(m+1)r^{m-1}.$

**2.** $\rho = a(\theta^2+1)^{\frac{3}{2}}/\theta^4; \rho = a(\theta^2+1)^{\frac{3}{2}}/(\theta^2+2); \rho = a/2.$

## PAGE 121-123.

**1.** $(a)\, \rho = 5\sqrt{5}/6.$ $(b)\, \rho = 5\sqrt{5}/22.$ $(c)\, \rho = -\sqrt{2}/2$ and $\rho = 5\sqrt{5}/18.$

$(d)\, \rho = 15a\sqrt{5}/14$ and $\rho = -\dfrac{3a\sqrt{2}}{2}.$

**11.** $x = 7$ and $x = 1.$

# CHAPTER XI.

## PAGE 126.

**2.** $256y^3 + 27x^4 = 0.$ **3.** $a^4/x^2 + b^4/y^2 = c^4/a^2.$

**4.** $y + \dfrac{1}{2}g\dfrac{x^2}{u^2} = \dfrac{u^2}{2g}.$

**5.** (i) $4x^3 + 27ay^2 = 0;$ (ii) $y^2 = 4h(a+h-x).$

**6.** $y^2 + 4a(x-2a) = 0.$ **7.** Two straight lines.

**8.** A parabola touching the axes.

## PAGE 128.

**1.** $27ay^2 = 4(x-2a)^3.$ **2.** $(ax)^{\frac{2}{3}} + (by)^{\frac{2}{3}} = (a^2-b^2)^{\frac{2}{3}}.$

**3.** (α) $x^2 + 4ay = 0,$ (β) $4x^3 + 27ay^2 = 0,$ (γ) $(p-1)^{p-1}x^p + p^p a y^{p-1} = 0.$

**4.** (η) $x^{\frac{2}{2-n}} + y^{\frac{2}{2-n}} = a^{\frac{2}{2-n}}$; (α), (β), (γ), etc. being special cases, their answers may be at once tested by this result.

**5.** (γ) $r^{\frac{n}{m-n}} = a^{\frac{n}{m-n}}\cos\dfrac{n}{m-n}\theta$; and the results of (α) and (β) may be verified by this result.

**6.** (α) $r^2 = a^2\cos^2\theta + b^2\sin^2\theta;$ (β) $r\cos\theta + a\sin^2\theta = 0;$

(γ) $x + a = 0;$ (δ) $r^{\frac{1}{3}} = (2a)^{\frac{1}{3}}\cos\dfrac{\theta}{3};$

(ε) The auxiliary circle; (ζ) $r^2 = a^2 \cos 2\theta$;

(η) $r^{\frac{2}{3}} = a^{\frac{2}{3}} \cos \frac{2}{3}\theta$; (θ) $r^{\frac{n}{n+1}} = a^{\frac{n}{n+1}} \cos \frac{n}{n+1}\theta$.

**7.** Similar loci to the results of 6 but of twice the linear dimensions.

**8.** (α) a parabola; (β) a point;

(γ) a conic with focus at the pole and of which the given circle is the auxiliary circle.;

(δ) a circle through the pole; (ε) a circle;

(ζ) a rectangular hyperbola; (η) an equiangular spiral;

(θ) $r^{\frac{n}{1-n}} = a^{\frac{n}{1-n}} \cos \frac{n}{1-n}\theta$.

**9.** (α) $\sqrt{x} + \sqrt{y} = \sqrt{c}$; (β) $x^{\frac{2}{3}} + y^{\frac{2}{3}} = c^{\frac{2}{3}}$;

(γ) $\frac{(m+n)^{m+n}}{m^m \cdot n^n} x^m y^n = c^{m+n}$.

**10.** (α) $x \pm y = \pm c$; (β) $x^{\frac{2n}{n+2}} + y^{\frac{2n}{n+2}} = c^{\frac{2n}{n+2}}$;

(γ) $\frac{(m+n)^{m+n}}{m^m n^n} \cdot x^{2m} y^{2n} = c^{2m+2n}$.

**11.** (α) $x^{\frac{1}{3}} + y^{\frac{1}{3}} = c^{\frac{1}{3}}$; (β) $x^{\frac{n}{2n+1}} + y^{\frac{n}{2n+1}} = c^{\frac{n}{2n+1}}$;

(γ) $\frac{(m+n)^{2(m+n)}}{m^{2m} \cdot n^{2n}} \cdot x^m y^n = c^{m+n}$.

**12.** $x^{\frac{mp}{m+p}} + y^{\frac{mp}{m+p}} = c^{\frac{mp}{m+p}}$. **15.** A circle.

## CHAPTER XII.

### PAGE 138.

**1.** A parabola with focus at the origin.

**2.** A conic with focus at the origin. **3.** A circle.

**4.** $r^{\frac{1}{3}} = \left(\frac{k^2}{2a}\right)^{\frac{1}{3}} \sec \frac{1}{3}\theta$. **5.** $r^{\frac{n}{n+1}} = \left(\frac{k^2}{a}\right)^{\frac{n}{n+1}} \sec \frac{n}{n+1}\theta$.

**6.** $x^m y^n = \left(\frac{k^2}{a}\right)^{m+n} \frac{m^m n^n}{(m+n)^{m+n}}$.

**7.** $x^{\frac{n}{n-1}} + y^{\frac{n}{n-1}} = \left(\frac{k^2}{a}\right)^{\frac{n}{n-1}}$. **8.** $(ax)^{\frac{m}{m-1}} + (by)^{\frac{m}{m-1}} = k^{\frac{2m}{m-1}}$.

## CHAPTER XIII.

### PAGE 148.

**14.** Area $=2ab$. **15.** $a^3/27$. **16.** $abc/3\sqrt{3}$. **17.** $4a^3/27$.

**18.** $p^p q^q a^{p+q}/(p+q)^{p+q}$. **20.** $3\sqrt{3}/8$.

**21.** $\left.\begin{array}{l}\text{If } a>b \text{ Max.}=a, \text{ Min.}=b\\ \text{If } a<b \text{ Max.}=b. \text{ Min.}=a\end{array}\right\}.$

**24.** If $a$ and $b$ are the sides the maximum area $=\frac{1}{2}(a+b)^2$.

**25.** $\left\{\begin{array}{l}\text{A Max. when chords coincide with Transverse Axis and Lat. Rect.}\\ \text{A Min. when chords are equally inclined to Transverse Axis.}\end{array}\right.$

### PAGE 154.

**5.** Max. value = 34, Min. = 33.

**8.** $x=-2, -1, 1, 2$ give Max. and Min. alternately.

**9.** At $x=1$, $y=$ Max.; $x=3$, $y=$ Min.

At $x=2$ and $x=4$ there are points of contrary flexure.

**10.** At $x=2$, $y=$ Min. At $x=\frac{4}{3}$, $y=$ Max.

### PAGE 155-157.

**1.** ($a$) Max. for $x=2-\frac{1}{\sqrt{3}}$; Min. for $x=2+\frac{1}{\sqrt{3}}$.

($b$) $x=1, 2, 3$ give respectively a Minimum, a Max., and a Min.

($c$) If $a>b$ $x=a$ gives a Min.; $x=\frac{2b+a}{3}$ gives a Max.

If $a<b$ $x=a$ gives a Max.; $x=\frac{2b+a}{3}$ gives a Min.

($d$) If $a>b$, the positive value of $y$ is a Max. when $x=(a+4b)/5$. The negative value is a minimum. Also when $x=a$, $y=0$ and there is a maximum ordinate for the portion of the curve beneath the $x$-axis, and a minimum ordinate for the portion above the axis. If $a<b$ the point $(a, 0)$ is an isolated point upon the curve.

**2.** ($a$) The greatest and least values are respectively $\pm\sqrt{a^2+b^2}$.

($b$) If $a>b$ $\left\{\begin{array}{l}\text{Max.}=a,\\ \text{Min.}=b.\end{array}\right.$ If $a<b$ $\left\{\begin{array}{l}\text{Max.}=b,\\ \text{Min.}=a.\end{array}\right.$

($c$) $r^2=\frac{a+b}{2}\pm\frac{1}{2}\sqrt{(a-b)^2+4h^2}$.

(*d*) Max. $= \dfrac{c^2}{a+b}$ when $\tan\theta = \pm\sqrt{\dfrac{a}{b}}$. (*e*) Min. $= a+b$.

(*f*) $\theta = \tan^{-1}\dfrac{\sqrt{3}}{2}, \dfrac{\pi}{2}, \pi - \tan^{-1}\dfrac{\sqrt{3}}{2}, \ \pi + \tan^{-1}\dfrac{\sqrt{3}}{2}, \dfrac{3\pi}{2},$

$2\pi - \tan^{-1}\dfrac{\sqrt{3}}{2}$ ... give maxima and minima alternately.

**3.** (*a*) $x = 1$ gives a minimum, $x = (+\sqrt{17}-1)/8$ gives a maximum and $x = (-\sqrt{17}-1)/8$ a minimum.

(*b*) $x = 0$ gives a minimum, $x = \pm\sqrt{3}$ give maxima.

(*c*) $x = n\pi + \dfrac{\pi}{6}$ give maxima, $x = n\pi + \dfrac{5\pi}{6}$ give minima.

(*d*) $x = e$ gives a maximum.

(*e*) The solutions of $x = \dfrac{k\pi}{n+1}$, where $k$ is any integer, give maxima and minima alternately, beginning with $k = 1$; omitting when $n$ is even those solutions for which $k$ is zero or a multiple of $n+1$.

**4.** (*a*) The roots of $\left(a - \dfrac{1}{r^2}\right)\left(b - \dfrac{1}{r^2}\right) = h^2$.

(*b*) Min. value $= 2c\sqrt{ab}$.

(*c*) Max. and Min. values respectively $= \pm 2\sin\dfrac{\alpha}{2}$.

(*d*) Max. and Min. values respectively $= 1 \pm \cos\alpha$.

**5.** $1/{}^{p-1}\sqrt{p}$. **6.** $\dfrac{ap}{p+q}, \dfrac{aq}{p+q}$.

**7.** A Max. when the segment is a semicircle.
A Min. when the radius is infinite.

**14.** If height of cone by $h$ and semivertical angle $= \alpha$, Max. Volume of Cylinder $= \dfrac{4}{27}\pi h^3 \tan^2\alpha$.

**20.** Half the triangle formed by the chord and the tangents at its extremities, or three-fourths of the area of the segment.

# CHAPTER XIV.

## PAGE 159.

**1.** $\log_b a$. **2.** $\dfrac{a}{b}$. **3.** $\dfrac{3}{2}$. **4.** $\dfrac{1}{2}$.

**5.** 1. **6.** $\dfrac{2}{3}$. **7.** 4. **8.** $\dfrac{1}{3}$.

**9.** $\dfrac{2}{5}$. **10.** $\dfrac{1}{4}$.

## PAGE 163.

**1.** $\alpha$. **2.** $\frac{2}{\pi}$. **3.** $0; \frac{1}{3}, \infty$. **4.** 1. **5.** $-\frac{3}{2}$.

## PAGE 165, 166.

**1.** 2. **2.** $\frac{1}{5}$. **3.** 2. **4.** $\frac{1}{2}$.

**5.** $-\frac{1}{\alpha}$. **6.** 4. **7.** $m - \frac{4m^3}{3}$. **8.** $\frac{1}{\sqrt{e}}$.

**9.** $e$. **10.** 1. **11.** If $n > m, \infty$; $n = m, \frac{A}{a}$; $n < m, 0$.

**12.** 1. **13.** 1. **14.** $\sqrt{a}$. **15.** $\frac{1}{6}$.

**16.** $a = -2$ ; Limit $= -1$. **17.** $a_1 = -4$ ; $a_2 = 5$ ; Limit $= 1$.

**18.** $a_1 = -4$ ; $a_2 = 3$ ; Limit $= 8$.

**19.** $a_1 = -\frac{1}{2}$; $a_2 = \frac{1}{2}$; $a_3 = 0$; Limit $= -\frac{1}{3}$. **21.** $\frac{4}{15}$.

**22.** $e^{\frac{1}{6}}$. **23.** $e^{\frac{1}{20}}$. **24.** (a) $e^{\frac{1}{2}}$; (b) $e^{\frac{1}{12}}$; (c) $e^{\frac{1}{30}}$.

## MISCELLANEOUS EXAMPLES.

**5.** (1) $e^{\frac{1}{3}}$; (2) $\alpha$; (3) $\frac{a}{e}$. **7.** $\frac{1 + \alpha^2}{\cos^2 \alpha}$

**9.** (i) $\frac{a}{3}$; (ii) $-1$; (iii) 1; (iv) $\frac{1}{\sqrt{2a}}$. **10.** $\frac{2a}{\pi}$.

**13.** $3(x-1)^2$. **18.** $\frac{108(x-1)^2}{(x+2)^5}; \frac{27}{8}$.

**23.** $\frac{(-1)^n n!}{2}\left\{\frac{1}{(x+2)^{n+1}} - \frac{1}{(x+4)^{n+1}}\right\}$.

**25.** $P \sin\left(x + \frac{n\pi}{2}\right) - Q \cos\left(x + \frac{n\pi}{2}\right)$,

where, $P \equiv x^m - {}^nC_2 m(m-1)x^{m-2} + {}^nC_4 m(m-1)(m-2)(m-3)$ $x^{m-4} - \ldots$ and $Q \equiv {}^nC_1 m x^{m-1} - {}^nC_3 m(m-1)(m-2)x^{m-3} + \ldots$

**42.** At the origin and at the points of intersection with $y = x\sqrt[3]{\frac{2b}{a}}$ and $y = x\sqrt[3]{\frac{b}{2a}}$.

**43.** Half a right angle. **46.** $\frac{\sqrt{15}}{4}$.

**57.** (i) $x \pm y = 0$; (ii) $x = 0$, $x = 2a$.

**58.** $x = 2y - 14a$, $x = 3y + 13a$, $x - y = a$, $x - y = 2a$.

**59.** $0, 1, -\frac{1}{2}$. **60.** When $y = \pm x\sqrt{n}$.

**61.** Maximum area $= 4r^2 \sin\alpha \cos^3\alpha$, where $r$ is the radius of the circle and $2\alpha$ the given angle.

**63.** The Centroid is at the centre.

**65.** $a$.

**66.** If $m$ be even $x = \frac{k\pi}{m+1}$ and $x = (2\lambda + 1)\frac{\pi}{2}$, where $k$ and $\lambda$ are integers.

If the several angles be arranged in order of magnitude we have Max. and Min. alternately, beginning with $x = 0$.
If $m$ be odd the solutions which give Max. and Min. are those of $x = \frac{k\pi}{m+1}$, and we have Max. and Min. alternately, beginning with $x = 0$.

**67.** $x = 0$ gives a maximum. Then the series of angles (arranged in order of magnitude) defined by $\sin x = 0$ and by $\cos x = \frac{\pm\sqrt{7} - 1}{6}$ given alternate maxima and minima.

**68.** Alternate Max. and Min. are given by $x = k\pi + \frac{\pi}{4}$. $k = 0$ gives a max.

**69.** If the breadth be $2\alpha$ the minimum length of crease is $\frac{3a\sqrt{3}}{2}$ and minimum area $= \frac{8a^2}{3\sqrt{3}}$.

**72.** $\begin{cases} a > b \text{ Max. if } x = \frac{a+2b}{3}, \\ a < b \text{ Max. if } x = a, \\ a = b \text{ gives a point of inflexion.} \end{cases}$

**75.** $y^2(x + 16a)^2 + 4\{6y^2 - (2a - x)^2\}\{y^2 - 3a(2a - x)\} = 0$.